D1268438

# Cassadaga

The Florida History and Culture Series

# UNIVERSITY PRESS OF FLORIDA

Gainesville * Tallahassee * Tampa * Boca Raton * Pensacola * Orlando * Miami * Jacksonville

# Cassadaga

*The South's Oldest Spiritualist Community*

EDITED BY John J. Guthrie, Jr.,
Phillip Charles Lucas, and Gary Monroe

PHOTOGRAPHY BY Gary Monroe

BOCA RATON PUBLIC LIBRARY
BOCA RATON, FLORIDA

Frontispiece: Christmas Candlelight Message Service, Colby
Memorial Temple, 1997.

Copyright 2000 by the Board of Regents of the State of Florida
"Seeking the Sweet Spirit of Harmony: Establishing a Spiritualist
Community at Cassadaga, 1893–1933," copyright John J. Guthrie, Jr.
Photographs copyright Gary Monroe unless otherwise specified.

Printed in the United States of America on acid-free paper
All rights reserved

05  04  03  02  01  00   6  5  4  3  2  1

Library of Congress Cataloging-in-Publication Data

Cassadaga : the South's oldest spiritualist community / edited by
John J. Guthrie, Jr., Phillip Charles Lucas, and Gary Monroe.
p.  cm. —(The Florida history and culture series)
Includes bibliographical references and index.
ISBN 0-8130-1743-2 (alk. paper)
1. Spiritualism—Florida—Cassadaga.  2. Cassadaga (Fla.)—History.
I. Guthrie, John J.  II. Lucas, Phillip Charles.  III. Monroe, Gary.
IV. Series.
BF1242.U6C375      2000
133.9'09759'21—dc21 99-38727

The University Press of Florida is the scholarly publishing agency for
the State University System of Florida, comprising Florida A&M
University, Florida Atlantic University, Florida International University,
Florida State University, University of Central Florida, University of
Florida, University of North Florida, University of South Florida, and
University of West Florida.

University Press of Florida
15 Northwest 15th Street
Gainesville, FL 32611
http://www.upf.com

JUL – – 2000

# CONTENTS

# FOREWORD

*Cassadaga: The South's Oldest Spiritualist Community* is the twelfth volume of a new series devoted to the study of Florida history and culture. During the past half century, the burgeoning population and increased national and international visibility of Florida have sparked a great deal of popular interest in the state's past, present, and future. As the favorite destination of countless tourists and as the new home for millions of retirees and immigrants, modern Florida has become a demographic, political, and cultural bellwether. Unfortunately, the quantity and quality of the literature about Florida's distinctive heritage and character have not kept pace with the Sunshine State's enhanced status. In an effort to remedy this situation—to provide an accessible and attractive format for the publication of Florida-related books—the University Press of Florida has established the Florida History and Culture series.

As coeditors of the series, we are committed to the creation of an eclectic but carefully crafted set of books that will provide the field of Florida studies with a new focus and that will encourage Florida researchers and writers to consider the broader implications and context of their work. The series will include standard academic monographs, works of synthesis, memoirs, and anthologies. And, while the series will feature books of historical interest, we encourage authors researching Florida's environment, politics, literature, and popular or material culture to submit their manuscripts for inclusion in the series. We want each book to retain a distinct "personality" and voice, and at the same time we hope to foster a sense of community and collaboration among Florida scholars.

In *Cassadaga: The South's Oldest Spiritualist Community*, editors John J. Guthrie, Jr., Phillip Charles Lucas, and Gary Monroe offer a probing analysis of one of Florida's most unusual communities. The small town of Cassadaga, located twenty-five miles north of Orlando, has been home to all manner of Spiritualists for more than a century. Today, as in the past, the homes and shops of mediums, readers of palms and tarot cards, and various other practitioners of "psychic science" line the town's streets. Visitors to this seemingly strange community may not know what to make of it, but they do know that they have strayed well beyond the boundaries of the Sunbelt mainstream. To the casual visitor,

Cassadaga may appear to be a homogeneous mass of Spiritualist activity, a string of indistinguishable psychics and occultists. In actuality, it is a complex network of subcommunities representing a broad array of countercultural lifestyles and beliefs. The largest of these subcommunities, the Southern Cassadaga Spiritualist Camp, is the focus of this anthology.

Founded in 1893, the Southern Cassadaga Spiritualist Camp began as a southern outpost of the New York–based Lily Dale Spiritualist Camp, one of the many experimental communities that dotted Victorian America. Despite continuing interest in Spiritualism, only a few of these nineteenth-century communities have persisted into the late twentieth century; indeed, as the editors point out, the Cassadaga camp "is the oldest religious community of its kind in the southeastern United States." It is also one of the first Spiritualist communities to give scholars the opportunity to examine its inner workings.

Beginning with Gary Monroe's photographic survey of the community and its inhabitants in 1994, the scholarly examination of the Cassadaga camp has grown into the multidisciplinary effort presented in this volume. In the seven chapters that follow, eight scholars representing a variety of disciplines explore the entire range of the Cassadaga camp experience, from its social and cultural roots to its guiding philosophy and architectural expression. Drawing upon archival research, oral histories, participant-observer accounts, and sophisticated theoretical constructs, the contributors to this fascinating anthology strip away the stereotypes and misconceptions that often have obscured the cultural meaning and human drama of places such as Cassadaga. The story that emerges from their labors is as revealing as it is entertaining. Far removed from the historical mainstream—but perhaps not so far from the common realm of human striving—the continuing saga of the Cassadaga camp reminds us that modern Florida is a repository of diverse cultures, religions, and peoples.

Raymond Arsenault and Gary R. Mormino, Series Editors

# PREFACE

EVERY RELIGION must confront the problem of death. Death forces questions about the purpose of life, the nature of human existence, and the ultimate fate of the individual. Since its beginnings in 1848, Spiritualism has provided answers to these questions for Americans who could find them nowhere else. In communication with the spirits of the dead, Spiritualists hope to witness evidence that departed friends and family are still present in their lives, that they continue to be concerned about those they have left behind, and that there is no interruption between the realm in which they currently reside and the earthly realm. Early Spiritualists rebelled against the orthodox Protestant view that those who died without a Christian conversion experience were not elected by God for salvation and consequently were damned to spend eternity in hell. While concurring with the general trend of liberal theology that viewed salvation as accessible to all people, Spiritualists went further than most Christians and rejected the ideas of hell and judgment altogether. Presenting a distinctive theology and religious practice, Spiritualism takes its place along side Mormonism and Christian Science and other American additions to the world's religions.

*Cassadaga* introduces a living Spiritualist community with roots reaching back into the nineteenth century. It opens a window to a past and present, encapsulating much of the course of alternative religious belief in America over the last century. And Cassadaga confounds expectations. A religious community that places spirit communication at the center of its very existence is a surprise. Devoted to a controversial faith assumed by many to have died out long ago, it is among the longest-lived and most successful American communities dedicated to an alternative religion—having outlived parallel efforts of both the nineteenth century and the 1960s. The community's location in the American South is another puzzle. A settlement committed to a heterodox religion often associated with radical social causes, Cassadaga prospers in a region known for its religious and social conservatism.

Challenging both spatial and temporal assumptions of American religious history, Cassadaga invites us to reconsider suppositions about the character of Florida's regional religious culture. The early days of the camp's history depict a community very much at home among its Protestant neighbors. At this point, it seems, Spiritualism flourished in Florida by blending in, by stressing its cultural sympathies with Protestantism rather than its rejection of the Christian doctrine of salvation. As the twentieth century progressed and the generation that came of age in the 1960s became a force in the life of Cassadaga, the community's approach to Spiritualism returned to the broader outlook of its nineteenth-century forebears. For many early leaders Spiritualism was an encompassing and eclectic faith that could incorporate diverse teachings from the world's religions. Both a selective appeal to Asian wisdom and the claim to special relationships with the spirits of dead American Indians echo significant strands of nineteenth-century Spiritualism. The centrality of healing to Spiritualist thought and practice at Cassadaga also hearkens back to the movement's early days.

Even the recent rejection of membership in national Spiritualist organizations parallels the movement's early suspicion of institutionalization. Having escaped established church structures and teachings to listen to the unfettered voice of Spirit to the unfettered human soul, many Spiritualists found it difficult to accept the voluntary constraints necessary to unite for the promotion of their movement. The conflict between the desire to protect spiritual freedom and individual conscience and the need to organize to promote the faith has plagued Spiritualism from its earliest days. The loose structure of the community of Cassadaga, like that of Lily Dale, its northern counterpart, reflects the costs and the benefits of Spiritualist outlooks. While both have provided the flexibility to accommodate their members' beliefs, neither has experienced growth commensurate with the popularity of their teachings. As a result, Cassadaga and Lily Dale retain the intimate scale and sensibility of turn-of-the-century Spiritual resorts.

The contributors to this volume invite us to explore this unexpected religious community from a combination of perspectives as revelatory as their subject matter. They provide a model for the study of religious communities by combining both historical and ethnographic approaches with the study of material culture, as well as photographic representations of the community. Perhaps the book is most innovative in combining insider and outsider perspectives, an approach rarely taken in the study of new religious movements. The use of both perspectives allows the authors to avoid the problem posed by so many historical treatments of religious communities—that they are unrecognizable to the living proponents of the religions they depict.

Their Cassadaga is at once surprising and familiar. To travel with them to Cassadaga is not only to travel back in time but also to see how America's past is present in its most modern religious developments. At Cassadaga the New Age does not appear as a foreign element on America's religious landscape but rather as a domestic product that is as American as the Bible Belt and as deeply rooted in our national religious longings.

Ann Braude
Director, Women's Studies in Religion Program
Harvard University, The Divinity School

# INTRODUCTION

THE SPIRITUALIST CAMP in Cassadaga, Florida, is the oldest religious community of its kind in the southeastern United States. In 1993, shortly before
Cassadaga's centennial, Gary Monroe approached the camp's board of trustees
and asked them to allow him relatively free rein to photograph residents and
visitors engaged in an array of activities within the community. The board enthusiastically approved his request, and Monroe began spending time at the fifty-
seven-acre camp and learning about the religion of Spiritualism. He quickly
realized the inherent difficulty of trying to represent the multifaceted character
of Cassadaga solely through still images. Monroe therefore invited several
scholars living in the area to join the investigation. The initial group then asked
other researchers from beyond the area to participate in the project. Our group
has grown to eight members. Together we set out to pursue the study in its
fullest dimensions and to produce an edited volume of articles and photographs.

This anthology offers a fresh and fair view of Spiritualism as practiced by the
Southern Cassadaga Spiritualist Camp Meeting Association (SCSCMA). One
should note that the camp retains a distinct identity apart from the township of
Cassadaga. Many people living in the immediate vicinity but outside the camp's
boundaries are Spiritualists, and some give readings. This group includes those
mediums who work out of the Cassadaga Hotel or in homes scattered around
the wooded village. But members of SCSCMA are quick to enumerate the significant differences between their brand of Spiritualism and the kind that appears outside the campgrounds. Spiritualists beyond the camp's perimeters, for
instance, embrace a wide variety of beliefs and rituals that seem odd, irrelevant,
or dubious to SCSCMA. These range from the psychic sciences and numerology
to palmistry and the reading of tarot cards. In contrast, Spiritualists affiliated
with the association believe in an "infinite intelligence," affirm that "communication with the so-called dead is a fact" supported by empirical evidence, and
govern their lives by the Golden Rule's admonition to treat others as one would
wish to be treated.

Despite these and other such stated beliefs, too much inaccurate and distorted information often permeates local conversations about Spiritualism at

Cassadaga. Rumors that "birds don't fly over Cassadaga," for example, or that "Spiritualists practice witchcraft and worship Satan" remain popular misconceptions about the community in the surrounding vicinity. Mindful of these distortions and misunderstandings, we embarked on this project intending to provide a more accurate portrayal of Cassadaga's past and present and to explore its rich humanity and culture.

In the opening chapter, Bret E. Carroll provides a broad historical overview of American Spiritualism, noting the religious, social, and cultural forces (including religious democratization, industrialization, urbanization, the growing pace of technological innovation, and the increasing cultural authority of science) that influenced its development. Covering the period of Spiritualism's emergence in the mid-nineteenth century to the 1890s, when SCSCMA was founded, this chapter sets the community in its larger historical context. Cassadaga must be understood not as an isolated or culturally marginal phenomenon, Carroll argues, but as an authentic expression of U.S. religious and cultural life.

Carroll pays special attention to New York State, where Spiritualism arose amid the spiritual ferment then transforming Victorian America, attracted a significant number of religious seekers, and spawned the Lily Dale Spiritualist Camp of which Cassadaga became a southern branch. Along the way, the discussion considers the inner tensions that the growing popularity of mediumship generated in the Spiritualist religion, the charges of fraud often brought against Spiritualism from outside and their effect on those inside, and the trajectory of the movement's institutional development from its relatively unstructured beginnings to the creation of formal organizations in the late nineteenth and early twentieth centuries. Above all, this chapter offers a nuanced description of Spiritualist beliefs and uncovers various dimensions of the religion's appeal.

In the second chapter, "Seeking the Sweet Spirit of Harmony: Establishing a Spiritualist Community at Cassadaga, 1893–1933," John J. Guthrie, Jr., explores the first four decades of Cassadaga's existence and reconstructs the camp's history during this period, using newspaper accounts, correspondence, church records, and other source material. Guthrie examines the relationships between the newly arrived Cassadagans and local Protestants as well as relations among camp members. He argues that, despite their unorthodox religious beliefs and practices, Spiritualists generally embraced U.S. traditions and values. Thus, Cassadagans reflected the middle-class culture of the mainstream to which they belonged. By this account, then, the Spiritualists appear as rather ordinary Americans who lived ordinary lives. This chapter was previously published in the summer 1998 issue of *Florida Historical Quarterly*.

In chapter 3, Phillip Charles Lucas describes and interprets the religious system of contemporary Cassadaga. Lucas's method is primarily phenomenological as he discloses the interrelated beliefs, practices, signs, and codes that comprise Cassadaga's religious worldview and employs "structured empathy" to render an alternative religious viewpoint as lived by its adherents. To accomplish his descriptive and interpretive task, Lucas draws on a combination of sources, including the literature published by the community, oral interviews of individual members, and participant observation of the group's religious services. Lucas is particularly interested in discerning the community's ritual life, its view of the future, its healing work, its understanding of gender roles, and its recent shifts in self-understanding. Along these lines, he probes the extent to which the Cassadaga community has assimilated New Age beliefs and practices and emphasizes how its religious system reflects larger trends in U.S. culture. Finally, his chapter examines generational tensions within the camp and Cassadaga's efforts to maintain a coherent self-representation and a sense of continuity with its past, given the group's present eclecticism and doctrinal flexibility.

In 1991 the National Register of Historic Places added Cassadaga's historic district to its list. The town contains a distinctive collection of buildings developed between the 1890s and 1920s. In chapter 4, Sidney P. Johnston guides readers through the district, highlighting important sites and buildings. In the process, he reviews the specific historical architectural styles apparent in the community, including bungalow, colonial revival, and frame vernacular, which allows him to place the community within its national and statewide context of popular trends. While detailing the town's architectural features, Johnston links them to the northern and midwestern backgrounds of its key figures. All this highlights Spiritualism's historically northern appeal and Cassadaga's resulting uniqueness vis-à-vis the surrounding culture.

Because Cassadaga is one of the few alternative U.S. religious communities in continuous operation since the nineteenth century, it is a historical treasure that can reveal much about the character of Spiritualism, U.S. religious culture in the nineteenth century, and changes in religious life since that time. While none of the founders is alive, some of their immediate successors still reside in the camp. These older Spiritualists are a living repository of stories about the original goals of the camp and the changes in Spiritualism since their youth. In order to uncover these rich personal histories, Ann Jerome Croce and Paul Jerome Croce in chapter 5 put together a group biography based on their interviews with four older Cassadagans. Although the chapter's themes vary with the character of each Spiritualist, the topics remain constant. These include daily life in the camp, the sources of residents' income, the camp's structures of authority, and the residents' views of social change, relationships with the surrounding community and with other religions, and perspectives on science and religion.

Another older and respected resident, the Reverend Eloise Page, has practiced mediumship in the community for more than forty years. She has taught many students, among them, for the last decade, psychologist and art critic Anne Barclay Morgan. Although Page is nearly ninety years old, she continues her teachings of natural law and visualization, the practice of reading for others, and the interpretation of symbols. In chapter 6, Morgan provides a student's perspective of Page's method of developing psychic abilities and paints a sensitive personal portrait of a medium who is widely acclaimed for her caring, generous, and compassionate nature.

Chapter 7 presents Gary Monroe's photographic images of the camp. Because of photography's inherently personal nature, Monroe has found little need to augment wondrously ambiguous imagery with more concrete text. In other words, he remains reticent about coupling written explanations with his photographs. Such imposed interpretations, Monroe fears, too easily rationalize complex understandings by putting one face on a myriad of possible meanings. As he puts it: "Coming to terms with the image is the responsibility of the viewer."

John J. Guthrie, Jr., Phillip Charles Lucas, and Gary Monroe

# ACKNOWLEDGMENTS

WE HAVE RECEIVED much assistance in bringing this anthology to publication. In acknowledgment of these debts, we wish to thank first the Cassadagans who welcomed us into their homes, told us their stories, and shared their beliefs and insights about the camp. We are especially grateful to the board of trustees and to the Reverend Janie Henderson and the Reverend Donna Bohrer, past president and vice-president of the board, respectively. During their terms in office we initiated the Cassadaga research project. When their terms ended, they passed their responsibilities to a new board headed by Barbara Joy Hines Bengtson. During her tenure, we have brought the project to completion, thanks to her quick responses to any request for aid made by our group. We also wish to thank Fran Ellison, Vince Owens, and the Reverends Jerry Frederich, Nick Sourant, Jonathan Ellis, and Steve Adkins for the valuable assistance they provided in making this book possible.

The Sunshine State is fortunate to have the Florida Humanities Council, which serves as the steward of Florida culture. The council encourages Floridians to learn about their state's history, cultures, and various communities. Simply put, the Florida Humanities Council believes in the value of thoughtful discussion and critical thinking when engaging Florida's rich cultural resources. The council funded our project in part through a grant from the National Endowment for the Humanities. We appreciate their generous support. And we extend special thanks to Joan Bragginton and Ann Henderson for their good suggestions.

We are also indebted to Robert Ellwood and Ann Braude for their helpful editorial suggestions. Finally, we thank our editor, Meredith Morris-Babb, at the University Press of Florida for believing in our project and guiding it through the process of publication.

In memoriam

JOHN J. GUTHRIE, JR., 1955–2000

without whom this project would not have come to completion

# ONE

# The Context of Cassadaga

## *A Historical Overview of American Spiritualism*

### BRET E. CARROLL

CASSADAGA is a small and picturesque central Florida town that is rich with history and resembles many other quaint American towns. A visitor to the place can stroll narrow streets lined with oak trees, admire homes that exude Victorian charm, and meet friendly people who, like most Americans, believe in a loving God and look forward to a happy afterlife. But Cassadaga is distinct from most American towns in that it is a community of Spiritualists. Because we have been encouraged by events of recent years to view small religious groups and communities with fear and mistrust, exploring Spiritualism's historical roots and situating it in its American context should foster greater understanding of the Cassadaga Spiritualist community, its religion, and its place in American life.[1]

However bizarre outsiders might consider Spiritualism and its adherents, the religion expresses the same spiritual longings that move people to join other religious bodies. Belief in immortality, curiosity about an afterlife, and the desire to establish communication with a higher spiritual world are as old and globally widespread as humanity. Archeological, anthropological, and historical evidence suggests that belief in communication between human beings on earth and beings in an afterlife or on a higher spiritual plane has always characterized, and continues to characterize, both Western and non-Western religions. Yet modern Spiritualism was a product of the particular circumstances of nineteenth-century America. In this respect, it is much like Mormonism, which emerged in the 1820s and has become a major worldwide religious movement, and Shakerism, which emerged during the late eighteenth century, flourished and produced several communities of believers in antebellum America, and continues to fascinate and impress Americans in spite of its debatable viability.

The United States of the early to mid-nineteenth century was the site of dramatic change. The political, economic, cultural, and religious life of the young nation, particularly of the Northeast and Midwest, were altered fundamentally, and in many places rapidly by a series of developments, including political and religious democratization; geographic expansion; the rapid growth of a market economy; urbanization; industrialization; the rising authority of science and an empirical method grounded in the study of observable phenomena; and such revolutionary developments as the railroad and telegraph. These changes were accompanied by a high level of cultural and religious ferment. In particular, experimental and sometimes radical religious, social, and scientific reform movements crowded the cultural landscape, especially where the transformation of American life was most pronounced. These movements promoted cosmologies and programs for action designed to impose order on a society whose changing nature made it seem fluid and even chaotic.[2] Many of them promised the achievement of the "millennium"—the utopian state foretold in the New Testament—beginning in the United States.

Western New York lay at the center of these developments. The opening of the Erie Canal in 1825, linking the Atlantic Ocean, the Hudson River, and the cities of the East with the newly settled West, sparked the growth of such new cities as Rochester and rapidly transformed the region. As a result, religious ferment there proved especially intense.[3] The fires of revivalism spreading over the northern and western United States—which emphasized personal experience of the divine and stimulated reform of both self and society—were so recurrent and strong there during the early decades of the century that the region became known as the "burned-over district." Mormonism was born there during the 1820s after a poor young man named Joseph Smith claimed special contact with the spiritual realm and gathered followers who considered him a prophet. William Miller attracted a following with his prophecies of the world's end in 1843. The region was dotted with communitarian experiments, including that established at Oneida by believers in the free-love ideology of John Humphrey Noyes, and those of the Shakers, whose communities experienced a burst of spirit communication during the 1830s. Lecturers and practitioners in the faddish new "sciences" of mesmerism and phrenology traveled the countryside, offering theories about the organization and workings of the human mind and seeking the cosmic mainsprings of human nature. A host of amateur physicians and self-proclaimed healers hawked an array of alternative medical treatments. The area was a center of radical abolitionist activity during the three decades preceding the Civil War, and the women's rights movement offered the first major articulation of its demands there at the Seneca Falls Convention of 1848.

It was in this hotbed of experimental religious, cultural, and social activity that modern Spiritualism emerged in the late 1840s. Most modern Spiritualists pinpoint the birth of their religion on the evening of March 31, 1848, in the small rural hamlet of Hydesville, close to both Rochester and the place where Joseph Smith was led to the truths of Mormonism by what he believed to be an angel guide. There, the young girls Kate and Margaret Fox, daughters of a poor farmer, claimed to hear strange knockings that responded intelligibly to their questions. The questions posed by the Fox family and others led them to believe that the girls were being used as instruments or "mediums" of communication by the spirit of a peddler who had been murdered and buried in their basement five years earlier. (A search conducted at the time turned up no remains, though a skeleton was allegedly found in 1904 behind a collapsed cellar wall.) Joined by their older sister, Leah Fox Fish, the Fox sisters soon claimed to summon a variety of spirits, attracted attention throughout the region—especially among radical Quakers[4]—and began to hold regular gatherings for curious investigators.

Many of these investigators sought out the Foxes for entertainment and novelty, or to recover personal relationships ended by death. Many others, however, came with the more serious religious intent of establishing definitive empirical proof of human immortality and of receiving enlightening spiritual instruction from inhabitants of a higher plane. Among the latter were Eliab W. Capron, a Quaker from the nearby town of Auburn, who became an early convert to the movement and its first important publicist and historian, and the Rochester Quakers and abolitionists Isaac and Amy Post. Isaac Post developed an alphabetic communication code that was quickly dubbed the "spiritual telegraph," because it resembled and seemed to extend the marvelous new communication technology that had emerged just a few years before.

In November 1849, the Fox sisters went public with their displays, hiring out Rochester's Corinthian Hall, charging an admission fee, and drawing widespread notice. The publicity generated in Rochester attracted the attention of rising showman P. T. Barnum, who invited the Fox sisters to exhibit their mediumship at his hotel in New York City during the summer of 1850, and the famous *New York Tribune* editor and reformer Horace Greeley, who endorsed the sisters and spread the word of the rappings in the pages of his newspaper. The favorable attention they received in the metropolis was followed by a national tour through such burgeoning western cities as Cleveland and Cincinnati. Interest and publicity continued, fueled by sensational newspaper stories and the resulting controversy. Within a short time, such literary luminaries as James Fenimore Cooper, Henry Wadsworth Longfellow, and Harriet Beecher Stowe were investigating the phenomena of the séance.

As word of the "Rochester rappings" spread and the Fox sisters became nationally renowned, others, mostly women, discovered their own mediumship and held their own séances. The "spirit manifestations" quickly developed into new forms as entranced mediums, claiming to be instruments of higher spiritual powers, began to practice spirit healing, speaking and writing, clairvoyance, drawing and painting, moving and levitating objects such as tables, and playing musical instruments. In the 1860s and 1870s, the mediumistic repertoire expanded to include spirit photography and visible spirit materializations. These new phenomena gradually pushed the Fox sisters, their humble rappings, and alphabetic communication into the background. But the sisters had spearheaded a new national fad and laid part of the groundwork for a new religion based on spirit communication.

Even before the Fox family was first disturbed by noises in the night, the philosophical and theological foundations of Spiritualist religion were being laid in another part of New York State by Andrew Jackson Davis.[5] Born in the Hudson Valley town of Blooming Grove, New York, Davis was the son of a ne'er-do-well father and a mystically inclined mother. The family moved about a great deal, finally settling in Poughkeepsie. There, the young Davis floundered as a shoemaker's apprentice until 1843, when he was introduced to the wonders of the trance by itinerant mesmerist J. Stanley Grimes. Intrigued, Davis sought local tailor William Levingston, an experimenter with hypnotism, who discovered that Davis made an excellent subject. In trances induced by Levingston, Davis experienced clairvoyant visions and suggested unorthodox medical remedies. The two men began to travel, attracting curious audiences in New York and New England. In Bridgeport, Connecticut, Davis caught the attention of a group of Universalists, including Dr. Silas Lyon and ministers Samuel Byron Brittan and William Fishbough.

As Davis's travels and contacts widened, so did his trance experiences. By 1844, he was claiming to receive wisdom from the spirit world through contact with the spirits of Emanuel Swedenborg, an eighteenth-century Swedish scientist-turned-mystic, and the ancient physician Galen. These experiences initiated his career as a religious seer and healer. By the close of 1847, Davis, working with Lyon as hypnotist and Fishbough as scribe, had delivered a series of trance lectures that were published that year as *The Principles of Nature, Her Divine Revelations, and a Voice to Mankind.*[6] This massive volume, the first of many books published by Davis over the next thirty years, contained his first and most influential statement of an ideology that he and his colleagues called "harmonialism."

Harmonialism drew, in both its worldview and its adherents, on a variety of contemporary religious, scientific, and social ideologies. Above all, it drew on the ideas and experiences of Swedenborg (1688–1772), who in 1743 had begun to undergo a series of profound mystical experiences that included strange dreams, trances, and clairvoyant visions. During these experiences, he claimed, departed spirits communicated with him and revealed to him the nature of the afterlife. Swedenborg described these visions in *Heaven and Its Wonders and Hell* (1758), which offered—in a sober and matter-of-fact style that reflected his scientific background—a thoroughly detailed portrait of heaven and hell, each consisting of three hierarchically arranged "spheres," with the pivotal sphere of earthly existence between them. After death, Swedenborg believed, the soul naturally gravitated to the sphere most suited to it, where it remained for eternity. Swedenborg divided his heavens into orderly communities and subcommunities of like-minded spirits drawn together by natural and mutual attraction, while his hells were places of chaos. He developed an elaborate theology in which God acted on the universe through spirit mediators. Swedenborg also devised, in the many other volumes that he published between the 1740s and his death, a new and complex method of scriptural interpretation. By the early nineteenth century, Swedenborg's teaching had spawned in the United States a fully developed sect called the Church of the New Jerusalem (or New Church), which would later contribute several members to the Spiritualist movement.[7]

Spiritualists derived several of their religion's central features and beliefs from Swedenborg's worldview and practices, including the concept of "correspondence" or parallelism between the spiritual and material worlds; a graphic vision of a spirit world arranged into seven ascending "spheres," where the departed soul assumes a position determined by its moral and spiritual state at the moment of physical death; and an understanding of spirits as essential mediators between God and human beings on earth. Foremost, Spiritualists took up Swedenborg's practice of communicating with the inhabitants of the spirit world and made the reception of inspirational spirit messages the central and distinguishing feature of their religion. In this, they departed from Swedenborg's example, democratizing a practice that he had warned should be strictly limited. Spiritualists also rejected key elements of Swedenborg's theology, adapting it to nineteenth-century American notions of progress and upward mobility. They regarded the afterlife not as the static state imagined by Swedenborg or as a place that included a hell of eternal punishment, but as an experience of gradual advancement through the spheres as the spirit was influenced and guided toward eventual perfection by higher ministering spirits. Despite and perhaps because of their deviations from Swedenborg, Spiritualists made him a crucial symbolic figure in their religion and believed him to be a frequent visitor to their séances.[8]

Another major component of Spiritualist ideology and practice derived from the heterodox medical practices developed by Viennese physician Franz Anton Mesmer (1734–1815) and elaborated upon by his students. Mesmer postulated the existence of an invisible but universally pervasive and scientifically demonstrable magnetic fluid called "animal magnetism," which bound the universe and its contents into a physical and spiritual whole. Mesmer believed that the manipulation of one's personal portion of the fluid during hypnosis—a practice that came to be called mesmerism—could induce physical and spiritual healing. As Grimes and other traveling lecturers and practitioners of mesmerism toured the United States during the 1830s and 1840s, animal magnetism became a national fad—and for those seeking scientific insight into the nature of the human mind and soul, a phenomenon worthy of serious examination. Following the lead of the prominent American scholar and Swedenborg disciple George Bush, who endorsed Davis and suggested that the mesmeric trance had been the mechanism of Swedenborg's communication with spirits,[9] Spiritualists incorporated the magnetic fluid into their cosmology and the trance into their practice. They looked to the fluid, acting in accordance with natural law, to explain the operations of deity on the universe, the ability of advanced spirits to influence and regenerate lower ones, and the ability of spirits to seize control of mediums and to produce the various phenomena of mediumship. They used the trance as the key mechanism of spirit contact and of spiritual and physical healing.[10]

A third important ideological element of Spiritualism was the communitarian philosophy of eighteenth-century French socialist reformer Charles Fourier (1772–1837). He had suggested that social and spiritual harmony required the reorganization of human society into small communities and the establishment of all human relationships—from economic ones to sexual ones—on natural forces of attraction. His followers in the United States attempted in the 1840s and early 1850s to apply his principles through the formation of experimental communities called "phalanxes," particularly in the Northeast and Midwest. Though most phalanxes were very short-lived and all had disappeared by the middle of the 1850s (the Fourierist Union Colony, established in 1870, evolved into the town of Greeley, Colorado), Fourier's ideas continued to influence American social reformers. Through prominent and glowing mention in Davis's *Revelations*, the ideas of the French social theorist entered Spiritualist thinking.[11] With the publication of *Revelations*, the combination of Swedenborgianism, mesmerism, and Fourierism to form the harmonial ideology—which comprised the heart of Spiritualist belief—was complete.

Spiritualist ideology stemmed from a number of other sources as well, particularly the new liberal and democratic Protestant theologies that emerged during the nineteenth century to challenge orthodox Calvinist assumptions of human depravity, limited salvation, and an angry God. From Transcendentalism, a radical offshoot of Unitarianism, came a rejection of the special divinity of Jesus—who was understood as a model and teacher for the human race—a belief in the basic goodness and divine potential of every human spirit, and an emphasis on inward contemplation as an essential source of religious insight.[12] From Universalism came a conviction that all human beings would eventually be saved by a good and merciful deity, though Spiritualists followed a schismatic group of Universalists called Restorationists in adding the qualification that nonrepentant souls would require a temporary postmortem punishment in the lowest sphere before beginning their upward ascent. Quakerism contributed to Spiritualism the belief that all people possessed an "inner light" by which the divine manifested its presence in the soul. From broader liberal currents and the growing philosophical emphasis on developmentalism came a rejection of the notion of sudden conversion in favor of gradual spiritual growth. Spiritualists adopted the free-thought conviction that God operated on the universe and could therefore be understood in terms of scientifically comprehensible natural law from which miraculous deviation was impossible. From traditional Christian orthodoxy, meanwhile, Spiritualists derived their belief in divine sovereignty, human dependence on the divine, the reality of an eternal afterlife, and the obligation of living one's life in accordance with a set of absolute moral standards represented by the life of Jesus. Spiritualists also defended their practice of spirit communication in terms of Christian historical tradition and biblical accounts of ancient mediumistic phenomena, although the movement was bitterly divided between those who sought to replace Christianity and the Bible with "modern revelations" from the spirit world (Davis led an iconoclastic "anti-Bible" convention in Hartford, Connecticut, in 1853) and the "Christian" Spiritualists who sought only to supplement Christianity and scriptural authority. Another religious influence on Spiritualism, often slighted, is Native American shamanism, which had become familiar to large segments of the American public and could now be interpreted in terms of the far more familiar Judeo-Christian tradition. (The appearance of "Indian guides" at Spiritualist séances was common in the nineteenth century and continues to be a feature of contemporary Spiritualism.) Later in the century, Spiritualism and related movements such as Theosophy increasingly incorporated Asian religious beliefs.[13]

Anxious to promote their new religion, Davis and other adherents of harmonialism capitalized on the sensation created by the Fox sisters. They joined their cause with that of the spirit manifestations by endorsing the controversial phenomena, explaining them in terms of the ideas and practices of Swedenborg and Mesmer, and emphasizing the potential of spirit communication to promote personal growth and enlightenment. The product of this union between harmonialism and the practice of spirit communication was the religion of "Spiritualism," a term popularized by Horace Greeley in the pages of the *Tribune*.[14] The new religion proved especially appealing to Swedenborgians, Universalists, Unitarians, Transcendentalists, Quakers, Shakers, and freethinkers, and to reformers from such contemporary movements as abolitionism, women's rights, marriage reform, Fourierism and other forms of communitarianism, and mesmerism.

Spiritualists found in their religion an answer to perennial spiritual longings that were given specific form by the antebellum American environment. Several features of American life had combined by the middle of the nineteenth century to produce both an enormous expansion of spiritual opportunity and a profound spiritual malaise. In a development termed by Nathan O. Hatch "the democratization of American Christianity," the republican ideology of the American Revolution had encouraged a questioning of traditional sources of religious authority and exalted the validity of the individual conscience. At the same time, intensifying currents of revivalism and Romantic idealism put a premium on personal religious experience and direct individual contact with the divine.[15] The eighteenth-century Enlightenment emphasis on reason, logic, and experimental investigation as the primary sources of knowledge had generated a respect for science that Spiritualists shared with most nineteenth-century Americans. But it had also encouraged a starkly mechanistic worldview that seemed to exclude the supernatural and stimulated a Romantic response that imagined a warmer and more organic cosmos. Scientists, who enjoyed growing cultural authority in an age of scientific and technological marvels, seemed to encourage scientific materialism by denying the empirical knowability, and often even the very existence, of spirit and the human soul. Religious liberals, who provided the bulk of Spiritualism's leadership, found it increasingly difficult to believe in a personal God and turned instead to abstract and impersonal notions of a natural-law deity. A professionalizing clergy, meanwhile, seemed to sacrifice spiritual vitality and moral leadership as it sought material comfort and the approval of society's elites. Competition among sectarian and denominational organizations in the aftermath of disestablishment, combined with the appearance of several would-be prophets in the democratic religious environment of the early nineteenth century, created a growing variety of belief systems that many in the United States found bewildering. Finally, the intensely competitive economic and political system taking shape in the young republic seemed to many observers to reward the ruthless pursuit of individual self-interest, creating vast economic inequities and sapping the moral and spiritual foundations of national life. Urbanization and industrialization, meanwhile, threatened the communal and republican values that had once contained individual ambition in a framework of mutual obligation.

These developments fostered in many Americans an uneasy feeling that their cosmos was cold, that their society had exchanged moral direction for excessive materialism, that they had lost control over their surroundings, and that they had become uncomfortably dependent on themselves alone. To these people, thirsting for a sacralized world and connection with a higher reality, Spiritualism offered a fairly consistent and comforting theology and cosmology.[16] It postulated a comforting hierarchy of invisible spirits who mediated between humanity and its distant deity—not unlike the hierarchy of saints and angels characteristic of Catholic belief—and served as crucial agents of divine activity and cosmic order.[17] Spiritualists believed that warm, friendly, and "familiar" spirits guided their consciences and their society in accordance with God's will, took a strong interest in their personal concerns, and soothed them with images of a domestic and sentimental cosmos. While they believed spirit communication to be empirically demonstrable and fully in accordance with inviolable natural law, they joined Romantic thinkers in challenging the mechanical cosmos and reason-based epistemology of the Enlightenment. In its place they posited a vital organic universe and intuitive, mystical, and nonrational sources of spiritual insight that were immediately available to every individual. Their democratization of religious power permitted them to tap the wisdom of the spirit world independently of institutionalized churches and ministers, and to seek religious truth from sources other than the Bible. It promised spiritual harmony, unity, and order among all human beings on the basis of fundamental and absolute religious truths, much as the Mormon prophet Joseph Smith had held up the doctrines of Mormonism against what he considered the confusing sectarian disputation of the period. Believers enjoyed a soothing religious ritual—the séance—that combined the hymns and prayers of conventional Christianity with alternative religious forms that were centered on the private home, encouraged close contact among worshippers, and removed spiritual seekers from the bustle of everyday life. In these gatherings, spirits often predicted the coming of a new and better millennial age, characterized by cooperative values, republican ideals, and social harmony, to be brought about through the combined efforts of spirits and mortals on earth, beginning in America. The spirit of George Washington was a particularly frequent bearer of such tidings. It is not difficult to understand why such ideas, practices, and promises appealed to many dissatisfied with the simultaneously exciting and troubling currents of nineteenth-century life.

Spiritualists found in the spirits' promise of a coming utopian age not only spiritual comfort but also a rationale for their continuing dedication to the variety of moral and social reform movements of the day, particularly abolitionism, women's rights, communitarianism, temperance, marriage reform, prison reform, and peace and Christian nonresistance.[18] Spiritualism was particularly important as a vehicle for women's rights activity since it offered women opportunities for both religious roles denied them by most other religious groups and healing roles denied them by the medical establishment.[19] Spiritualist reformers occupied the same range of positions on these issues as did non-Spiritualist reformers—some were moderate, others quite radical—and moderates within the movement often strained to distance themselves and the movement from the radicals. Especially troubling to many Spiritualists was the widespread association of their movement with those notorious reformers who rejected the legal trappings of traditional marriage and urged romantic attachments based on mutual attraction in the name of women's rights and "free love." Spiritualists nevertheless agreed, both among themselves and with non-Spiritualist reformers, that the competitive nature of the country's political, social, and economic life generated chaos that needed to be tempered by religious principles of love, harmony, and order. They therefore worked both with each other and with non-Spiritualists as they followed their religious commitments into various forms of social activism. Indeed, their belief that the moral forces of the spirit world were assisting their efforts revitalized their hopes, which were sagging as the antebellum reform impulse began to wind down in the 1850s.[20]

The mounting cultural authority of science in nineteenth-century America, and the concern among many Americans that the relationship between science and religion might not be harmonious, made the Spiritualists' claim that science supported their beliefs an especially important source of the movement's appeal.[21] Seeking scientific grounding for their religion, they claimed that séance phenomena represented definitive empirical proof of human immortality. They welcomed and even encouraged scientific investigations of mediumship and complained that the scientific establishment had unnecessarily expelled spirit from its domain. They sought to eliminate supernaturalism from religious belief by insisting that spirit was a form of matter that behaved according to natural law and was amenable to scientific analysis. Spiritualist leaders were anxious to enlist scientists in their cause and were especially pleased by such conversions as that of the prominent Philadelphia chemist Robert Hare, who had at first dismissed spirit manifestations as fraud and delusion. Hare lent his scientific credentials to the cause by becoming a publicist for the movement; he published *Experimental Investigation of the Spirit Manifestations* in 1855, launched a speaking and demonstration tour on which he repeated his experiments and unsuccessfully attempted to persuade the American Association for the Advancement of Science to address the topic.[22] S. B. Brittan, a Spiritualist editor and early associate of Davis, made a similar effort, petitioning Congress to appoint a scientific committee to investigate the manifestations. Convinced that the existence of spirits had been established and that the future of religious belief in a scientific age depended upon their success, Spiritualists like Hare and Brittan bristled when the scientific establishment rejected what seemed to them to be indisputable fact. At a time when Americans marveled at the mysterious phenomena of electricity and magnetism, postulated invisible fluids to explain them, and were amazed at new inventions like the electromagnetic telegraph, the notion that science and technology might illuminate the spiritual world did not seem farfetched.

There were, of course, other reasons for Spiritualism's appeal. It provided consolation for those whose loss of friends and relatives to the common occurrence of premature death left them wanting scientific assurance that the soul survived the dissolution of the physical body, the certainty of future reunion with loved ones in the afterlife, and an opportunity to chat with the departed in the meantime. (The greater control we now have over the occurrence of premature death has by no means eliminated this need for reassurance.) Indeed, Spiritualism was an important expression of a Victorian "cult of death" as "manifested in a 'rural cemetery' movement" and elaborate mourning rituals during the 1840s and 1850s.[23] It also promised new sensations to those whose experiences with accelerating advances in science and technology, and with the emerging industry of popular entertainment, left them continually hungry for novelties. The Americans who gaped at the unusual phenomena of the séance—the tables that rose from the floor, the concerts played on floating instruments by invisible hands, the entranced mediums who delivered spirit messages, and the actual appearance of spirits before their eyes—undoubtedly found good theater.[24] Still, these sources of Spiritualism's appeal should not overshadow its fundamentally religious content and purposes. Believers have consistently understood the physical phenomena as little more than the starting point of belief, signposts to something higher, doorways to the profound spiritual knowledge that regular contact with advanced spirits would provide.[25]

The new religion attracted considerable negative attention and developed a disreputable public image from the start. Sensing (correctly) that Spiritualism was potentially and often practically inimical to the authority of Scripture and established clergy, ministers from several denominations branded it necromancy and witchcraft. Other critics associated Spiritualism with the notorious free-love movement—which used the harmonial ideology to develop new understanding of sexual relations—and held it up as a stimulus to immorality. Still others in this age of Barnum accused mediums of practicing commercially driven fraud and "humbug," and a series of scientific investigations—including one by a team of professors from the University of Buffalo Medical School in 1851 and another by a team of prominent Harvard scientists in 1857—added fuel to such charges with their negative and critical conclusions. A particularly damaging wave of well-publicized debunkings occurred in the 1860s, 1870s, and 1880s, highlighted by the unfavorable 1887 report of the Seybert Commission[26] (which investigated Spiritualism under the auspices of the University of Pennsylvania at the bequest of wealthy Philadelphia Spiritualist Henry Seybert) and the 1888 confession by the Fox sisters to having produced the rappings with their toes. Metaphysically inclined Spiritualists bemoaned the emphasis on the physical phenomena of mediumship but were frustrated. Debunking ranging from sensational exposés by Harry Houdini to the recent activities of the Amazing Randi continued in the twentieth century and remains a major obstacle to both Spiritualism's public acceptance and its hopes for scientific verification.

Despite the negative publicity—and perhaps in part because of it—the Spiritualist movement grew rapidly during the early 1850s. Serious believers and more casual investigators of mediumistic phenomena formed séance circles throughout the nation, mostly in the Northeast and Midwest and to a lesser degree—because of its association with abolitionism and other radical reforms—in the South.[27] Many of these circles proved to be enduring and effectively met their members' spiritual needs. By 1851, more than 150 regular circles were functioning in New York City and 60 in Philadelphia, with thousands of others nationwide.[28] By the middle of the decade, New York and Boston had emerged as especially important centers of Spiritualist activity; each had large numbers of public mediums and private circles, one or more lecture series, publishing houses, and Spiritualist periodicals. Smaller cities, such as Rochester, Buffalo, Providence, Cleveland, Cincinnati, and St. Louis, became secondary centers. By 1860, the movement had spread as far as New Orleans, Texas, and San Francisco. While activity tended to concentrate in urban areas, it could also be found in rural settings ranging from New England and New York State, where the movement showed great strength, to Iowa and Wisconsin in the Midwest to Tennessee and Georgia in the South. The movement crossed not only geographic lines but also lines of class, race, and ethnicity. Even so, the majority of its leadership was white, Protestant, and middle class.[29]

Spiritualist leaders took pride in numbering among the converted not only prominent scientists like Hare but also important public officials—including John W. Edmonds, a judge on the New York Court of Appeals, and Nathaniel P. Tallmadge, a former governor of Wisconsin and U.S. senator—whose conversion lent stature to the movement. Attempts to measure the number of Spiritualists in the nineteenth century are problematic if not impossible because of the lack of formal Spiritualist organizations and the varying motives and levels of interest among those who attended séances. Contemporary estimates varied widely. The only safe conclusion is that "there were several hundred thousand men and women who were to one degree or another interested in spiritualism."[30] Like Mormonism, Spiritualism became an American export, spreading into France, Latin America (especially Brazil, where it remains popular), Canada, Australia, New Zealand, South Africa, and other countries.

Resistance to large-scale organization was one of Spiritualism's most salient features, particularly during its early history.[31] Spiritualists of the 1850s tended to be fiercely independent, considering the individual conscience a more reliable source of truth than institutions, creeds, and clergy. They resisted what they considered the stifling and antidemocratic encrustations of organized Christianity, arguing that religious organizations, doctrines, and leadership hierarchies inevitably hardened into authoritative structures that frustrated spiritual growth and spontaneous religious feeling. They were outspokenly determined, most of them insisted, to avoid replicating the formalistic rigidity that they felt had enervated previous religious movements. The only important attempt by Spiritualists of the pre–Civil War period to form a national organization—the Society for the Diffusion of Spiritual Knowledge (SDSK), formed and led in New York City in 1854 by a group of wealthy, socially prominent, and self-consciously Christian Spiritualists—folded amid a tide of hostile essays and letters. In its resistance to large-scale organization, Spiritualism stood in sharp contrast to other new and "alternative" religious movements of the nineteenth century—such as Mormonism, Shakerism, the New Church, and, later in the century, Christian Science—which built tightly organized institutional structures around authoritative texts, creeds, and leaders.

Still, the new movement was by no means entirely lacking in structure and organization; the very attempt to form the SDSK was perhaps as important an indicator of trends in Spiritualism as the SDSK's rapid demise.[32] The Spiritualists' universe was above all an organized and orderly place, and they were determined to replicate that cosmic order in their earthly religious lives. The ideology and practice of Spiritualism, grounded in the cosmic visions of Swedenborg, Mesmer, and Fourier, as well as in the social and political concepts of republicanism, positively encouraged the formation of small communities of like-minded believers. Furthermore, while Spiritualists believed in theory that all people had equal potential for spiritual inspiration and looked forward to a time when every person would be able to establish direct contact with the spirit world, they also believed that some people were especially well endowed with powers of mediumship and might serve as attractive centers for small groups of followers. The result was a movement arranged into small but well-structured circles displaying strongly cohesive qualities as their members sought to forge bonds of religious community.[33]

Circles of religious Spiritualists, typically composed of a dozen or so people, tended to endure and to meet on a regular basis, at scheduled times and places, for the purpose of conducting a more or less formalized religious ritual that combined innovative elements with those of conventional Christian worship. On the one hand, they met not in churches but rather in dimly lit rooms in the homes of mediums. Spiritualists looked to these mediums, usually women, rather than to ordained clergy, usually men, as their liaisons with the spirit world and as spiritual teachers with important religious authority (women continue to occupy a large number of pastoral positions in Spiritualist religious organizations and communities).[34] Unlike participants in traditional Christian services, they hoped through close contact around a small table to establish enlightening communion with spirits whose passage from the limitations of earthly existence to a higher plane qualified them to offer profound spiritual wisdom. Yet the séance ritual retained the familiar practices of opening and closing benedictions, an appropriately reverential deportment, prayer, singing of hymns, delivery of homiletic messages, selective membership, a sense of congregational belonging, and sometimes readings from Spiritualist texts. Some Spiritualists, emphasizing the religiously inspirational functions of the circle, compared séance meetings to the revival meetings that had become a fixture of American religious life. (On the connection between Spiritualism and revivalism, see Carroll, *Spiritualism*, 127–129.)

Spiritualism's small-scale organizational thrust and conventional features make comprehensible the eventual formation of formal Spiritualist institutions and large-scale organizations, beginning gradually in the 1850s and accelerating in the latter decades of the nineteenth century. If national organizations did not take shape during the 1850s, smaller associations on the local, state, and regional levels, such as the New England Spiritualist Association and the Ohio and Wisconsin State Spiritualist Associations, did emerge. To be sure, these organizations never won the allegiance of all, or even a majority, of the Spiritualists in their respective geographic areas, but their existence indicates the organizational impulse that was at work in this as in most religious movements.[35] State and regional Spiritualist conventions, too, met on a fairly regular basis beginning in 1852. These were often wracked by internal conflict—attendees were in most cases unable to agree on specific religious doctrines or social reform commitments, or to create permanent convention structures—but were nonetheless similarly suggestive of Spiritualism's organizational tendencies.

An equally telling sign of developments to come was the appearance in the 1850s of Spiritualist churches, which were more institutionalized forms of the private circle meeting, and the gradual establishing of procedures (generally relaxed) for ordaining mediums as ministers, which resulted in the ordination of James H. Powell as the first Spiritualist minister in 1869.[36] The federal census listed 17 Spiritualist churches in 1860, 95 in 1870, 334 in 1890, and 455 in 1906, with membership in the latter two years numbering in the tens of thousands— a sign of a growing impetus toward church organization among Spiritualists. The census suggests that these churches tended to be urban, to spread in tandem with the general westward thrust of the movement, and above all to be evanescent (the large majority of the 1906 churches had lasted for fifteen years or less). Lacking centralized leadership and an authoritative set of writings, Spiritualist churches were "distinctly congregational," with authority resting firmly in the hands of the individual church rather than in an overarching organization.[37] Lacking money, they usually did not own real estate and met in rented rooms, halls, and private homes; less than one quarter of the 95 churches in 1870 or the 455 in 1906 had edifices, and almost none of those buildings had been erected by Spiritualists themselves.

The religious practices of Spiritualist churches throughout the nineteenth and twentieth centuries, like those of the private circles, have in many ways resembled those of conventional Protestant groups. The Bible has typically been consulted as an authoritative religious text, and services have usually included an invocation, prayers, hymns, and a sermon or lecture. At the same time, Spiritualist church services have been unique in their doctrinal content, the often entranced state of the person delivering the sermon or lecture, and the practice of receiving spirit messages through a medium. Spiritualists in urban areas began in 1853 to hold regular, large-scale, and formalized public Sunday services that transferred the ritual of the private circle to a larger public setting. Boston Spiritualists, for example, flocked to the Melodeon, and their New York counterparts to the Stuyvesant Institute, then Hope Chapel, and finally Dodworth's Hall. Like the meetings of the circle and private church, these gatherings involved a general order of ritual that combined conventional practices with the reception of spirit communications. They also included readings from Spiritualist works and a featured speaker, male or female. These and other regularized religious practices, including midweek message and healing services and personal development classes, have become standard among most Spiritualist groups.[38]

The outdoor summer camp meeting was another practice that brought together large numbers of Spiritualists—in this case thousands of them—in an institutionalized setting. Camp meetings, like Spiritualist churches, first appeared during the 1850s, usually gathering for a few days at scattered locations and attracting relatively small numbers. Though there was a large meeting in Chautauqua County in western New York in September 1858, highly popular and more permanent camps emerged only in the 1870s and after. In its early days, the environment of the summer camp was more festive than solemn—drawing complaints from serious believers like S. B. Brittan—and therefore bore only a remote resemblance to the outdoor camp meetings of Protestant revivalism. Private consultations with mediums and lectures by popular Spiritualist speakers, moreover, seem to have been more typical than the more communal religious practices of holding circles and formal religious services. Before the nineteenth century ended, however, the camps were becoming more formalized institutions, adding increasingly well structured religious activities to popular lectures and lighter fare. In any case, the gathering of Spiritualists in these camps highlighted shared Spiritualist beliefs and enhanced bonds of community, therefore providing "an important sense of coherence and cohesion" among believers.[39]

The largest of the late-nineteenth-century camps was Lake Pleasant in Massachusetts. Consisting of tents when it was established in 1874, it grew by 1890 to include five hundred cottages, a grocery store, and a hotel, and offered band concerts, dancing, and refreshment stands as well as a variety of mediums, fortune tellers, magnetic and electric healers, and inspirational Sunday lectures. But while Lake Pleasant was the largest of the Spiritualist camps, the most famous was the Cassadaga Lake Free Association, established in Chautauqua County, New York, in 1879 and renamed Lily Dale in 1906. At its height in the early twentieth century, this eighty-acre camp encompassed several hundred cottages, indoor and outdoor meeting places, a hotel, a store, a post office, a library, athletic fields, and a fire department. Visitors to the camp could find an abundance of mediums, teachers, astrologers, palmists, and healers. It became the leading Spiritualist mecca of the early twentieth century—particularly after the Fox cottage was removed to the site in 1916 as a sort of shrine—and still flourishes today.

During the latter part of the nineteenth century, similar camps appeared in warmer climates to provide winter havens for northern Spiritualists. Among these was the Southern Cassadaga Spiritualist Camp Meeting Association, established in Florida in 1894 as a counterpart to the New York site and explored in the chapters that follow. Spiritualist camps, like Spiritualist religion more generally, faced the perennial problems of financial weakness and unfriendly press reports of fraudulent mediumship and free love, and most eventually disappeared after seasons of poor attendance or natural disaster forced them into chronic debt or complete suspension. Lily Dale, Florida's Cassadaga community, and the other remaining camps—most of which have evolved into permanent Spiritualist communities—still face public skepticism but continue to be an important source of vitality in the movement.

Some groups of Spiritualists also attempted to institutionalize their religious lives and dedication to social reform through communitarian experiments similar to those of other American reformers.[40] In some cases, previously existing experimental communities became hotbeds of Spiritualist activity when their leading lights embraced the new religion in the early 1850s. Prominent examples are Hopedale, created in Massachusetts in 1841 by Adin Ballou, a former Universalist minister, abolitionist, and Christian nonresistant, and Modern Times, established on Long Island in 1850 by philosophical anarchists Josiah Warren and Stephen Pearl Andrews.[41]

Other intentional communities were created by Spiritualists under what they considered spirit directives, specifically for the purpose of holy living based on Spiritualist principles. One of the best known of these was the short-lived community of Harmonia, located near the village of Kiantone in western New York. It was established by John Murray Spear, a charismatic and enigmatic medium who embarked on a mission of religious benevolence after several decades of activity as an abolitionist, prison reformer, and Universalist minister. Chosen by Spear in 1852 because he thought that the spring water in the area had healing powers, the spot would become the site of a model summer community patterned after the harmony of the cosmos and directed through Spear by his spirit guides. The residents, never many in number, probably experimented with communal property arrangements and certainly indulged their penchant for such architectural innovations as octagonal and oval houses. The public responded with ridicule and charges of sexual immorality, fueled by rumors of Spear's extramarital affair with an amanuensis and then of the woman's pregnancy. The community dissolved in 1858 amid public disapproval, internal dissension, financial difficulty, and Spear's increasing interest in other projects. (Similar problems beset and destroyed contemporary non-Spiritualist communitarian ventures as well.)[42]

Another attempt at a Spiritualist utopia, even more short-lived, was the Mountain Cove Community, formed in 1851 in what is now West Virginia by a group of migrants from the Spiritualist hotbed of Auburn, in western New York. Convinced by their spirit guides that their southward journey had led them to the spot of the actual Garden of Eden and seeking under spiritual inspiration to recover the Edenic state on earth, James L. Scott and a group of followers set up an agricultural community on what they considered a "Holy Mountain." Scott, soon joined by Thomas Lake Harris, quickly attempted to establish complete autocratic control over the community and divine stewardship over the property of its residents. Like Kiantone, Mountain Cove was plagued by internal tensions and lack of funds. It collapsed in 1853.[43] In the latter decades of the century, Spiritualists joined other communitarians in founding communities in the newly developing and relatively permissive states of the West, particularly California. Thomas Lake Harris, for instance, established the mystical Fountain Grove community near Santa Rosa in 1875, and, in the 1880s, John B. Newbrough tried to attract urban religious seekers of the East to the Shalam colony in New Mexico.[44]

One of the most effective methods of establishing community and structured relationships among Spiritualists was the creation and distribution of periodicals, the first of which appeared in 1847 when Davis and the original harmonial group established the *Univercoelum and Spiritual Philosopher*. Such periodicals proliferated quickly in the years that followed. Wherever the movement gained a sufficiently strong foothold, Spiritualist newspapers emerged to announce, solidify, and, if possible, expand its presence by offering philosophical essays, reports of the latest developments, schedules of upcoming events, and listings of available mediums. The Northeast was home to the bulk of the early periodicals, and, in the larger cities such as Boston and New York, one could find several at any one time. But Spiritualist papers were also published during the 1850s in Philadelphia, Cleveland, Cincinnati, Chicago, St. Louis, and New Orleans, as well as in Vermont, Wisconsin, and Georgia. Later in the century, they appeared in California and other western states. Spiritualist colonies and camps issued their own newspapers to publicize their existence and to cement bonds of community among their members; Hopedale's *Practical Christian,* Mountain Cove's *Mountain Cove Journal,* and the Cassadaga Free Lake Association's *Cassadagan* (1892–1897) and *Sunflower* (1890–1909) are a few examples. Most Spiritualist papers suffered from chronically low subscription rates and folded early, but there were occasional and important exceptions. The *Spiritual Telegraph,* published in New York from 1852 to 1860, was the longest-lived and most widely circulated periodical of the 1850s, while two later papers—Boston's *Banner of Light* (1857–1907) and Chicago's *Religio-Philosophical Journal* (1865–1907)— flourished for several decades, reached large Spiritualist audiences, and became important institutions in the movement.[45] The Cassadaga Association's *Sunflower* also enjoyed a long life, contributing to the stability of the association that published it. Spiritualists persisted in establishing periodicals despite their frequent unprofitability—more than seventy-five different titles appeared during the 1850s alone, with several hundred more appearing during the following decades—because they served a function crucial to the movement. However financially unsuccessful, they succeeded in creating what one historian has called "reader communities" that helped to compensate for the movement's lack (particularly in its early decades) of strong formal organizations by serving as a clearinghouse for information and communication.[46]

The movement's increasingly powerful organizational thrust found its most decisive expression in the formation and proliferation of permanent state, and eventually national, associations, beginning in the final decades of the nineteenth century.[47] It first began to gain momentum in the 1860s in response to a decline in enthusiasm brought on by the damaging Harvard report of 1857 and the onset of the Civil War, and accelerated amid a broader cultural trend toward large-scale institutionalization in American life.[48] Spiritualists in several states of the Northeast and Midwest (as well as California) created formal associations in 1866, 1867, and 1868, and by the middle of the following decade most states in those regions had operating organizations. While these state institutions lacked, and were not meant to have, effective governing power over their membership, they did circulate information, formulate policy for approval or disapproval by local churches, and push for fair treatment by the government and the press.

The move toward an overarching national structure in the late nineteenth century was more halting—"rather painful and not wholly successful" as one commentator has accurately summarized it.[49] Serious efforts began at a national Spiritualist convention held in Chicago in 1864, the first of an annual series that indicated the movement's strengthening structural thrust. There, a resolution to form a national organization and central committee was introduced. The resulting debate was stormy, and the resolution was defeated, but pro-organizationists at the 1865 convention in Philadelphia succeeded in establishing the National Organization of Spiritualists. Throughout its short life, the organization was weak, lacking money, authority over local churches, and the ability to draw lower-level organizations into affiliation with it. It did, however, manage to keep the annual conventions going. The American Association of Spiritualists, organized to replace it at the 1868 convention in Rochester, was only slightly stronger. It was resisted not only by the anti-organizationists outside of it but also by conservatives and purists within it who were alienated by its commitment to reforms they considered extraneous to Spiritualism proper—including women's suffrage, opposition to war and capital punishment, and temperance—and by the election to its presidency in 1871 of Victoria Woodhull, the outspoken feminist, socialist, and free-love advocate. The association expired in 1873, and the move toward national organization subsided for a time.

Two important and particularly demoralizing developments of the later 1870s and 1880s decisively renewed the push. One of these was the emergence of competing religious movements, especially Christian Science and Theosophy. Growing numbers of middle-class Americans whose spiritual searching for religious alternatives to conventional Christianity might have led to Spiritualism turned instead to these two new movements. Both were launched by people—Mary Baker Eddy in the case of the former, and Helena Petrovna Blavatsky and Henry Steel Olcott in the case of the latter—who had been influenced by Spiritualism, offered worldviews that resembled that of Spiritualism in important respects, and successfully capitalized on Spiritualism's vulnerability to charges of fraud by publicly distancing themselves from the movement. Theosophy and especially Christian Science also offered well-organized institutional structures that made them effective competitors. The other important new challenge to Spiritualism during the late nineteenth century was the appearance during the 1880s of psychical research societies—most notably the American Society for Psychical Research, organized in 1885—that used scientific methods to seek nonspiritual explanations for mediumistic phenomena as well as for telepathy, hypnotism, clairvoyance, and other paranormal phenomena. Psychical research expanded considerably in the half century that followed.

Faced with these new threats, as well as with the perennial problems of financial weakness and sensational exposés of fraud, Spiritualists organized in an attempt to define their religion, solidify their membership, seek federal recognition and legal protection from a hostile press, and enhance their fund-raising ability. In the long run, they focused increasingly on personal spiritual development and decreasingly on the phenomena that had made them vulnerable to debunkers and the inroads of psychical research. In short, they were struggling to establish and preserve their position on the American religious landscape.

The most important result of their organizational efforts was the formation of the National Spiritualist Association (NSA). The NSA was created in 1893 by a convention of Spiritualists in Chicago, where the movement was strongest, the Psychical Science Congress was gathering, and the World Parliament of Religions was being held. The convention was led by former Universalist ministers James M. Peebles and Harrison D. Barrett. Head of the Cassadaga Lake Free Association and, later, editor of the *Banner of Light,* Barrett was chosen as the organization's first president. Empowered by its constitution to compile statistics, arrange for the education of lecturers and teachers, and raise revenue, the NSA won the loyalty of most state and local Spiritualist organizations by 1906. It avoided internal squabbling more successfully than had its predecessors by focusing on organizational, educational, and advisory activities, and leaving divisive questions of theology, politics, and reform to the consciences of individual members. (It did adopt a formal though loosely worded creed in 1896.) It was therefore able to exercise considerable informal influence during the early years of the twentieth century, and it effectively spearheaded the passage of Spiritualism from the home circles and stage demonstrations of the nineteenth century to the relatively ecclesiastical character it has assumed in the twentieth. Rivals to the NSA soon emerged, but it remains the largest of the approximately fifty existing national Spiritualist organizations.[50]

The existence of so many different organizations suggests that the Spiritualists' drive to organize did not result in the degree of institutional unity and success enjoyed by other American denominations. The individualistic nature of Spiritualist religion prevented the NSA from becoming a strong governing body capable of articulating an authoritative Spiritualist creed. As an institution with little formal authority, the association could do little to strengthen local churches against instability and lack of financial resources. The NSA also struggled to maintain its own unity amid a growing concern among some of its members— a concern that had driven Andrew Jackson Davis from affiliation with the movement by the 1880s—that it focused its attention on séance phenomena and scientific research to the neglect of inner spirituality and religious philosophy. Several members withdrew from the NSA over this matter in 1907, forming the Progressive Spiritual Church in an attempt to "lift spiritualism above mere psychic research, to establish it upon a sound religious basis, and to secure its recognition among other Christian bodies."[51] Another internal dispute in the NSA led to the formation of the rival National Spiritualist Alliance a few years later. Still other Spiritualists sought a more authoritative institutional structure than existing organizations provided, and in the twentieth century small groups formed such highly centralized institutions as the Churches of Spiritual Revelation Association and the Spiritualist Episcopal Church.

Beset by financial weakness, internal division, competing religious philosophies, debunking and charges of fraud, and scientific explanations for psychic phenomena, Spiritualism has experienced shifting fortunes over its century and a half of existence. It never regained the level of popularity it enjoyed during the 1850s, though the early 1870s and 1920s witnessed revivals of interest, in both cases fueled by a desire for communication with wartime casualties and in the latter case by the energetic worldwide promotional activity of famous convert Arthur Conan Doyle (1859–1930).[52] The most recent revitalization of interest occurred during the 1960s as part of a broader fascination with alternative spiritual expressions, and spirit "channeling" is one of the several elements that constitute the eclectic New Age movement.

The two twentieth-century Spiritualist revivals, those of the 1920s and 1960s, witnessed a resurgence of the division between Spiritualists who consider themselves "Christian" and defend the supreme authority of the Bible—including such conservative bodies as the NSA—and those, including the residents of Florida's Cassadaga community, who supplement the Bible with alternative revelations from the spirit world.[53] In addition, twentieth-century Spiritualism has divided over the question of reincarnation, which began to enter the debate in alternative religious circles as Indian and other Eastern religious philosophies became increasingly influential in the late nineteenth century. Both sources of tension in the movement owe much to the appearance of new Spiritualist works that have departed further from traditional Christian belief than early Spiritualist texts, been accorded scriptural status by some Spiritualist groups, and added reincarnation to the more longstanding Spiritualist themes of spiritual evolution, a higher reality than the physical, and other worlds. One of these, John B. Newbrough's *Oahspe* (1882), tells of humanity's origins on a now lost Pacific continent and predicts a coming utopian age. Another, Levi H. Dowling's *Aquarian Gospel of Jesus Christ* (1907), contains alleged events in the life of Christ, including a trip to India, not found in the New Testament. More recent is the anonymous *Urantia Book* (1955), which discusses the spiritual organization of the universe, the religious history of earth, and the life of Jesus. Each of these works is still in print and widely read by Spiritualists.

Whether self-consciously "Christian" or not, Spiritualist churches, communities, and other organizations continue to attract Americans dissatisfied with conventional religious life. About 150,000 Americans today claim Spiritualism as their religion.[54] These include the residents of Florida's Cassadaga, now the oldest active religious community in the southeastern United States. Along with contemporary proponents of Scientology, Transcendental Meditation, UFO cults, and New Age religion, the Spiritualists of today testify to both the enduring individualistic thrust in American religious life, by which believers seek to cultivate inner spirituality and a personal faith, and the continuing American quest for spiritual order and cosmic connection in a complex and changing world.

## Notes

1. Spiritualism in the United States has attracted increasing scholarly attention in recent decades. See Braude, *Radical Spirits*; Carroll, *Spiritualism*; and Moore, *In Search of White Crows*. Two older studies are still useful; see Lawton, *Drama of Life after Death*, and Podmore, *Modern Spiritualism*.

2. An excellent recent statement of this view of antebellum religion and reform is Abzug, *Cosmos Crumbling*. Spiritualism has been interpreted in this light in Carroll, *Spiritualism*.

3. Cross, *The Burned-Over District*, is still the best treatment of religion, reform, and the social and economic factors influencing them in western New York in the early to mid-nineteenth century.

4. The early involvement of radical Quakers with Spiritualism is discussed in Braude, *Radical Spirits*, 12–15.

5. On Davis, see the following, all by Delp: "Andrew Jackson Davis and Spiritualism,"

"Andrew Jackson Davis," "Andrew Jackson Davis's *Revelations,*" and "The Harmonial Philosopher."

6. Davis, *The Principles of Nature.*

7. On Swedenborg, see George F. Dole and Robert H. Kirven, *A Scientist Explores Spirit* (New York: Swedenborg Foundation, 1992); Cyriel Odhner Sigstedt, *The Swedenborg Epic* (New York: Bookman Associates, 1952); Signe Toksvig, *Emanuel Swedenborg, Scientist and Mystic* (New Haven: Yale University Press, 1948); and George Trobridge, *Swedenborg: Life and Teaching,* 5th ed. (New York: Swedenborg Foundation, 1992). There is no published scholarly analysis of Swedenborg's influence in the United States, but see Richard Kenneth Silver, "The Spiritual Kingdom in America: The Influence of Emanuel Swedenborg on American Society and Culture, 1815–1860" (Ph.D. diss., Stanford University, 1983). The Church of the New Jerusalem, a sect founded on his writings, has been examined in Block, *New Church in the New World,* and Swank, "The Unfettered Conscience"; its connection with Spiritualism is addressed in Carroll, *Spiritualism,* 29–33, and Swank, "The Unfettered Conscience."

8. On the Spiritualist conception of the afterlife, see Carroll, *Spiritualism,* 60–84 (which also examines the Spiritualist adaptation of Swedenborg, 21–25), and Lawton, *Drama of Life after Death,* 35–132.

9. Bush, *Mesmer and Swedenborg.*

10. On mesmerism, see Darnton, *Mesmerism and the Enlightenment,* and Fuller, *Mesmerism.* On the association between Spiritualism and mesmerism, see Carroll, *Spiritualism,* 18; Fuller, *Mesmerism,* 83, 95–100; and Moore, *White Crows,* 9.

11. Fourier's thought has been examined in Beecher, *Charles Fourier,* and Riasanovsky, *The Teaching of Charles Fourier.* On Fourierism in America, see Guarneri, *Utopian Alternative.* On the connection between Fourierism and Spiritualism, see Carroll, *Spiritualism,* 18–19, and Guarneri, *Utopian Alternative,* 348–53.

12. Moore has criticized Spiritualists for "transforming a concern for man's inward spiritual nature into an empirical inquiry into the nature of spirits" in their attempt to garner scientific support, but I have suggested that Spiritualists both explored inner spirituality and sought scientific confirmation of their beliefs. See Moore, *White Crows,* 7, 19, and Carroll, *Spiritualism,* 110–11.

13. Whether Spiritualism ought to be considered a part of the Christian tradition or an alternative to it has been a topic of debate among religious historians. Spiritualism's "alternative" features have been emphasized by Frankiel, *California's Spiritual Frontiers,* and Judah, *Metaphysical Movements in America,* while its fundamentally "Christian" nature has been suggested by Butler in *Sea of Faith,* 253–54, and "The Dark Ages of American Occultism, 1760–1848," in *The Occult in America: New Historical Perspectives,* ed. Howard Kerr and Charles L. Crow (Urbana: University of Illinois Press, 1983), 72. I have taken a middle position in Carroll, *Spiritualism,* 8–10.

14. Isaacs, "Nineteenth-Century American Spiritualism," 102–3.

15. Hatch, *Democratization of American Christianity.*

16. Moore (*White Crows,* 42) has denied that Spiritualism offered a coherent belief system, but I agree with Mary Farrell Bednarowski, Ann Braude, George Lawton, and Alex Owen that Spiritualists did articulate a coherent religious worldview. See Bednarowski, "Nineteenth-Century American Spiritualism," 4, 22; Braude, *Radical Spirits,* 6,

32–55; Carroll, *Spiritualism,* 6 and passim; Lawton, *Drama of Life after Death,* ix; and Owen, *The Darkened Room,* xviii.

17. Comparisons of Spiritualist religion to Catholicism—which proved similarly attractive to antebellum Protestants troubled by the austerity of Protestant theology—have been drawn by Carroll, *Spiritualism,* 79–81, and Lawton, *Drama of Life after Death,* 578.

18. On the connection between the philosophies of Spiritualism and abolitionism, see Perry, *Radical Abolitionism,* 213–22, 276–78. On Spiritualism and free love, see Perry, *Radical Abolitionism,* 213–16, and Spurlock, *Free Love,* 2, 97–98, 138, 140, 143–44, 151, 171, 196–98. On Spiritualism and women's rights, see Braude, *Radical Spirits.*

19. Braude, *Radical Spirits.*

20. This waning of the antebellum reform impulse has been noted by Higham in *From Boundlessness to Consolidation.* A direct relationship between this development and the emergence of Spiritualism has been suggested in Carroll, *Spiritualism,* 102 ff., and Moore, *White Crows,* 88.

21. This dimension of Spiritualism is at the heart of Moore's interpretation in *White Crows,* as well as of Bednarowski, "Nineteenth-Century American Spiritualism." On science and religion in antebellum America, see Conser, *God and the Natural World,* and Hovenkamp, *Science and Religion in America.*

22. Hare, *Experimental Investigation.*

23. On the Victorian fascination with death, see Curl, *Victorian Celebration of Death;* Douglas, *Feminization of American Culture,* 240–72; and Morley, *Death, Heaven, and the Victorians.*

24. On this point, see Moore, *Selling God,* 125–27.

25. On this point, see Carroll, *Spiritualism,* 125–27.

26. *Preliminary Report of the Seybert Commission.*

27. Spiritualism in the nineteenth-century South has received little scholarly attention. The most thorough treatment of which I am aware—Delp, "Southern Press"—focuses on hostility rather than adherence to Spiritualism in the antebellum South.

28. Carroll, *Spiritualism,* 124–25.

29. See Braude, *Radical Spirits,* 28–31, and Butler, *Sea of Faith,* 255.

30. Brown, "Spiritualism in Nineteenth-Century America," 112.

31. On this point, see Braude, *Radical Spirits,* 163–73, and Moore, *White Crows,* 13–14.

32. Most historians have emphasized Spiritualism's antiorganizational and anti-institutional tendencies; see Braude, *Radical Spirits,* 163–73; Isaacs, "Nineteenth-Century American Spiritualism," 221–37; and Moore, *White Crows,* 13–14.

33. This point is argued at greater length in Carroll, *Spiritualism,* 123–25, 152–62. The practices of Spiritualist circles are explored on 129–40.

34. On the authority of the Spiritualist medium, see Braude, *Radical Spirits* 82–98, and Carroll, *Spiritualism,* 143–51. Braude focuses largely on the ways in which Spiritualism empowered women in nineteenth-century America.

35. One scholar has called structural tendencies "the stuff of religious life"; see Stein, "Shaker Gift and Shaker Order."

36. The data in this paragraph are derived from Bureau of the Census, *Religious Bodies,* 1:102–4, 402, 565; 2:269.

37. Brown, "Spiritualism in Nineteenth-Century America," 154.

38. On Spiritualist church services, see Brown, ibid., 156–58; Carroll, *Spiritualism*, 156–57; Isaacs, "Nineteenth-Century American Spiritualism," 213–14; and Lawton, *Drama of Life after Death*, 189–252.

39. Moore, *White Crows*, 67; on Spiritualist camps, see also Braude, *Radical Spirits*, 173–75; Brown, "Spiritualism in Nineteenth-Century America," 165–74; Carroll, *Spiritualism*, 157–58; Lawton, *Drama of Life after Death*, 292–371 (he includes a list of the camps on 599–600).

40. I examine the relation between Spiritualism and broader communitarian ideology in Carroll, "Spiritualism and Community," and in *Spiritualism*, 162–76.

41. On Hopedale, see Ballou, *Hopedale Community*; Padelford, "Adin Ballou," esp. 277–80; and Spann, *Hopedale*. On Modern Times, see Spurlock, *Free Love*, 107–38, and Wunderlich, *Low Living and High Thinking*.

42. On the Kiantone community, see Duino, "Utopian Theme with Variations"; Isaacs, "Nineteenth-Century American Spiritualism" 251–55; and Miller, "Utopian Communities." Spear's life, including his activities at Kiantone, are examined in Lehman, "Life of John Murray Spear." Spear left a brief autobiographical chronicle of his activities, *Twenty Years on the Wing*.

43. On the Mountain Cove community, see Carroll, "Spiritualism and Community" and *Spiritualism*, 162–76; and Isaacs, "Nineteenth-Century American Spiritualism," 243–47.

44. See Fogarty, *All Things New*, 31, 185–89.

45. The *Religio-Philosophical Journal* moved to San Francisco in 1895 and shortened its name to the *Philosophical Journal*.

46. On Spiritualist periodicals and their function, see Braude, "News from the Spirit World," and Carroll, *Spiritualism*, 159–61.

47. On the formation of these institutions, see Brown, "Spiritualism in Nineteenth-Century America," 180–92, 202–7.

48. On the trend toward large-scale institutionalization in American life, see Bledstein, *Culture of Professionalism*, and Higham, *From Boundlessness to Consolidation*.

49. Brown, "Spiritualism in Nineteenth-Century America," 153.

50. For a list of fifty-four existing Spiritualist organizations, see J. Gordon Melton, ed., *Encyclopedia of American Religions*, 5th ed., s.v. "Spiritualism."

51. Quoted in Brown, "Spiritualism in Nineteenth-Century America," 205.

52. Spiritualist church membership figures have been interpreted by some scholars as suggesting a decline in the early twentieth century and a subsequent rise after the First World War, but Rodney Stark and William S. Bainbridge have questioned both those figures and the conclusions that have been drawn from them. See Stark and Bainbridge, *Future of Religion*, 253–54.

53. The program for the 101st Annual Meeting of the Southern Cassadaga Spiritualist Camp Meeting Association states that community residents "understand that God-truth has been given to mankind down through the ages and that these truths have been recorded in books known as Bibles."

54. Kyle, *The Religious Fringe*, 28.

# TWO

# Seeking the Sweet Spirit of Harmony

## *Establishing a Spiritualist Community at Cassadaga, 1893–1933*

### JOHN J. GUTHRIE, JR.

IN MARCH 1899, J. Clegg Wright, a prominent Spiritualist from Amelia, Ohio, wrote to Emma J. Huff, a medium who had helped organize Cassadaga's most recent Spiritualist camp meeting at the time, that he planned to attend the following year's Spiritualist convention in Florida. Congratulating her for having a "fairly good meeting this year," he added: "It must be a hard region in which to sow the seed of progressive thought. The South Land is behind. It is cursed by the heel of old religion—a monstrous tyrant. He puts the eyes out of all his subjects."[1] Wright's letter reveals much about the attitudes that many northern Spiritualists held toward the region in which the emerging religious community at Cassadaga had taken root. To some Spiritualists who had never traveled below the Mason-Dixon Line, Florida looked like a stereotypical southern state full of people whose values contrasted sharply with those of northerners. Wright's letter provokes numerous questions concerning Florida's "spiritual frontier" at the turn of the century.

One outpost of that frontier, the Spiritualist camp at Cassadaga, founded in 1894 by northerners, is the oldest such community in the South. Spiritualists who found themselves "marginalized" in their native North might have expected to harmonize even less with southern religious culture, which was dominated by Christian evangelicalism and fundamentalism. Yet despite their unorthodox faith, they were steeped in a set of Protestant American traditions that ranged from capitalism to republicanism. Spiritualists at Cassadaga would in fact fit nicely into the mainstream of American middle-class culture.

Although this chapter explores, through newspaper accounts, church records, and other contemporary documents, the Cassadaga Spiritualist community's first forty years, the seeds of the settlement were sown some forty years earlier. In 1847, Andrew Jackson Davis, a founder of modern Spiritualism, wrote: "The great movements of the day are all advancing the public to [a] desirable consummation." Advocates for the abolition of slavery, the repeal of capital punishment, the prohibition of alcohol, and other social reforms, Davis suggested, would help establish a universal system of happiness representing "the harmony of all created things, and typify the . . . majesty of the Divine Creator." Although Spiritualists displayed similar reformist concerns, they often remained loath to adopt the radical path blazed by extremists. Instead, they recommended a course of gradual reform taken one step at a time. A more radical approach, they feared, would prove impracticable and destructive. The more moderate worldview of Spiritualists became apparent following John Brown's raid on Harpers Ferry in 1859. With tempers raging in both the North and the South, leading Spiritualists advised restraint. An editorial in the *Spiritual Telegraph and Fireside Preacher* renounced the use of force and implored all Americans to sit down "and reason together." Such moderation led abolitionist Parker Pillsbury to denounce Spiritualists as dead weights in the cause of freedom and progress.[2]

Because of such ridicule, Spiritualists gradually became alienated from a significant number of antebellum reformers. Even within Spiritualist ranks, conflicts proved long and bitter. Between 1872 and 1893, personal feuds stirred animus and undoubtedly contributed to Spiritualism's failure to maintain solidarity at the national level.[3] In the spring of 1877, for instance, a group of Spiritualists in Chautauqua County, New York, arranged to hold a camp meeting on Willard Alden's farm on the eastern shore of Cassadaga Lake. Alden furnished a grove for the Spiritualist gathering, free of charge. In September the meetings convened for six days, and most Spiritualists who attended considered the event sufficiently successful to warrant a ten-day meeting in 1878. Alden, however, died the following winter, and his heirs wanted a percentage of the gate receipts as payment for the use of the family's property. Because of these money matters, a spirit of unrest plagued the next two summer seasons. In August 1879, a faction of the Spiritualists proposed securing new grounds and organizing a camp meeting independent of the Aldens'. To that end, they chartered the Cassadaga Lake Free Association and purchased land adjacent to the Alden farm for holding their annual meetings. For several summers the two sites competed with each other. Eventually the Cassadaga Lake Free Association purchased the twenty-three-acre Alden grove. With this merger, the site now known as Lily Dale became the foremost Spiritualist camp in the United States.[4]

Dedicated to free thought, free speech, and free investigation, Spiritualism questioned hierarchical traditions while placing great trust in human reason. Not surprisingly, Spiritualists often had considerable difficulty reaching consensus over their internal affairs. In the early 1890s, for example, Spiritualists embarked on an effort to achieve national consolidation by forming the National Spiritualist Association (NSA). In the midst of these attempts, a Spiritualist from Buffalo, New York, Joseph W. Dennis, complained that Lily Dale was attempting to control the NSA convention and make it a "sideshow" for its particular interests. To support his claim, Dennis reported that several years earlier Moses Hull, a celebrated Spiritualist leader and convert from Seventh-Day Adventistism, had lectured in Alden's Grove in opposition to the Lily Dale faction. As a result, "the Lily Dale crowd" had directed much animus at Hull and his friends. Dennis also questioned the competence and integrity of Harrison D. Barrett, a man who would later become president of the NSA. Barrett was widely known among Spiritualists for his work in their cause.[5]

Lily Dale resident Emma J. Huff refuted Dennis's charges. She claimed that the "Powers of Light" had announced that the time had come for a new regime to select a place for concentrating "the forces that shall evolve and project the knowledge that shall bless every child of Earth." She believed that "wise and good spirits [were] working . . . to bring this about and they had chosen . . . Lily Dale to be a Mecca." Inasmuch as Lily Dale represented the world spiritually, she further contended, the convention stood for "the whole body of Spiritualists" who love the cause and not for a narrow faction confined to Chautauqua County. Although Huff agreed that Barrett lacked "business ability," she believed that he "held the spirit of truth in his heart" and would provide valuable service in the general work of Spiritualism.[6]

Against this backdrop of national organizational infighting, medium George P. Colby announced in January 1893 that the National Spiritual and Liberal Association would soon meet at DeLeon Springs, in Volusia County, Florida. The organizers expected at least one thousand people to attend, including some of the most distinguished Spiritualists in the nation.[7] Many Volusians no doubt viewed the approaching Spiritualist convention as an economic opportunity worth exploiting. If a thousand people attended the inaugural session in 1893, it seemed reasonable to expect even larger crowds at future meetings. Because of this, many locals worried less about the convictions of Spiritualists and more about their money. In short, they believed that expenditures by Spiritualists on goods and services would help bring prosperity to the county.

The novel Spiritualist organization then assembling in Florida confronted an external but timeworn menace to their religion. Before the initial meeting could convene, talk and allegations of fraud provided grist for the local rumor mill. In late nineteenth-century America, Spiritualism as a religious belief remained unpopular and was "universally denounced by the [mainstream] churches." In general, mainstream religionists claimed that Spiritualism was a lie practiced by frauds. Whatever the grounds for such allegations, impostors had plagued Spiritualism's good reputation since its birth. As historian Ann Braude put it, once mediumship demonstrated a potential for monetary gain, "fraudulent mediums imposed themselves on the public, and some indeed profited from deception."[8]

Small wonder, then, that some locals cast a dubious eye on the Spiritualists visiting Florida in 1893. Yet in response to such skepticism an editorial in the local *Volusia County Record* claimed: "We have as much respect for a person who is sincere in his spiritualistic ideas as we have for those happy in the enjoyment of any other religious belief. Because fraud and impostors have crept into the teachings of Spiritualism it affords no argument to denounce all those who are enjoying the comforts and promises they sincerely find in its doctrine. Firmly . . . fixed in the belief of Spiritualism can be found people among the best in their communities." The paper extended to the Spiritualist outsiders the hand of fellowship and hoped that the people of Volusia County would always treat them with large measures of charity and tolerance.[9] The editor's favorable response to their visit may have surprised some Spiritualists. The southern press in the past had generally attacked Spiritualism as subversive of Christian morality. In the process, southern newspapers had linked Spiritualism with abolitionism, women's rights, and other antebellum social reform movements that had emanated from the North and that had little appeal throughout the South.[10]

On January 29, 1893, Harrison D. Barrett of Lily Dale, New York, called the DeLeon Springs meeting to order. After a brief address of welcome, Barrett congratulated his listeners for "basking in the glorious sunshine in the open air in the bright sunny South," instead of "shivering around their coal stoves in the bleak North." He then introduced George P. Colby, who delivered a lecture titled "What came ye out into the wilderness to seek?" Speaking before an engrossed audience, Colby provided great "satisfaction even to those of orthodox proclivities." The same crowd also responded enthusiastically to Mrs. M. C. Thomas, "favorably known throughout the South as a . . . lecturer of great power," and A. B. Clyde, "the great silver-tongued orator from Ohio." Such an array of talent, a reporter pointed out, would afford locals "an excellent opportunity to investigate Spiritualism."[11]

The reporter's prediction rang true, for local interest in the meetings grew steadily. In February an excursion train from nearby DeLand brought in three hundred people who joined a crowd of three hundred already gathered to hear the various speakers scheduled for a Sunday meeting. Colby's lecture that day proved "especially fine," containing "poetic imagery from first to last."[12]

Such oratory aside, many visitors came to the meetings merely to satisfy their curiosity about Spiritualism. A correspondent for the *Record*, for example, went to investigate the authenticity of Dr. W. S. Rowley, a "spirit telegrapher" from Cleveland. Using an ordinary battery with a Morse Key sounder, Rowley gave one of the "most remarkable demonstrations ever witnessed in a public assembly." According to the journalist, unseen operators ticked off long messages from the spirit world without Rowley's hands ever touching the key. Although some scoffed at the phenomena, the reporter believed what he saw. If the critics are "so blind they will not see and so deaf they won't hear," he claimed, then "it is their misfortune, and their ignorance is deserving the heartfelt pity of all intelligent people."[13]

While convening in DeLeon Springs, the Spiritualists' association appointed a committee to select a permanent location for their winter camp. Members of this committee visited St. Petersburg, Tampa, Tarpon Springs, and other points on the west coast of Florida, hoping to find a regular site for their annual meetings. Similarly, they looked at St. Augustine, Daytona, and New Smyrna on the east coast. The association agreed to decide where to locate the camp at the next meeting of the board. Meanwhile, fearing that the Spiritualists would choose a different site, civic leaders of DeLeon Springs met to discuss raising $2,000 in municipal bonds to encourage the Spiritualists to locate permanently within their town limits. Following a brief debate, they quickly raised $750 and then moved resolutely to secure pledges for the balance.[14] With an eye on economic development and monetary reward, these locals apparently welcomed the Spiritualists with open arms and urged them to locate the camp in their community.

After canvassing the state for a more favorable permanent location, the trustees of the National Spiritual and Liberal Association settled on DeLeon Springs. Apparently several factors influenced the board's decision. John B. and H. H. Clough had generously donated twenty-five acres of land to the association; sales of lots from the parcel would provide needed revenue for the organization. In addition, the citizens of DeLeon Springs remained united in their efforts to make northerners feel both welcome and appreciated in the community. To that end, they promised to erect a large auditorium in the near future.[15]

Sweetening DeLeon Springs's offer further, the Clough brothers proposed building an extravagant two-hundred-room brick hotel "at the earliest moment." This structure, combined with private boardinghouses and restaurants, would furnish ample accommodations for northern guests as well as for visitors from the South. All this, one DeLeon Springs booster observed, "will add much to the natural advantages of our lucky neighbors, and advance the 'boom' several degrees."[16]

Yet despite the efforts of community boosters, and regardless of the association's announcement, the Spiritualist colony did not take root in DeLeon Springs. The Spiritualists instead established a permanent site on George Colby's property about three-fourths of a mile south of Lake Helen and six miles from DeLand. Colby had usually remained silent when Spiritualist leaders discussed a permanent location for the camp, and only after the board had considered all possible options did he suggest that organizers visit his property. According to Colby, spirits had selected the place twenty years earlier when he was living in Wisconsin. His Indian spirit guide, Seneca, subsequently advised him to go south and to help establish a great spiritual center where thousands of believers could congregate. Following this "imperative command," Colby went to Florida, traveled south up the St. Johns River, and landed at Blue Springs in Volusia County. The morning after he arrived, Colby fell into a trance. Spirit guides then allegedly led him "through the pathless wilds" to where the Spiritualist colony would settle. As Seneca had prophesied, Colby viewed a "Promised Land" of lakes and high bluffs. In 1880 he filed a homestead claim for seventy-five acres. Four years later the government granted him title to the land destined to become a mecca for Spiritualists.[17]

When Colby filed his claim, "Florida was very much a frontier state," according to historian Samuel Proctor. It was "isolated from the rest of the South, and it would remain so for many decades." This proved particularly true for Volusia County. The Seminole Wars and poor transportation links with outlying areas, among other factors, had impeded population growth, and in 1860 the federal census counted only twelve hundred people living in the county. Most residents were yeoman farmers who owned between one hundred and two hundred acres of land and lived in sparsely settled areas. During the Civil War, the Volusia wilds became a favorite refuge for Floridians trying to avoid service in the Confederate Army. Not until the 1870s, when the infusion of northern money spawned considerable growth, did the county begin emerging from the frontier. In 1870, for

*George P. Colby. Courtesy of the Southern Cassadaga Spiritualist Camp Meeting Association.*

example, an entrepreneur from Ohio, Mathias Day, launched a settlement that became Daytona. Six years later a thirty-eight-year-old industrialist from New York, Henry Addison DeLand, founded the community that bears his name. These efforts and those of other northern developers more than doubled Volusia County's population in ten years, from 3,294 in 1880 to 8,467 by 1890.[18]

Demographics aside, only mediums Emma J. Huff and Marion Skidmore had bothered to accept Colby's invitation to visit his remote piece of land. Both women had played crucial roles in founding and maintaining the Lily Dale Assembly in New York.[19] They assumed similar roles in establishing Cassadaga. In fact, since the inception of Spiritualism, women have played important parts in leading and organizing the religion. Women attained the special status of medium because their attributes harmonized with the nineteenth-century ideology of domesticity. Séances usually took place in the medium's home, a setting that was widely regarded as "women's separate sphere." Female mediums thus outnumbered their male counterparts, and Spiritualism offered a unique opportunity for women to assume a "public role in American religious life."[20]

Colby's property made a powerful impression on Huff and Skidmore. To these influential mediums, the "lovely site" radiated spiritual harmony. Still, Huff insisted that in order for the camp to succeed, Henry Flagler's railroad must serve it. Six years earlier Flagler had purchased "the thirty-six-mile Jacksonville, St. Augustine, and Halifax Railroad" to serve as the first leg of his Florida East Coast System. However, since Flagler did not own the line to Lake Helen, Huff's enthusiasm waned. Yet, fortunately for the two mediums, Flagler purchased the line three weeks after their visit to Colby's property. In March 1894 the Spiritualist camp at Cassadaga became a reality. Members formed a nonprofit stock company—the Southern Cassadaga Spiritualist Camp Meeting Association (SCSCMA)—and began planning camp activities for the following winter. In December, George Colby topped the Cloughs' gift at DeLeon Springs by donating thirty-four acres for a permanent meeting site.[21]

The association aimed "to form an educational center where the highest truths of Spiritualism [could] be taught." It pledged to do this, "not only for the benefit of their friends in the South," but also for Spiritualists who wished to escape the rigors of northern winters. Meanwhile, the association drafted a set of bylaws to govern its internal affairs. Article 12 highlights one of the camp's more enduring folkways—sobriety. This bylaw prohibited selling, or distributing for free, alcoholic beverages within the camp. With this measure, Cassadaga went dry twenty-six years before the Baptists, Methodists, and Women's Christian Temperance Union succeeded in their quest to prohibit alcohol statewide. This attitude of Spiritualists toward liquor approached that of the more conservative elements of Florida society. In any case, on February 8, 1895, after months of preparation, the association opened its first season, and one hundred people attended the three-day event held at Colby's home.[22]

The next year, hoping to draw larger crowds to its second season, the association extended a cordial invitation to all who were interested in Spiritualism, regardless of caste or color. If their cause favored caste, custom, or selfish power, Cassadagans feared that they would fail to meet the salient principle upon which their faith was founded, namely, "Universal Brotherhood." Thus camp leaders requested all to come and experience the spiritual harmony that the faith promised to deliver. In this respect, the camp made an effort to reach out and touch the African-American community in the vicinity. Even so, most blacks initially shied away from Cassadaga. They disappeared from the streets after sunset, mused one observer, and watched the Spiritualists attending the meetings with much reticence. According to a local white's biased account, African-Americans evidently feared northern Spiritualists as "ghosts or goblins." In 1897, however, Professor William F. Peck addressed a large delegation of blacks and told them that the spirit world "had been chiefly instrumental" in bringing slavery to an end. As he put it, Spiritualists were their best friends. Peck claimed that abolitionists Wendell Phillips, William Lloyd Garrison, Elijah Lovejoy, and the "sainted" Abraham Lincoln had all followed the principles of Spiritualism.[23]

At the turn of the century, most southern whites probably would have excluded Phillips, Garrison, Lovejoy, and Lincoln from their pantheon of heroes. And although Peck's actions would not have necessarily violated southern racial taboos, white Floridians would have likely bristled at the sight of a white professor lecturing to a black audience. Furthermore, Florida law then mandated segregation of the races, so Peck might have unwittingly violated several Jim Crow statutes. Race relations in the area, therefore, could have stirred animosity between some locals and the seemingly more tolerant Spiritualists at Cassadaga. Yet Emma Huff reported that the people of the South had cordially received the "Spiritualist Yanks." Besides respecting the rights of the Spiritualists, native Floridians had also extended many favors to the community that enabled the newcomers to plant deep roots in Volusia County.[24] For example, local businesses often gave Cassadagans reasonable terms for purchasing building material on credit.

Regardless of such goodwill, allegations of fraud again disrupted the harmony between the Spiritualists and the local community at the end of 1896. The controversy stemmed from an incident that involved two popular practitioners at the camp—the materializing medium O. L. Concannon and his wife, Edella, a platform test medium. A materializing medium produces a variety of physical phenomena from spirit, which range from rappings and levitating tables to the manifestation of ethereal persons and the emission of ectoplasm. A platform test medium operates on a stage and relays spirit messages to his or her audience.

Although details surrounding the episode in question remain sketchy, according to one eyewitness, when O. L. Concannon performed a séance in Boston, a member of the audience called him a phony. Although some excitement ensued, the accuser failed to produce either a wig or the garment that led to his allegations. Nevertheless, the issue followed the Concannons to Cassadaga. One editorial in the *Record* attempted to vilify the Concannons without maligning the entire community. "There are too many sincere and earnest believers in the faith," it said, "to have [Cassadaga's] plans upset by the exposure of frauds such as Concannon." Some locals, however, defended the Concannons. In a letter to the *Record*, Mrs. J. F. Leavitt wrote, "If this account is proven a mistake, will the Christian world be as ready to deny as they were to circulate the story, I wonder?"[25]

This time the association moved quickly to keep a minor problem from erupting into a serious crisis. In doing so, it dealt directly with the issue by conceding that some mediums worked almost entirely for selfish ends. Their moral natures, according to camp spokesperson Emma Huff, had "never been quickened to perceive the ethical side of Spiritualism," the *Record* reported on December 19. Still, she did not mean that they lacked psychic power. According to Huff, some "genuine mediums" not only had powers sufficient to produce manifestations to satisfy their insatiable greed, but also remained weak enough to attempt a counterfeit. Yet such shams, she claimed, would be detected in the end and "subjected to the penalty that falsehood [must endure] when coming in contact with true spiritual power." Every movement toward unknown heights, Huff continued, would always battle the "countless enemies who strive to clog the wheel of [progress]." God had his devil, Jesus had his Judas, and "Spiritualism has its jokes and frauds." For a time Huff's rhetoric managed to silence the accusations of fraud leveled at the camp by certain locals.

In 1897 both Concannons participated fully in the annual meeting, and it appeared that the worst of the controversy was behind them. In the early months of the year, newspaper accounts lauded their work. The March 13 *Record* reported that eleven Cassadagans had signed a testimonial confirming the authenticity of the manifestations conducted by the Concannons. While such support must have comforted the couple, the *Record* of April 3 quoted "a reliable source" who reported that O. L. Concannon had an experience in Palmetto, Florida, similar to the Boston episode. Apparently a group of skeptics disrupted and harassed Concannon during a séance. This event had also inspired a non-Spiritualist to pen a letter on behalf of the Concannons to the *Record,* which was published in the same issue. Although she was not personally acquainted with these mediums, she wrote, "Their doctrines should be respected by those who attend their worship. If they believe them frauds and do not agree with them in their belief, they are not compelled to attend their séances, and should they do so, they should be ladies and gentlemen enough to behave themselves. It is to no one's credit to attend anything that is morally and socially correct, and make a disturbance."

All the while, within Cassadaga support for the Concannons remained steadfast. At the season's closing ceremony, as the *Record* also reported on April 3, Edella Concannon "gave the spirit descriptions" with such accuracy that many eyes welled with tears. According to Eber W. Bond, a future president of the association and former executive officer of the Ohio Spiritualists' Association, she was a comely instrument for the spirit world to employ. "May she ever be faithful to her guides," he added, "and strengthen her well earned reputation for genuine medium tests."[26]

In perhaps the final word on the Concannon matter, four months later, on August 7, the *Record* published an unsigned letter whose author, alluding to the Concannons, wrote: "Public opinion used to burn heretics and witches for being eccentric, and now people are often cruelly persecuted for having ideas of their own, even in supposedly liberal and enlightened communities. We should do all we can to make the world we live in better and brighter, and a good way to do so is to serve on our own shortcomings, rather than on other peoples'." The following spring a guest lecturer at the camp reaffirmed that Spiritualists had little tolerance for impostors by strongly denouncing "those mediums who practice[d] fraud at their séances." With that, the issue faded away. No longer distracted by accusations of fraud, Spiritualists at Cassadaga returned to their ordinary routines, supporting Braude's observation that the historical weight of Spiritualism falls more with the masses of faithful followers who made it a popular movement, than with a few sensationalized frauds.[27]

Despite the controversy surrounding the Concannons, Cassadaga had flourished in 1897. In March the town dedicated a new auditorium. For the occasion residents decorated its rostrum with flowers, roses, and especially orange blossoms and hung flags of the world's nations across the top of the stage, spreading like a fan from the central "Old Glory." Spiritualists proudly and conspicuously displayed the flag of the United States as an emblem of the American creed. "True Americanism," they believed, "embraced the principles of human brotherhood and sisterhood."[28]

After speeches by Peck and Colby that emphasized the importance of permanently establishing a Spiritualist center in the Deep South, Caroline Twing of Westfield, New York, made a stirring appeal for funds to pay for the auditorium. The spectators responded quickly. At a time when $150 would have purchased a five-acre orange grove of 125 trees less than four miles from the DeLeon Springs Railroad Depot, Twing's audience donated more than $100 for the cause. Such generosity encouraged Cassadagans to anticipate "great improvements" in the coming year.[29]

In February 1898, with expectations soaring, Hubbard H. Brigham formally opened that season's meetings, urging everyone in attendance to feel at home in Southern Cassadaga. A subsequent invocation by Abbie E. Sheets of Michigan appeared to bring the heavenly powers in such close rapport, mused one member, that "a sweet spirit of universal harmony prevailed." At the time, "human sorrows and antagonisms were forgotten and all the world [was] kin in this peaceful atmosphere of divine perception." In the season's finale, Sheets praised the good work they had accomplished and implored her listeners "to live the life of moral elevation which was the basis of the spiritual religion."[30]

That season's remarkable success promised well for 1899. The association formed a class to study "the Vedantic philosophy as given by the Swami Vivekananda, [a] representative from India at the World's Congress of Religions." In addition, the management considered extending its meetings from January through March in 1899.[31]

In late 1898 the *Volusia County Record* published four letters written by "Nero," a Christian who reflected on the Spiritualists at Cassadaga. The content and tone of the letters suggest that Nero wanted to bridge a gap between Spiritualism and Christianity. One aspect the two faiths shared was their relatively shallow roots in the county. To be sure, the Spanish had brought Catholicism to Florida in the sixteenth century and four Methodist Episcopal ministers had ridden the Volusia circuit in the 1840s. But no Christian churches existed in the county until 1870, when members of the Methodist Episcopal Church finally managed to construct for $100 two crude buildings with a combined seating capacity of one hundred worshippers. During the next few years, itinerant ministers held infrequent services in those churches. In 1880 thirteen DeLand residents met and organized the town's First Baptist Church. The next year Rev. A. L. Farr led the congregation in constructing a temporary place for worship. Three years later they erected a more spacious building that could accommodate eight hundred people and cost nearly $16,000. By 1887, the Baptists, Methodists, Episcopalians, and Presbyterians had all constructed churches in DeLand. In nearby Lake Helen, moreover, John P. Mace built the First Congregational Church in 1889. Three years later a Baptist congregation, originally organized at Lake Winnemissett, relocated and built a church in Lake Helen. Apparently, Protestants had only a twenty-three-year lead over Spiritualists in establishing a permanent material presence in the county.[32]

In Nero's first letter, published in the *Record* on November 5, 1898, he wrote that he found Spiritualism "a sect who believe a good deal as I [save one] distinction," that Jesus was the only son of God. From Nero's perspective, Spiritualists believed in the Christ within themselves, the fatherhood of God, and the brotherhood of man. While noting that all Spiritualists did not "practice all they preach," Nero also admitted that "our church folks don't always [measure] up to my standard of what they should be, or always follow the teachings of . . . Christ." Nero claimed to have known some of the Cassadagans for years. The only negative thing he could say about them was that they did not belong to his church. And since the U.S. Constitution guaranteed religious freedom, he decided to "allow his neighbors to worship God after the dictates of their own conscience as long as they did not disturb [others]." On that tolerant note, Nero said he would "go down and hear some of their lectures this winter." Of course, he would do so, he wrote, only if his wife raised no objections.

She disapproved vehemently, as Nero's letters published in the *Record* on November 26, December 18, and December 24 testified. Initially, however, Nero disregarded her objections and regularly visited the Spiritualist grounds during December. On his first sojourn to Cassadaga he noticed that the community seemed to be expecting more people than in previous years. The first buildings erected by the now ubiquitous Yankees, said Nero, had undergone some much needed repairs. He also dropped by the village library hoping to read some of the "fine books" on its shelves. Nero's spouse, learning of this, became outraged. "Infidels could read Christian works with profit," she fumed, but Christians could not benefit from reading the works of infidels. That abruptly ended Nero's ventures to Cassadaga.

A year later the prospect for full attendance at the upcoming meetings had never seemed better. Because the association had secured "some of the best talent on the Spiritual rostrum," guests had booked most cottages and rooms for the 1900 season, the *Record* reported on November 25, 1899. Material changes proved equally significant. Workers had nearly completed construction of the Webster Sanitarium, "one of the finest buildings in the county." For Cassadaga, then, the new century seemed promising. Two decades had elapsed since "beneficent spirits" had purportedly led George Colby to the site where he and others would form a center for the work of the spirit world. Even so, the wise guides never led the faithful to believe that the avenue to success would follow an unimpeded course. Spiritualists knew that to overcome the many barriers that "ignorance has always placed in the highway of progressive thought," they needed patience, strength, and fortitude, the *Record* reported on January 27, 1900.

The obstacles that Spiritualists confronted in establishing Cassadaga tested their mettle. Considering the initial economic disadvantages—the limited public finances of the state following the "Freeze of 1895," and disappointing private funding because of the prolonged national recession of the 1890s—the camp succeeded against great odds. For every stumbling block, Spiritualists at Cassadaga found a comparable amount of aid. For example, Cassadagans received a great deal of assistance from the railroads and other businesses in the vicinity. According to the January 27, 1900, *Record* the Florida East Coast Railway sold tickets at half-fare on Saturdays, good for the return trip on Mondays during the season. Such courtesies made it possible for the association to bear the financial

Cassadaga, Fla.    OLD  HOTEL

*The Cassadaga Hotel, c. 1900. Courtesy of the Southern Cassadaga Spiritualist Camp Meeting Association.*

burden that the meetings entailed each year. By 1900 Huff could assert, as the *Record* reported on February 10: "Be assured that we have found no enemies in the South and if we have had foes they have been those supposed to be of our own households." With a little more labor and a small sum of money, she claimed, they could make Cassadaga one of the most attractive places in Florida.

By mid-February a new season was in full bloom. Mediums on the grounds gave private readings daily. Materialization, slate-writing, and healing represented the diversity of mediumship found inside the camp. A highlight of the season came with an invited speech from the platform by the Reverend Getty, a Christian minister, quoted in the *Record* on March 17. Getty claimed that Spiritualism differed very little from his own religion. He could see merit in all faiths and beliefs. While he looked to Christ crucified, he said, Spiritualists looked "to the Christ within themselves for being children of God." This speech explains in part why the association considered the first season of the new century a major success.

*Cassadaga Spiritualists in 1904;* center front, *medium J. Clegg Wright. Courtesy of the Southern Cassadaga Spiritualist Camp Meeting Association.*

As Cassadaga grew over the next few years, Spiritualists came out in larger crowds, arriving at the camp earlier than in previous seasons. At the same time, lectures and demonstrations by Colby, Huff, Peck, and others drew perhaps more appreciative audiences. The town's visitors also found a wider array of middle-class social activities in which to engage. If tea parties or the bazaar failed to satisfy them, weekly hops offered young and old the opportunity to dance away the nights.[33]

Such changes, however, did not alter Cassadaga's fundamental objective "to plant progressive ideas in the hearts of humanity." George N. Hilligoss, a new speaker visiting the camp in 1902 and future president of the association, reaffirmed that mission. It is, he preached, "the celestial love or good in man, which prompts all to conquer selfishness and unfold spiritually. When we have reached that state of love, then Spiritualism will no longer be stigmatized by society, [instead] the most learned men will embrace this truth and acknowledge that Spiritualism is the only religion whose followers . . . prove what they teach."[34]

The agenda of the Progressive Era—roughly the first two decades of the twentieth century—included women's suffrage, prohibition of alcohol, immigration restriction, monetary reform, and government regulation of the market. Of these, Cassadagans endorsed women's suffrage, temperance, and government intervention in the economy.[35]

A comedy performed by Cassadagans in 1909, reported by the *DeLand News* on March 5, reflected Spiritualists' interest in reform politics. The characters in the play, *Mrs. Jarley's Wax Works,* represented "American types." A "bloated bondholder" dressed in fine evening attire and holding a gold-headed cane, thundered, "Money is power!" The show's host, Mrs. Jarley, responded that "if a form without brains could talk that way, what might not a man with brains do?" Taking her cue, a suffragist demanded the ballot for women, as a ponderous William Howard Taft shouted for the GOP. A Spiritualist playing the nationally known cartoon character Mr. Dooley declared, "I told Hennery, [William Jennings] Bryan would have been elected if the women could have voted." Carry Nation appeared, waving her hatchet and exclaiming, "The saloon must go!" Jarley then "brought the house down" by remarking "Mrs. Nation meant well and had been of great help to glass manufacturers." The audience roared with laughter. In politics as in religion, Spiritualists disarmed their critics with subtlety.

Whatever their politics, the Cassadagan Spiritualists' regard for patriotism, republicanism, and other American traditions must have eased their acceptance by local Protestants. At the camp, they sang "My Country, 'Tis of Thee" for opening day ceremonies and continued to decorate the platform with flags of all nations surrounding the American flag. A news item reported that a scheduled speaker had "fought for his country in days that tried men's souls." Another visitor to the village had used "his tongue and pen for human justice" as a member of Congress for several terms. The camp reserved one week in February 1909 to pay tribute to the Civil War. On Wednesday of the weeklong celebration, a large crowd gathered in the auditorium to hear old veterans of both the Union and Confederate armies reminisce about the war. Two days later, Cassadaga closed the celebration by honoring the Lincoln centenary. C. P. Pratt read the Gettysburg Address, followed by J. Clegg Wright, who gave a personal memorial that lauded "the service rendered our nation by the arisen statesman Abraham Lincoln."[36]

By 1910 the Cassadaga Assembly had become much more than a series of tent meetings. Many fine cottages, as well as an auditorium, the pavilion, Harmony Hall, and other structures that accommodated the winter season, all stood as monuments to the efforts of early Cassadagans to fulfill Colby's dream of establishing a "Spiritualist Mecca" in Florida. Before the decade ended, even the Reverend Blocker, Lake Helen's Baptist preacher, complimented the Spiritualists for their work at Cassadaga.[37]

In 1915 the association selected Joseph Slater as president. He would hold the office for the next decade. Many Cassadagans identified Slater as the driving force behind the town's development. A piece on Slater in the *Cassadagan* of January 27, 1939, would quote a community member who claimed that "perhaps no more beloved figure exists today in the memory of older residents of the camp." Slater was "very active" in the Methodist Church before his conversion to Spiritualism in 1906. In that year he had journeyed to Cassadaga with a friend whom the association had scheduled to lecture. The community made such an impression on Slater that he built a home on the grounds before departing for Ohio. In 1912, he retired from business and returned with his family to Cassadaga, where they would permanently settle. The welfare of the village then

*Spiritualists gathered in front of a house in Cassadaga, c. 1904. Courtesy of the Southern Cassadaga Spiritualist Camp Meeting Association.*

became a principal concern of Slater's life. From 1915 to 1925, his tenure as president, he devoted time, money, and labor to Cassadaga's sundry developments. Years later, many residents would still recollect the "energetic way in which he helped lay sidewalks, took charge of burning scrub around the grounds, or performed other tasks around the camp."

Despite the apparent satisfaction with Slater's leadership, dissent brewing in 1918 would eventually disrupt camp harmony. In early March, police arrested George "Doc" Dimmick on the charge of cursing coresident Melvin J. Holt. Born in New Hampshire, Dimmick came to Florida as a thirty-year-old master carpenter in 1882. He settled in New Smyrna and worked for years on Flagler's East Coast Railway. Dimmick had his first spiritual experience in the 1880s, through the materializing medium Concannon. At about that time, he befriended George Colby, who would remain his close associate over the following four decades. Dimmick eventually moved to Cassadaga, where residents praised his talents as a spiritual healer. At any rate, the criminal court fined Dimmick for his profanity, and he cheerfully paid the penalty, since he had "gotten his money's worth." A few weeks later the dispute escalated. Joined by Joseph F. Snipes and several others, Dimmick hired an attorney to bring proceedings against Slater, Herbert Hollely, William Critchley, and several others, with the intention of ousting them from their positions as trustees of the camp. Dimmick's group alleged that the defendants had unlawfully usurped their office as trustees of the association because they had been elected illegally.[38]

Judge James W. Perkins heard the case in chambers. As the lawsuit unraveled, Perkins ruled against the defendants and gave them until April to show the court what authorized them to hold office. At the association's annual meeting earlier that spring, an election had been held to choose trustees for the coming year. Stockholders cast sixty-two ballots; Dimmick, Snipes, and the other plaintiffs received forty votes, the defendants, twenty-two. But the defendants had apparently violated the association's charter by allowing stockholders to cast one vote for each share of stock held, instead of one vote per stockholder as stipulated in the bylaws. The defendants claimed to have won the election 329 to 308 (62 ballots, 637 shares of stock). Four days prior to the election, moreover, the board of directors had illegally issued to Slater one hundred shares of stock, the plaintiffs charged, "with the . . . express purpose of controlling the . . . election." That stock had enabled Slater's faction to dominate the board of trustees. Since the plaintiffs claimed to have legally won the election, they argued that they deserved the franchises, offices, privileges, and powers that the association had bestowed on its trustees. Litigation continued for at least another twenty months and, although no evidence of its outcome has surfaced, that Slater remained camp president until 1925 suggests that his side prevailed.[39]

In 1919, with the inflation induced by World War I, the prices of "articles of comparative necessity" soared in Cassadaga to all-time highs. Cassadagans complained of profiteering by certain merchants who were taking advantage of the town's relatively remote location to charge outrageous prices for food and other consumer goods. Responding to allegations of price gouging, an operator of a general store said that he had to charge a large advance on all his goods, particularly kerosene, since Standard Oil had recently raised its price four times. Yet the town's leading progressive and self-appointed consumer advocate, Joseph F. Snipes, produced a letter from the president of Standard Oil that refuted the merchant's claims. While prices over the previous two years had generally increased, according to the letter, the cost of petroleum products had remained unchanged. "Such profiteering, in smaller or larger degree, is a subject of public interest, domestic economy, and self-defense," Snipes grumbled in a March 5, 1919, article in the *Deland News*.

Yet automobile prices fell during these years. So Cassadaga found itself positioned to exploit an emerging market in tourism as automobile ownership rose during the 1920s. Because of its location on the northern edge of the citrus belt, according to one booster quoted in the same *Deland News* piece, Cassadaga's climate was ideal, "with just enough of occasional tang in the winter air to make it delightful." In addition to its excellent weather, Cassadaga offered a variety of modern conveniences. The community had facilities for piping pure artesian water "without a particle of sulfur" into every home in the camp. A municipal plant at Lake Helen provided affordable electricity for Cassadaga. The same plant manufactured ice and brought this highly valued commodity directly to customers in the village. To a considerable extent, the Spiritualist town had entered the modern era. "From humble beginnings, the place had grown into [a] community with all the advantages of a city," an observer noted, "and every passing season swings the gates wider toward a still more radiant future."[40]

While Cassadagans awaited a "more radiant future," the local chapter of the Ku Klux Klan made itself known to county residents in November 1920 by parading openly in nearby Daytona. The Klansmen intended their public demonstration to intimidate black voters enough that they would not cast ballots in the upcoming election. The following spring, during a campaign of terror directed against Catholics and African-Americans, Klansmen burned two black theaters and a Catholic church in Daytona. When not resorting to arson, the "Invisible Empire" menaced the county by beating innocent people, who often died from the thrashings. Despite mountains of evidence implicating members of the Klan, their crimes frequently went unpunished because the organization had coerced local authorities into looking the other way.[41]

Granted, the Klan met formidable resistance from the *Daytona Morning Journal,* the American Legion of DeLand, and the politicians of Daytona and DeLand. Yet in 1922 the Klan's candidates for judicial, municipal, and legislative office swept the June primaries, carrying Daytona, DeLand, and Ormond. Internal discord, however, would shorten the Klan's victory celebration. "When the mayor of DeLand [a Klan member] refused to heed the wishes of the local Klan leader, the Klan summoned him to a meeting in the woods at which he was tried for mutiny." In spite of (or perhaps as a result of) such intimidation, the mayor and his friends withdrew from the organization. Their actions prompted many of the county's leading citizens to also quit the Klan.[42]

But the exodus of its respectable community members did not mean that the Klan's days in central Florida were numbered. In 1923 Orlando hosted a statewide "Klanvocation to mark the inauguration of Florida as a self-governing realm in the Invisible Empire." Eighteen months later a Klan newspaper reported that a unit of the organization had infiltrated the campus of Stetson University, operating as the Fiery Cross Club. In the spring of 1925, moreover, the hooded knights boasted that DeLand Klansmen assisted local authorities in enforcing prohibition, despite "harassment by corrupt politicians, rum rings and a few unscrupulous Romans." And as late as 1926 the *Tampa Tribune* reported that floggings by Klansmen continued to occur in Volusia County.[43]

Cassadaga escaped the Klan's wrath during the 1920s. That the terrorist group did not so much as burn a cross in the Spiritualist community defies explanation, considering the crimes committed by the Klan and the victims who suffered their drubbings. The revived Ku Klux Klan of the 1920s pledged to return the nation to a fantasized past of cultural purity—that is, "one hundred percent Americanism." Acting on these distorted notions, Klansmen attacked bootleggers and wayward whites, as well as racial, ethnic, moral, and religious "deviants." One could speculate that because Cassadaga went "dry" before either state or national prohibition became law, and since the Spiritualists manifested a strong sense of patriotism, the Klan looked elsewhere for more appealing targets to terrorize. Perhaps the Spiritualists seemed too ordinary, too typically American, to tempt the Klan. Yet the town's progressive ideas on race and gender coupled with its unorthodox faith made Cassadaga a "sitting duck" for the Klan in its "fight against ignorance and superstition." What saved the tiny community from the Klan's abuse remains a mystery.[44]

In 1923 Cassadaga's "more radiant future" began unfolding. In July the association razed the old auditorium and started constructing a new one.[45] In January 1924, the camp dedicated the new auditorium in the inaugural ceremony of the thirtieth annual convention at Cassadaga. By then, guests had booked every room at the Cassadaga Hotel for the season, and camp officials scrambled to find accommodations for the overflow. The tiny community was experiencing spillover benefits from the Florida land boom that began in the mid-1910s and came to a halt in 1925, its economy rising and falling with the fortunes made and lost in Florida land transactions.[46]

As the boom accelerated toward its peak, the Cassadaga Spiritualist Camp formally opened for the 1925 season on January 4. The town had no vacancies because northerners had booked all available cottages and rooms, only one of many indications that this would be the most successful season in the history of the community.[47] On the platform, Oscar Edgerly and Mable Riffle drew the largest and most enthusiastic crowds. Since his debut in 1885, Edgerly had earned much acclaim among Spiritualists as a trance speaker, and Jamestown, New York's, *Evening Journal* for July 20 reported on a speech in which he elaborated on one of his recurring themes, "the Civic and Religious Responsibilities of Spiritualists." Civic responsibility referred to citizenship, patriotism, and the individual's relationship to government. Like many ordinary Americans in the 1920s, Spiritualists took great pride in the republic and embraced the notion of civic virtue. Edgerly believed that "the desire for [the nation's] welfare dwells in our hearts." Since Americans possessed both liberty and independence, he declared, they suffered no influence other than their own conscience. "If you profit by your inspirations, and register them at the ballot box," Edgerly said, "you are performing your civic duty." He told his listeners to exercise their sovereignty as voters with discretion. Let no man or party own you and, Edgerly advised, "exercise your franchise for the greatest good of the greatest number." If Spiritualists followed his counsel, he believed, they would better appreciate their independence, transcend the political and religious chains of the past, and rise to new heights by becoming nobler characters.

Mable Riffle's Sunday evening séances attracted the largest crowds ever recorded at the auditorium. Typically for forty minutes at a time, the "great message bearer" would roll out "name after name, fact after fact, in an endless stream that delighted her audience, confounded critics, and filled investigators with wonder." Moreover, a voluntary offering at one of her séances surpassed any other in the camp's history and the sale of tickets doubled that of the previous season. Given such success, Cassadagans held high expectations for 1926.[48]

By the mid-1920s, the physical isolation of Cassadaga from other groups and the fact that Spiritualists did not actively proselytize had helped ease their acceptance by locals. And Cassadagans' mainstream, white, middle-class progressive values, ranging from capitalism to republicanism, perhaps enhanced their esteem in the county. Spiritualists also had friends who wielded influence over high public offices. In May of 1926, to illustrate the point, Anna Louise Fletcher, the wife of Florida's U.S. senator, Duncan U. Fletcher, defended Spiritualism before a House subcommittee hearing on legislation to limit the activities of mediums in the District of Columbia. To the subcommittee, Mrs. Fletcher announced that she had personally investigated Spiritualism for more than twenty-five years. Declaring that her mother was a natural medium, Fletcher testified that she had never met a dishonest medium. Indeed, some of the most important Spiritualists had gathered in her home to perform séances. At these circles, she said, she had received messages inscribed on slate from her deceased father in his own handwriting. She challenged anyone in the room to deny the authenticity of her communications with her father's spirit. Proponent of the legislation and renowned magician Harry Houdini had earlier claimed he could and would duplicate what transpired at séances. Undaunted by such claims, Fletcher said she had pledged many years before "to help the cause of Spiritualism at any time and in any place that I could."[49]

Making good on her promise, Fletcher published *Death Unveiled* before the year ended. A record of facts gleaned from careful investigation, the book underscored Fletcher's favorable opinion of Spiritualism. According to a Spiritualist newspaper, the *Progressive Thinker,* the text deserved "a careful perusal, coming as it does from one who occupies an influential place in Washington, D.C." In the meantime, Senator Fletcher maintained "careful ties to Jacksonville's First Baptist Church," lest his wife's interest in Spiritualism cause him political embarrassment. As it happened, the subcommittee rejected the fortune-telling bill because the members viewed it as an encroachment on liberties guaranteed by the First Amendment.[50]

On Christmas night 1926, fire swept through the Cassadaga Hotel, leveling it and two adjacent buildings. Only a heroic effort by the fire department prevented the flames from consuming the eastern side of the village. Justin and Reid Williams, who lived next door to the hotel, were the first to detect the fire. They roused the guests, many of whom had only enough time to snatch a few clothes in their hurried flight from the burning building. Their hasty departure made a difference—all guests survived the inferno. Without a hotel and with a new season approaching rapidly, the camp had to improvise. The association used Brigham and Harmony Halls to provide rooms for visitors, while Spencer House served as a dining hall. Despite the creative ways in which Cassadagans responded to the disaster, their efforts proved little more than a stopgap. The camp needed a hotel.[51]

"Every great system," wrote Evangelina P. Bach, the camp's corresponding secretary, "has its central figure, its leader, its inspirer, its cause of success." When fire destroyed the Cassadaga Hotel, Edward F. Loud was the camp's central figure, elected president of the association earlier that year. Under his leadership over the next two years, growth, development, and beautification efforts transformed the community, as the *DeLand Daily News* reported on the two-year anniversary of the fire, December 26, 1928. Merchants, realtors, journalists, and businesspersons agreed: "Cassadaga is doing things all the time—having a boom after the boom."

Loud had experience with financing "big business." One of the last of Michigan's lumber tycoons, Loud had earned a fortune in timber at the turn of the century. He and his father had staked claims in the virgin forests along the Au Sable River. Their timber holdings, in turn, made the H. M. Loud Company one of the richest firms of its kind in Michigan. Although the business suffered considerable losses from the Panic of 1907, Loud's fortune still afforded him a comfortable retirement in Cassadaga. As president, Loud immediately set about implementing a plan to make Cassadaga "the greatest Spiritualist Assembly in the world." Under his administration, the community laid more than three thousand linear feet of concrete sidewalks, added more electric street lights, and improved the roads. Residents built twenty-one dwellings ranging in price from $1,000 to $25,000. With this growth came a new store, a barber shop, a Woman's Club house, and a beautiful new pavilion on the lake. But the greatest of all the construction projects was the modern hotel. Besides forty rooms equipped with baths, the well-furnished hotel had a dining area that could seat 150 persons, ample parlors, and the best heating system available.[52]

The new hotel was Loud's greatest legacy to the town. When the old hotel burned and Cassadagans had little hope of building a new one, Loud stepped in and inspired many of them to donate money to the cause. At his urging, residents contributed $22,135 to a hotel fund. Subsequently, the assembly authorized a bond issue, and the "friends of Cassadaga" purchased $29,000 worth of the notes. Because of such charity, the community managed to build a hotel that "would be a credit to [any] large city."[53]

At the launch of the 1929 season, great enthusiasm permeated the community. On January 23, the *Deland Daily News* reported a number of developments.

The hotel was experiencing a three-fold increase in the number of guests booked on opening day compared to the previous year. Perhaps even more significant, Cassadagans anticipated having telephone service, provided by the Bell Company, by the end of the month. Two years earlier the association had appointed Lizzie Bears to chair a committee for securing telephone service for the town. Bears eventually signed up more than sixty subscribers from Cassadaga and Lake Helen. In another communication effort, the association produced an attractive descriptive circular about Cassadaga, which was mailed to various chambers of commerce throughout Florida to inform the public that Volusia County had the second most important Spiritualist assembly in the nation and the only one in the South. The *DeLand Daily News* on January 7 quoted George Colby's opening-day speech, in which he captured the essence of the community's spirit by saying "there is only one person here today." What he meant by this, he explained, was that "by the harmony, interest and earnestness this great assemblage are welded into one unit as the drops of water are blended into a pool of water."

Because 1929 marked Cassadaga's thirty-fifth anniversary, the association invited some well-known Spiritualists from various parts of the United States to participate in its celebration. The speakers booked for the occasion were Elizabeth Harlow Goetz of Philadelphia and Rev. Henry Ward Beecher Myrick of Indianapolis. Many of the faithful considered Goetz the foremost woman Spiritualist. A former president of the Lily Dale Assembly, she had also served as a trustee of the NSA. Goetz believed that Spiritualism gave people the liberty to think profoundly about their lives. What is more, like many Spiritualists, Goetz was a rationalist who greatly admired Thomas Paine. In one lecture, she went so far as to suggest that Cassadagans should set aside the last Sunday in January as a memorial for "this great benefactor." Paine, she said, "gave his life, his pen and his pocketbook to establish this [land] as a free nation." When her time to enter the spirit world came, Goetz said, she hoped she would see Paine and "be permitted to worship at his feet." These comments not only reveal the Spiritualists' staunch belief in individualism and independent thinking, but also reflect the close connections that they maintained with republicanism.[54]

Myrick came late to Spiritualism. For thirty-five years an evangelist, he had preached in a Campbellite church and had baptized hundreds of people. Even after converting to Spiritualism he retained his evangelical fervor. "The preacher who undertakes to propagate Spiritualism," Myrick asserted, "ought to be a man of good repute." Still, he realized that in spreading the word a Spiritualist preacher often endured much hostility. From his personal experience of riding the circuit, Myrick had learned that Christian audiences needed little or no persuading to join the church. Spreading Spiritualism proved much more difficult. When Myrick held up the philosophy and phenomena of Spiritualism, skeptics would denounce it as "the work of the devil." So he had to prove everything. But because Myrick could not prove every proposition of his faith, he had a medium attend his meetings "to give proof to the audience." Despite dealing with detractors, Myrick maintained a friendly attitude toward all religions. As he put it, "I did not come from a Christian pulpit into Spiritualism to condemn anybody." Instead, he wanted to retain all the good things in the Bible—the splendor of mercy, the nobility of forgiveness, and the grandeur of self-denial. "Let us adopt a commonsense principle," he suggested in one speech, "and say everything good is ours, and we are going to practice it to the best of our knowledge and ability." At Cassadaga he declaimed, "The world owes us nothing and we have no right to be here unless we can do some good."[55]

Perhaps inspired by Myrick's speech, one Sunday in February 1929, President Loud spoke of his goals for Cassadaga. "If Cassadaga only had an endowment fund," he said, "how much easier the work would be for those who have the affairs of the Association to administer and how much more could be done for this cause we are striving to promote." In his dreams Loud saw an endowment of $100,000 for the camp. Although some residents remained skeptical about the figure, Loud said that the association had acquired a substantial sum of money. Moreover, the endowment's benefactors made a provision calling for the surrender and retirement of about $10,000 in the association's bonds. Other contributors informed Loud that they would cancel their bonds "when they or their immediate descendants" no longer needed the interest payments to supplement their household income. After disclosing these developments to his audience, Loud noted that they had already raised nearly $25,000 for the foundation. He therefore saw no reason to solicit additional funds. Rather, he asked his listeners to think about it. Should they decide to contribute "in this great effort for the up[lifting] of Cassadaga and the advancement of Spiritualism," he would gladly speak with them in private.[56]

To achieve Loud's ambition, the association included a bequest form in its program for 1929. Emphasizing the community's previous contributions for the good of Spiritualism, the program noted that Cassadaga wanted to broaden the scope of its work then in progress. Simply put, the association hoped that some members would remember Cassadaga's accomplishments when drafting their wills.[57]

As the 1929 season came to an end, Cassadagans—like many Americans who did not possess psychic abilities—foresaw neither the stock market crash nor the Great Depression. When the economic crisis hit Florida, per capita annual income dropped from $510 to $478 in 1930, and to $392 in 1931.[58]

In a financial pinch, the camp at Cassadaga failed to "make good" on its obligations to the bondholders who had financed the new hotel. In 1931, for example, the hotel earned $2,000 in rental income for the association. But instead of paying the money to the bondholders, the camp used it for other purposes. Such actions prompted former president Loud to address a meeting of the association's stockholders on March 26, 1932. Loud reminded his audience that five years earlier Cassadagans and their friends had joined in a rushing, mighty, effort to conceive, finance, build, and furnish a new hotel. "It should never be forgotten," he declared, "that it was bondholders' money that enabled the project to be completed." Since the association told the bondholders that all rental income would service the interest on the notes, according to Loud, those who purchased the bonds had first claim on any hotel earnings.[59]

Some residents, however, considered the hotel a financial burden to the camp because the association paid the taxes and insurance on the building. From their perspective, the camp lacked the funds to cover expenses along with the interest on the bonds. In response, Loud argued that without a hotel Cassadaga would have received far less revenue from gate receipts, collections, and various other functions. Noting again that the hotel generated $2,000 for the camp in 1931, he said, "It would be a wild flight of the imagination to call [the hotel] a hardship." After painting a gloomy picture of the crisis confronting Cassadaga, he admonished the community to pull together under effective leadership, so the camp could weather the storm. "I plead once more for harmony," Loud concluded, "for I want to see Cassadaga live, grow, and prosper." Yet the members of the association who considered the hotel a burden prevailed. In 1933, when the association could pay neither its taxes nor the debt it owed the bondholders, the Cassadaga Hotel was sold; it remains privately owned six decades later.[60]

That same year, Cassadaga lost its founder, George P. Colby. In January 1933, after living in New Smyrna for several years, Colby had returned to Cassadaga because of his declining health. The camp provided him with an apartment, and many residents accommodated his needs. Nonetheless, by June Colby had become feeble. Following a short stay in a hospital where he had suffered a stroke, the octogenarian died in Cassadaga the morning of July 27, 1933. His death marked the end of an era that had spanned nearly four decades of Cassadaga's history.[61]

*   *   *

THE LOSS OF the hotel and Colby's death notwithstanding, by 1933 the Spiritualists' mission to establish a permanent religious community in Florida had become a reality. For the most part, the local population tolerated its new neighbors and provided the kind of support that assured Cassadaga's initial success.
Volusians accepted the Spiritualists at Cassadaga for both economic and cultural reasons. Since the Spiritualists had the time and money to spend the winter months in Florida, some natives thought Cassadagans' cumulative expenditures on construction materials, furnishings, food, and other items would
stimulate the local economy. For instance, in 1933 when the Great Depression
had reached its nadir, the *DeLand News* ran an editorial on January 6 touting
Cassadaga's positive economic impact. "The arrival of two-thousand guests at
Cassadaga for the winter season means much to DeLand merchants. While they
are settled some seven miles from this city many of them do most of their trading
here. Countless others seek recreation in this city, particularly at the picture
houses." The paper concluded that "the Cassadaga Spiritualist Assembly is an
asset to DeLand and is gladly welcomed each winter season." The opportunity
for financial gain, therefore, helped mitigate any rancor that locals held toward
the Cassadagans.

Finally, as Emma Huff had noted at the turn of the century, conflicts within
the camp posed a greater danger to Cassadaga's survival than external threats. In
fact, locals directed little animus toward the community. Because most of the
county's white residents came originally from the North, culturally they shared
much with the Spiritualists.[62] Reared in Anglo-Saxon Protestant households
steeped in capitalism and other American traditions, many Spiritualists had
backgrounds and experiences familiar to the locals. Thus the cultural traits that
linked the two groups in the material world proved stronger than the religious
differences that divided them. Rather than perceiving Spiritualists as radical
utopian communitarians who professed to communicate with the dead, locals
viewed them as a group of ordinary people who came to the county seeking their
version of the American dream. In the last analysis, their mainstream values
help explain why the community has thrived as a Spiritualist mecca in central
Florida for over a century. The Spiritualists aspired only to congregate in sweet
harmony with like-minded people in a mild climate.

# Notes

1. J. Clegg Wright to Emma J. Huff, Amelia, Ohio, March 25, 1899, Vince Owens Collection, Cassadaga, Florida (hereinafter Owens Collection). I wish to thank Eileen Kiser, Christine Spillar, Vince Owens, and Nick Sourant for their valuable research assistance, and Kurt Cumiskey, Kari Frederickson, Len Lempel, and Frank Wetta for commenting on earlier drafts of this chapter.

2. Davis, *The Principles of Nature,* 778, 690, 692, 742; Delp, "American Spiritualism," 86, 87, 91.

3. Delp, "American Spiritualism," 94.

4. Downs and Hedley, *History of Chautauqua County,* 421–25; Joyce LaJudice, compiler, "Lily Dale Chronicle: History as It Happened" (Lily Dale Assembly, 1984, photocopy), 26–31, Owens Collection.

5. Joseph W. Dennis to Emma J. Huff, Buffalo, New York, November 21, 1893, Owens Collection; *Light of Truth Album,* vii.

6. Emma J. Huff to Joseph W. Dennis, Lily Dale, New York, October 1893, Owens Collection.

7. *Volusia County Record,* January 14, 21, 1893.

8. Braude, *Radical Spirits,* 30–31.

9. *Volusia County Record,* January 14, February 4, 1893.

10. Delp, "Southern Press."

11. *Volusia County Record,* January 14, February 4, 1893; *Light of Truth Album,* iii.

12. *Volusia County Record,* February 11, 1893.

13. Ibid., February 18, March 4, 1893.

14. Ibid., February 18, 25, 1893.

15. Federal Writers' Workshop Project, "Southern Cassadaga's Spiritualist Camp," 5 (hereinafter FWWP); *Volusia County Record,* March 25, 1893.

16. *Volusia County Record,* March 25, 1893.

17. FWWP, 3–5; *Volusia County Record,* September 2, 1895; *Florida Times-Union,* September 2, 1895; Henderson, *The Story of Cassadaga,* 12–15.

18. Gannon, *New History of Florida,* 268, 272; Schene, *Hopes, Dreams, and Promises,* 59, 71; Dietrich, *Urbanization of Florida's Population,* 204–5.

19. Vaught and LaJudice, *Lily Dale Proud Beginnings,* 12–13; Downs and Hedley, *History of Chautauqua County,* 421–24.

20. Carroll, *Spiritualism,* 150; Braude, *Radical Spirits,* 82–116.

21. Gannon, *New History of Florida,* 269; FWWP, 7. See also Akin, *Flagler.*

22. *Volusia County Record,* December 14, 1895; Henderson, *The Story of Cassadaga,* 15; SCSCMA, "By-Laws of the Southern Cassadaga Spiritualist Camp Meeting Association," January 15, 1895, Book of Records, Owens Collection; *The Southern Cassadaga Spiritualist Camp Meeting Association, General Statement 1903* (DeLand: Painter, 1903) 3; Alduino, "Noble Experiment in Tampa," 6; Guthrie, *Keepers of the Spirits,* 26–32.

23. *Volusia County Record,* January 11, 1896, February 11, 1893, April 3, 1897.

24. See Shofner, "Custom, Law, and, History"; *Volusia County Record*, December 5, 1896.

25. *Volusia County Record*, February 15, 29, December 5, 26, 1896.

26. On Bond, see *Light of Truth Album*, 11.

27. *Volusia County Record*, August 7, 1897, February 26, 1898; Braude, *Radical Spirits*, 31.

28. Downs and Hedley, *History of Chautauqua County*, 424.

29. *Volusia County Record*, March 13, April 3, November 6, 1897.

30. Ibid., February 12, March 26, 1898; *Light of Truth Album*, xvi.

31. *Volusia County Record*, December 31, 1898.

32. Schene, *Hopes, Dreams, and Promises*, 60, 83, 90; *Daytona Beach News-Journal*, April 28, 1957. For an example of how Spiritualists interacted with the "religiously informed" elsewhere, see Frankiel, *California's Spiritual Frontiers*.

33. *Daytona Beach News-Journal*, February 2, March 30, December 21, 28, 1901; February 8, 1902; June 6, 1903; February 27, 1904; January 25, February 1, 1902; *DeLand Daily News*, January 22, 1909.

34. *Volusia County Record*, December 21, 1901; January 25, 1902.

35. *DeLand News*, January 29, 1909. For an overview of the Progressive Era in Florida, see Gannon, *New History of Florida*, 266–86. For the contradictions within progressivism, see Grantham, *Southern Progressivism*; Link, *The Paradox of Southern Progressivism*.

36. *DeLand News*, February 5, 12, 19, 1909; *DeLand Daily News*, January 22, 1909.

37. *DeLand Daily News*, January 22, 1909; *DeLand News*, November 4, December 16, 1910.

38. Ibid., January 29, 1939; *DeLand Daily News*, March 27, 1918.

39. *State of Florida, ex rel. Charles T. Ford, George A. Dimmick, Joseph F. Snipes, A. B. Gaston, F. W. Mack, Charles Coolidge and T. Babcock v. Joseph Slater, Melvin J. Holt, E. P. Sully, Herbert Hollely, William Critchley, E. E. Hopkins, and A. Cowcroft* (Seventh Judicial Circuit Court of Volusia County, Florida 1918).

40. *DeLand News*, March 5, 1919.

41. Chalmers, "Ku Klux Klan"; *Daytona Morning Journal*, June 16, October 2, 4, 5, 1921; March 4, June 4, 1922; *New York Times*, June 18, 1922; Lempel, "Race and Politics," 14–15.

42. Chalmers, "Ku Klux Klan," 211, 212, 214, 215.

43. Ibid; *Washington National Kourier*, February 9, 1925; *Fiery Cross*, March 13, 1925; *Tampa Morning Tribune*, September 14, 1926.

44. Chalmers, "Ku Klux Klan," 211. On the Klan, see MacLean, *Behind the Mask,* and Jackson, *Klan in the City.*

45. SCSCMA, *Twenty-Ninth Annual Convention Program*, 1, Owens Collection; *DeLand Daily News*, December 12, 1923.

46. *DeLand Daily News*, December 26, 1923. On the real estate boom, see Frazer and Guthrie, *Florida Land Boom.*

47. *DeLand Sun News*, January 2, 7, 1925.

48. Ibid., January 29, February 11, 18, 1925; *DeLand Daily News*, February 4, 1925.

49. *Tampa Morning Tribune*, May 22, 1926; House Subcommittee on Judiciary of the Committee on the District of Columbia, *Fortune Telling*, February 26, May 18, 20, 21, 1926, 49–51; *Progressive Thinker*, December 1926, 3.

50. Flynt, "Religion at the Polls," 470, and *Duncan Upshaw Fletcher.*

51. *Cassadagan,* February 14, 1939.

52. *New York Times,* January 20, 1952; *DeLand Daily News,* December 26, 1928.

53. *DeLand Daily News,* December 26, 1928.

54. Ibid., January 4, 16, February 1, 1929; Lily Dale Spiritualist Association, *Official Program,* 1925, 18. Since the advent of Spiritualism in antebellum America, its followers have admired Paine. See, for example, Hammond, *Pilgrimage of Thomas Paine.*

55. *Jamestown (New York) Evening Journal,* July 1, 6, 1925; *DeLand Daily News,* January 16, 1929.

56. *DeLand Daily News,* February 7, 1929.

57. SCSCMA, *Thirty-Fifth Annual Assembly Program,* 13, Owens Collection.

58. Tebeau, *A History of Florida,* 400–401.

59. Edward F. Loud, "Address," speech delivered at the annual stockholders meeting of the Cassadaga Spiritualist Camp Meeting Association, Cassadaga, Fla., March 26, 1932, Owens Collection.

60. Ibid.; *Daytona Beach News Journal,* April 28, 1957.

61. Henderson, *The Story of Cassadaga,* 16; *DeLand Sun News,* July 27, August 2, 1933.

62. McCluskey, "Mary McLeod Bethune's Impact"; Fitzgerald, *Volusia County,* 99–100.

# THREE

# On the Threshold of a New Age

## Cassadaga as a Contemporary Therapeutic Community

### PHILLIP CHARLES LUCAS

A VISITOR walking through the small Florida town of Cassadaga for the first time is likely to feel some confusion about the community's religious beliefs and practices.

On the southwest corner of Stevens Street and County Road 4139 sits the Cassadaga Spiritualist Camp Bookstore and Information Center. In the center's vestibule, leaflets advertise lessons in rainbow shamanism, advanced mediumship, astral projection, psychic development, trance channeling, psychometry, healing angels, Reiki healing, and skotography (the photographing of spirit entities). In the bookstore proper are book displays on subjects such as numerology, tarot, runes, dreams, meditation, UFOs, Eastern mysticism, Edgar Cayce, "A Course in Miracles," angels, alternative medicine, and the philosophy of Spiritualism. The visitor will also find tables of incense, candles, jewelry, and assorted New Age CDs and tapes. Across Stevens Street from the bookstore stands the historic Cassadaga Hotel with its Lost in Time café and bevy of palm readers, tarot specialists, and psychic advisors. An assortment of jewelry and paraphernalia such as Australian aboriginal rain sticks and Native American dream catchers are available for purchase in the hotel's gift shop.

Crossing County Road 4139 and heading down Stevens Street past the local post office, one might stop at the Sunflower Deli and Gift Shop for various health foods or continue next door to the Purple Rose Metaphysical Stuff store with its assortment of Native American artifacts, crystals, incense, candles, and jewelry, as well as various tarot and fortune-telling decks. Psychic readings are offered in an anteroom. Crossing Stevens Street again, one passes Sydney's Psychic Corner of Cassadaga, which offers tarot readings, handwriting analysis, and past-life regression. At the Universal Center of Cassadaga bookstore next door, a visitor can request a psychic reading or browse among books on ESP, reincarnation, ancient civilizations, palmistry, and crystal healing. Farther south down Stevens Street in the direction of Spirit Pond, one passes the Eloise Page Meditation Garden, the camp bookstore, and quaint Victorian-style houses with signs advertising mediums for hire. Where Stevens Street and Seneca Street intersect stand the Colby Memorial Temple and a small gazebo, the Caesar Forman Healing Center. More walking along the smaller streets of the town reveals more mediums for hire and, in a forest clearing, a stone circle that is used for Native American medicine wheel ceremonies.

In 1993, I was this confused visitor, wondering what the hodgepodge of signs, symbols, rituals, and accouterments revealed about the religious beliefs and practices of Cassadaga. As a scholar of alternative religions in contemporary America, I was drawn to uncover, describe, and interpret the religious system of the community and to do so on its own terms. I have attempted, to the extent it is possible, to see the world through the eyes of the camp's inhabitants. This search has entailed many hours of oral interviews with mediums, students, and visitors, participant observation at various rituals and classes over a five-year period, and a close perusal of such primary sources as advertising leaflets, annual programs, teaching materials and curricula, and lecture transcripts. The work of other scholars of Spiritualism has provided a historical and cultural backdrop to my interpretive labors.

Throughout my description and analysis, I have sought to uncover how Cassadaga as a religious community has evolved beyond traditional Spiritualism in its teachings, ritual life, and range of interests. In many ways, this development has been a generational shift, as older camp leaders have given way to those who came of age during the countercultural explosions of the 1960s and 1970s. In spite of the intracommunity tensions this shift has engendered, the expansion beyond traditional Spiritualism has been deemed necessary by camp leaders if the community is to attract new members and survive in Central Florida's competitive religious marketplace. While examining the changes that have taken place in recent years, I also argue that Cassadaga continues to value and express its long tradition of Spiritualist belief and practice and that its emerging new style and sense of mission perhaps represent the future of American Spiritualism.

# The Core Beliefs of Camp Members

The Southern Cassadaga Spiritualist Camp Meeting Association (SCSCMA) consists of fifty-seven acres where residents own homes (on land leased from the association), attend church services and workshops, and provide counseling and guidance in their roles as mediums and ministers.[1] The association does not own or run the Cassadaga Hotel and distances itself from the psychic readings and Spiritualist services taking place on its grounds. The same holds true for the various bookstores, gift shops, and readings parlors that stand across County Road 4139 from the camp's bookstore and information center. The Spiritualist services held until 1996 under the auspices of the Christian Church of Spiritual Science in the Cassadaga Hotel were unrelated to the religious ceremonies held in the camp itself. The SCSCMA is an independent Spiritualist community that is unaffiliated with any larger Spiritualist association. In 1981, the camp withdrew from the nation's largest and oldest Spiritualist umbrella organization, the National Spiritualist Association of Churches, because the national organization began exerting various pressures on the camp—particularly with regard to its certification of mediums, as unofficial camp historian Vince Owens told me in our interview.[2] In this chapter, my concern lies with the religious system of SCSCMA and its members.

Although Cassadagans firmly promote openness to alternative religious ideas and respect for other traditions, there does appear to be a core of beliefs that is generally subscribed to by the community. The first of these concerns the nature of "Infinite Intelligence," which is the way the first of the camp's Nine Principles—a statement found in the church's hymnals and shared with other Spiritualist churches—articulates the idea of a supreme being or God. Infinite Intelligence is understood by camp members to transcend the anthropomorphic images of most mainline Christian denominations. It is an impersonal creative source that is "all inclusive, omnipotent, omnipresent, and manifested through all forms of life and matter."[3] The word "matter" is important, because camp members also believe that all natural phenomena are expressions of the divine being. God, according to this view, is an "all pervading mind and intelligence that is in and of all things animate and inanimate."[4] This sense of the divine at work in all facets of nature enhances members' appreciation for the physical universe and especially for the great laws that govern natural phenomena. In many ways, this conception of God resembles Deism's supreme being, who sets in place immutable laws to which all natural phenomena must conform. As Bret Carroll's article in this volume makes clear, Spiritualists see no contradiction between religion and science and fully accept the workings of the natural order as divinely inspired and governed. The camp's conception of deity also has a strong panentheistic element, however, in that the divine being is seen as a force or energy that infuses the natural order yet also transcends it.

This conception of divinity was elaborated during my interviews with members. Rev. Jerry Frederich, a camp medium who lives in Daytona Beach, spoke of God as a "governing intelligence" and "mind" that was in "every bit of molecules in the whole universe" and that could be accessed or "downloaded" to receive important information. He also saw God as a "law of balance" and "love without ego."[5] Rev. Eloise Page described God as a "universal intelligence that we can tune into. We're part of it. But because of our personality we limit ourselves." Through meditation, Page asserted, humans could expand themselves and become attuned to the infinite mind that is God.[6] Another teacher at the camp, current president Steve Adkins, described God as "pure thought and pure impersonal love." For him, Spiritualism's disavowal of a personal God was necessary "because to put a face on God is to limit God's potential."[7] Medium Donna Bohrer summed up her understanding of God by stating: "I perceive it being an energy that permeates the universe. It's the reason why the universe doesn't just disintegrate."[8] Although members from conventional Christian backgrounds sometimes struggled with the idea of an impersonal deity—especially because it seemed to imply an uncaring nature—they had come to appreciate that an all-pervading energy and intelligence does not play favorites and does not single anyone out for punishments or rewards. Indeed, the whole idea of "chosenness" falls away with this conception, for all persons have the same opportunities to harmonize with the divine being.[9] Members emphasized their appreciation for the freedom within Spiritualism to define God according to their own understanding and experience. A distaste for unchanging dogma and doctrine was a commonly expressed theme in my interviews.

A second core belief at Cassadaga concerns the fate of humans after the death of the physical body. Teaching materials in the camp unanimously confirm that the human personality survives physical death in a conscious state and that it is possible to recognize other personalities in the afterlife. As one lesson expresses it, "We will meet, we will recognize and hold communion with loved ones" in heaven.[10] Camp members believe that persons in the afterlife state continue to progress and that souls live in conditions suited to their own level of spiritual development. The higher the development, the freer the spirit is to travel and to teach others in the heaven worlds. Evolved spirit beings travel as quickly as the mind can conceive of a place or state. They have heightened capacities and can therefore "accomplish much more than mortals do."[11] Moreover, if certain tasks remain uncompleted at the time of physical death, there is an opportunity to finish these tasks "from the Spirit side, through some mortal, who is attracted to us."[12]

Cassadagans understand the process of dying in terms that resonate with Western esoteric traditions such as Theosophy and Rosicrucianism. They believe that a person has both a physical and an etheric body (a kind of subtle blueprint for the physical body). The latter can disconnect from the physical body to travel into the spirit realm. This "body of light" connects to the physical body by a "silver cord," a kind of etheric umbilical cord. At death, the silver cord is severed, and the etheric body is free to enter the spirit world permanently.[13] Within the etheric body is what Steve Adkins termed "the spark of the infinite," the divine image which is the true identity of each person. This spark of pure awareness needs a special kind of body to function in the spirit world and thus converts the etheric body into a "causal" body. As the causal body evolves to higher levels, the personality becomes more aware of its deeper identity and more capable of serving those on lower levels of awareness—including those still in physical incarnation. Many residents accept a multitiered picture of heaven wherein people serve as overseers or helpers to individuals, groups of people, whole continents or nations, the planet earth, and finally the solar system, in ascending sequence. Spirit beings retain a strong interest in loved ones they have left behind on earth and in people who work in their areas of special interest such as science or music.

Many of the younger members I interviewed believe in reincarnation, or multiple earthly incarnations, while acknowledging that this is not an officially accepted Spiritualist doctrine. Spiritualism has tended to reject the reincarnationist perspective until recently, when it officially adopted a more neutral position. Although most Spiritualist churches still do not allow ministers to discuss reincarnation from the platform during worship services, SCSCMA does permit such discussion, William Deep, a camp member who lives in Orlando, told me.[14] To most of the Spiritualists I spoke with, acceptance or rejection of reincarnation was not a critical issue, since "the basis of Spiritualism is spirit communication, which says nothing about whether you or the spirit you are communicating with have been reincarnated in the past."[15] Moreover, reincarnation does not directly contradict Spiritualism's foundational belief in the survival of the individual personality after death and in the soul's progressive evolution throughout eternity. Nevertheless, I was struck by how many of the mediums I interviewed had adopted a reincarnationist perspective. This is one area of camp belief that has clearly been influenced by the increased American interest in Eastern religious philosophies since the mid 1960s.

Camp members hold closely to Spiritualism's traditional beliefs concerning heaven and hell. Principle 8 of the Nine Principles states: "We affirm that the doorway to reformation is never closed against any human soul here or hereafter. . . . Man can change his way of thinking, acting, and living. . . . Eternal damnation has no place in the philosophy or religion of Spiritualism."[16] The radical rejection of hell as a place of eternal torment was part of Spiritualism's earliest identity and reflected a broader questioning of traditional Christian afterlife doctrines that took place during the early 1800s in America. Like the Universalist movement of the same era, Spiritualists embraced an optimistic and merciful view of human destiny that left open the possibility of repentance and self-reformation at any stage of the soul's eternal journey. The camp's teaching materials maintain that the doctrine of eternal punishment was not part of early Judaism but rather the invention of Christian priests bent on frightening the laity into servile submission.[17] Adkins affirmed in our interview that human nature was originally good rather than sinful and that following Spiritualist principles help in the restoration of that goodness. This attitude resonates well with contemporary America's culture of recovery, whether from substance abuse, criminality, depression, or any of a host of psychosocial dysfunctions. The belief that self-transformation is never beyond human possibility, even in the hereafter, conforms to the experience of many Americans who have "recovered" from difficult conditions.

Members elaborated on their view of heaven and hell in ways that disclosed the community's basic code of ethics. Several stated that heaven and hell were states of mind and being, rather than places, and that the only heaven or hell a person would experience was that of their own making. By following the Golden Rule and treating others with love and respect, Spiritualists believe they are creating conditions of love, peace, human solidarity, and enlightenment for themselves and others in the afterlife. As the Reverend Frederich expressed it, "when we pass over into the world of spirit, we very much create the situation that we progress into." During a "life review," souls experience the effects of their words and actions as if they were on the receiving end.[18]

This focus on personal responsibility is the cornerstone of ethical thinking at Cassadaga. Barbara Joy Hines Bengtson, a former president of the association, told me in our interview: "Each person is responsible for their own lives. You cannot simply defer that responsibility or delegate it to any church or priest or minister. We must each ultimately be responsible for ourselves and walk in that responsibility. . . . It's not simply a matter of do as you will and right before you pass you'll cover my sins for me. . . . No loopholes, no blanket coverage."[19] The subtext for the camp's ethic of responsibility is a rejection of the traditional Christian doctrine of the "vicarious atonement," the teaching that through the shedding of his blood on the cross, Christ took away the sins of the world—paid them off, in effect, for those willing to believe in him. As Hines Bengtson expressed it, "I think there's going to be a big surprise for many people who believe that. . . . I don't think that we can just go out and sin and sin and dump it on him [Christ]. It doesn't make sense." SCSCMA members feel unburdened by the complex systems of law that guide followers in such traditions as Orthodox Judaism and Islam. For Cassadagans, William Deep said in our interview, Jesus' summation of Jewish law in the Gospels, "Love God and love your neighbor as yourself," is all the guidance a person needs to live the good life.

Related to this rejection of orthodox Christian doctrine regarding the crucifixion of Christ is the Cassadaga community's ethos of self-empowerment and self-validation. Although God's grace is real and can be felt when a soul chooses to be of service to others, all human advancement comes through personal effort, Hines Bengtson told me. Belief in saviors or gurus is discouraged at Cassadaga, and members are proud that their religion does not require them to take anything on pure faith. Rather, they are encouraged to search, explore, and question, and to test their own principles; they validate only those teachings that can be proven and experienced personally. Participants are urged to develop their own psychic and spiritual faculties and to make contact with the spirit world personally, without the mediation of priests or outside authority figures.[20] This empirical, pragmatic attitude concerning the spiritual life has long been a hallmark of Spiritualism, a tradition that has its roots in nineteenth-century Christian anxieties concerning the ascendancy of science as a master interpretation of the world. Spiritualists have throughout their history sought to reconcile religion and science by demonstrating empirically the survival of the human personality after death. This empirical attitude extends to all facets of spiritual unfoldment at the camp.

With regard to the future, camp members expressed a kind of progressive millennial perspective that envisioned a greater spiritual awareness developing within the current generation and the potential for real human progress on a number of fronts. None of my respondents foresaw an imminent catastrophic apocalypse, and most rejected various disaster scenarios, whether related to tectonic upheaval, meteors slamming into the earth, environmental meltdown, or a shifting of the earth's poles. In keeping with their ethos of personal empowerment and responsibility, members affirmed that what happens in the future is for humans to decide. As Hines Bengtson put it, "Each person must choose for themselves . . . it is changing with every breath we exhale, with every thought we think . . . it's up to humankind." The Reverend Donna Bohrer stated that the present period is characterized by an intensification of transformative energies in the earth and by religious revivals of many stripes. As a prerequisite for planetary transformation, however, people must experience an inner transformation of consciousness: "I don't think you are going to get people to change their lifestyles unless you change how they see themselves, how they see the world and where they fit in. You are not going to get somebody to give up their five-bathroom house just because you say it's not good for the earth. . . . If you are going to change the world outside, you have to change people inside first, and one would hope that spiritual communities would help people do that."

Camp president Steve Adkins expressed his belief that a new race of metaphysically minded people would gradually replace the present race of machine builders and technocrats. As for impending catastrophe, Adkins rejected the doom and gloom prophecies of many groups and speculated that any earth changes would evolve slowly and in harmony with natural law. Again, human choice would be the predominant factor influencing what kind of future people experienced: "I feel that whatever people expect is where they're going to be drawn to. If they expect revolution and disruption, they're going to draw themselves to the places where that's going to occur. If people expect hope and inspiration, they're going to be drawn to those places." In the main, Cassadagans placed little emphasis on millennial hopes and fears, preferring to focus their energies on providing healing and guidance to clients and church members, and on individual practices of self-realization and self-empowerment.

Asked about the ultimate purpose of human life, the community expressed a range of opinion and belief. For Hines Bengtson, the purpose of life is to serve others and to return to a conscious union with the divine being. The material world provides individuals with valuable learning experiences: "It's like an oyster and the grit—through the friction and density of this incarnation we're able to work out things that could take eons and eons on other planes. So we choose to come here. It's like a schoolhouse, an experiential playground. We choose to come here and we choose to try to accomplish certain things." At the highest level of human evolution, Hines Bengtson believes that spirits come and go at will between earth and heaven with an "ascended" body.

For another medium, Jerry Frederich, the purpose of life is ascension—a term that connotes an overcoming of the limitations of earth's gravitational pull and a returning of the soul to the "God-mind" after fully realizing the "spark of God within us." Ascended beings form a kind of heavenly hierarchy who return to earth when needed to assist in human spiritual evolution. Discourse within the camp concerning ascension and ascended beings resonates with a perennial esoteric tradition that posits the existence of highly evolved humans who have achieved a level of spiritual development comparable to that of the ascended Christ. These beings are intimately involved in assisting and guiding spiritual aspirants on earth. Contemporary alternative religious movements such as the I AM Activity and the Church Universal and Triumphant promote ascension as the goal of human life and claim to receive guidance from various "ascended masters." William Deep summed up the view of most camp members I interviewed when he explained that the goal of human life is to return to one's true home in the spirit world. The means of return, he added, is by serving others so that mental and emotional healing can take place and all people can return to their heavenly home together.

Although a number of individual interpretations of Spiritualist ideas exist and are tolerated at Cassadaga, I found a remarkable degree of agreement concerning the community's core beliefs and convictions. This seeming consensus is initially puzzling, given the independent thinking that is fostered at the camp and the group's longstanding refusal to proselytize for new members. However, the principle of affinities would dictate that only people who already hold compatible beliefs would be drawn to investigate seriously the camp and its religious principles. Those who actually join the church and seek certification as mediums would have learned through sermons, workshops, and ministerial training to see the world through the community's eyes and would therefore be gradually socialized to accept the core beliefs that make Spiritualism a distinct brand of alternative American religion.

These core beliefs, to summarize, include the acceptance of an impersonal God that manifests throughout the natural order in various laws and processes. Spiritualists view God as an energy and an intelligence with which humans can achieve harmony and which they can "access" for knowledge, healing, and creative inspiration. Like the mysterious Tao in Chinese Taoism, this divinity far transcends human understanding, including the conventional concepts and anthropomorphic images of orthodox Christianity. Camp members believe that the human personality, with all its distinctive characteristics, survives physical death as a kind of subtle body that continues to learn and progress in the afterlife. Although many different levels or states of consciousness exist in the spirit world, spirits are not relegated to any particular state for all of eternity. Rather, as lessons are learned and growth occurs, spirits move forward to greater service and responsibility within the divine economy. For many Cassadagans, this can include reincarnation into physical bodies on earth.

The essential ethical code of the community includes both the Golden Rule and the Christian command to love and serve God and one's neighbor unconditionally. This ethical striving encompasses a strong focus on personal responsibility for one's thoughts and actions, and a rejection of the idea that one can avoid the consequences for transgressions through faith in a savior or redeemer figure. The opportunity for reform is always present, but the reform process entails learning lessons in the "school of hard knocks" and tangible restitution for harm inflicted on others. Camp members downplay faith-based knowledge and take pride in the empirical verification of their principles. Experience, investigation, and testing provide the means to reliable knowledge both in this world and the next. This ethic of self-validation is related to an ethic of self-empowerment that is also important in the camp. Members believe that the future is created by human action and thought in the circumstances of each day. Although hopes for a more spiritual and enlightened future exist, the details of that future are not seen as predestined by God. Rather, they are fluid and ambiguous. The ultimate purpose of life, for the Spiritualists I interviewed, is to achieve a thorough integration with the divine being. This is accomplished by loving service to others, by inner attunement with one's deepest self, and by developing the capacity to move between the spirit and earth realms in an "ascended" body of light. The pathway to this self-unfoldment, for many Cassadagans, is mediumship.

## Mediumship and Healing at Cassadaga

Mediums play a vital religious role at Cassadaga. Such persons are trained and certified by the camp to communicate with the spirit world, to counsel and guide both church members and nonmember clients, and to act as agents of physical and spiritual healing. As has been true throughout Spiritualism's history in America, the medium's vocation is open to both genders, but women predominate. The 1994–95 camp program listed sixteen women and seven men as approved mediums.[21] The following year the list had grown to eighteen women and seven men, and the next year to eighteen women and six men.[22] Although all persons are believed to possess the potential for mediumship, women have been considered superior mediums because Spiritualists have traditionally viewed them as having more passive temperaments, more sensitivity to spirit vibrations, and a natural capacity for various levels of trance. Feminist scholars have effectively "problematized" such Victorian gender stereotypes, and current research and analysis emphasize that Spiritualism's appeal for women had mainly to do with the opportunities for religious leadership and the forums for public advocacy of various reform causes that Spiritualism provided them.[23]

According to Spiritualist literature, a medium serves mainly as a messenger of ideas, words, symbols, and other forms of communication from discarnate spirits to persons on earth. Messages can last anywhere from a minute to an hour, depending upon the setting, the purpose of communication, and the ability of the medium.[24] During Cassadaga's Wednesday evening services, for example, messages are given in a public setting and usually last for no more than three to four minutes. Private readings in a medium's parlor, on the other hand, can last anywhere from twenty minutes to a full hour. The mediums I interviewed each spoke of personal spirit guides who act as their gatekeepers to the spirit world as well as their protectors and teachers. These guardian spirits develop characteristic means of letting the medium know that the channels to the spirit world are open for communication. In a sense they can be said to run interference with the various spirit beings who wish to communicate through the medium. In traditional Spiritualism, Barbara Joy Hines Bengtson told me in our interview, each medium was thought to have a special band of spirit guides that included a Native American, a physician, a philosopher, and a joy guide—a kind of inner child who brings joy and spontaneity into the medium's life. Cassadaga's mediums work with such bands, but usually have a main guide or "control." Medium Jim Watson described his spirit guide as a seven-foot Native American named White Bear, who was revealed to him during his training as a medium. For Watson, White Bear has become a continuous presence that he talks to as he would any good friend. William Deep's spirit guide appears to him as a monk in a long brown robe with a rope around his waist. Several mediums said they had first encountered their guides during childhood or adolescence and that coming to Cassadaga had validated their mediumistic experiences and helped them develop a closer relationship with their personal spirit teachers.

Mediums use various modes of communication to receive messages from their spirit guides. Some hear an actual voice, while others simply sense a presence and message, which they communicate to their client. In some of the auditory communications, a lecture or speech is given word for word to the medium. Mediums such as Eloise Page receive visual symbols, which they interpret intuitively according to a tested scheme of correspondences.[25] According to medium Steve Adkins, all Spiritualists accept as fact the proposition that discarnate spirits are "willing and anxious" to communicate with loved ones on earth and that a spirit's unfoldment in the afterlife often is contingent on helping earthbound family members or those with whom they have some kind of special mentoring relationship.

The camp's mediums make a clear distinction between spirit mediumship and "psychic readings" and place a greater value on the former means of communication. Spirit mediumship entails raising one's vibrations and awareness so that spirits from higher dimensions can use one as a sounding board. The medium is a passive receiver—often likened to a telephone wire—who is personally uninvolved in the message process. Psychic reading, on the other hand, is an active sensing by the psychic of a client's etheric field. This field can be likened to an extrasensory tapestry that contains various kinds of information about the person's past and future. These readings involve no trance and no communication with spirit intelligences.[26] During their training, mediums learn to distinguish between these two modes of information retrieval, and to seek greater development of spirit mediumship proper. Not only is the information communicated from spirits believed to be clearer and less tainted with personal biases, but it is also considered primary proof of personal immortality—something of fundamental importance to all Spiritualists. Still, mediums at Cassadaga do not wholly discount psychic ability or the helpful personal guidance that is often given during psychic readings.

After discussing this point with mediums and observing both kinds of readings, I have concluded that, for many mediums, the distinction between these two categories is less clear in practice than it is in theory. One indication of this is the often heard statement that "all mediums are psychics, but not all psychics are mediums." This seems to be a tacit admission that camp mediums can receive information from both psychic reading and spirit communication, and that often the real source is a matter of interpretation. Barbara Joy Hines Bengtson admitted that her primary spirit guide might in reality be a part of her own corporate awareness—but "far enough removed from human perception to seem as a separate entity." The distinction between spirit mediumship and psychic reading may be largely a function of the camp mediums' need to establish a market advantage over the "psychic" readers who earn their livings on the camp's periphery.

Related to psychic and mediumistic information retrieval is the issue of spirit discernment. Although most mediums scoff at the idea of Satan and his demonic host, they concede that some spirit entities are unreliable and foolish. Some mediums frankly stated that simply because persons had passed over to the spirit world did not mean that they automatically became wise spirit guides. As medium Steve Adkins reflected, "I think that you have certain spirits that are in the lower astral planes that try to communicate out of confusion or try to communicate because they have not risen very far out of their psychic vibration, but no spirit can do anything in this physical realm without using a person to work through." SCSCMA mediums emphasize the importance of developing a means of discerning between a vengeful and deluded spirit entity, a busybody spirit who simply wants to dispense advice to all and sundry, and a higher spirit whose motive is to bring messages of healing and consolation. Because spirit beings in theory tend to gravitate toward mediums who are similar in temperament and intention, student mediums are encouraged to follow a disciplined program of self-improvement and self-purification.[27]

Unspoken but recognized in several written sources and in many of my interviews was the danger of spirit possession and the need to protect oneself from spirit attacks. As medium William Deep observed, "The problem with being a medium is that you can be wide open and if you're not on your guard you can be wide open to things that you'd rather not be open to." Particularly when mediums expose themselves to the "dense" atmosphere of places such as bars or gambling casinos, their auras are believed to be penetrable and "open for attachment." To prevent such negative attachments, medium Jerry Frederich told me, the mediums employ a host of protective practices—they may visualize angels and force fields, burn candles and incense, employ the Native American practice of "smudging" with sage, recite the Lord's Prayer, or play sacred music.

SCSCMA mediums undergo a thorough certification process that usually lasts between four and six years. The academic rigor and professionalism of this training has been augmented during the 1990s, both to improve the quality of mediumistic service for clients and to weed out unscrupulous mediums who come to the camp with questionable certification from other organizations. In addition to various classes and workshops, mediums must provide evidence of their ability to communicate with the spirit world before becoming SCSCMA certified.[28]

As detailed in the association's educational literature, those seeking certification as a medium must first become camp members and find a "certifying evaluator." This person is a SCSCMA-approved medium who acts as a kind of mentor and advocate for the student. After writing up a plan of study in consultation with the evaluator, the student submits the plan to the certification committee for review. When the plan is approved, the student begins taking classes in the religion, science, and philosophy of Spiritualism, the distinctions between mediums and psychics, the phases of mediumship, the human aura, the methods and ethics of spiritual healing, performing as a platform speaker at worship services, the history of ancient Spiritualism, Spiritualism in the Bible, natural law, parapsychology, spiritual metaphysics, comparative religions, pastoral ethics, and the psychology of teacher/student, medium/client, and healer/client relations. Students submit a progress report to their certifying evaluator every six months. When, any time after the first year of training, the evaluator deems that the student has developed the requisite skills to begin public work, the evaluator submits a written recommendation to the certification committee. Upon the committee's recommendation, the board of trustees usually gives its approval for the student to begin working in the camp as a probationary medium.[29]

SCSCMA-trained mediums remarked that the most important part of their education was the continual practice of giving readings and learning to bring through verifiable facts from the spirit world. Much of this practice entailed a growing sensitivity to subtle energies and changes of vibration as well as confidence in their inner contact with spirit beings. As one student, Don Zanghi, commented, "The training for mediumship isn't so much gathering left-brain knowledge as it is the unfolding of the spiritual part, the unfoldment of your psychic abilities . . . so there is a lot of meditation, a lot of practice getting messages, a lot of drills and exercises . . . basically it is to go deeper than yourself, to make the connection where spirit resides and make up a guided meditation or visualization that will take you to that point."[30] Many classes include scientific experiments designed to fine-tune the medium's extrasensory capabilities and to convince the students that such perception is both possible and natural.[31] This emphasis on the scientific verification of spiritual phenomena, as we have seen, is a distinguishing feature of Spiritualism and owes as much to the fraud scandals that threatened the religion's survival in the late nineteenth and early twentieth centuries as it does to the desire for certainty in religious matters during an increasingly scientific age.

Following a minimum of two years' study the student submits a final progress report to the certification committee along with general letters of recommendation and a letter from the certifying evaluator detailing the student's demonstrated competencies. The committee then refers these materials to the board for final action. According to camp policy, final certification by the board comes upon demonstration that the student is a "test and message" medium who possesses "psychic powers of an evidential and edifying nature," or a medium "through whose instrumentality physical phenomena can be produced."[32]

Physical phenomena, which have been downplayed by Spiritualists over the past fifty years because of embarrassing instances of fraud, result from the "process whereby someone, in Spirit, usually known as a spirit operator (as compared to a spirit communicator) works or operates through the mental *and* physical energies of the medium and causes something physical to happen on the Earth plane." Physical phenomena are objective and thus can allegedly be seen or heard by all persons present when they happen. Although the explanations for these phenomena vary, the traditional view is that spirit operators use excess "etheric matter" in the medium's etheric body to produce various physical manifestations. Such manifestations include the movement of objects such as tables or chairs, direct vocal sounds (often given through a small conical device known as a trumpet), the materialization and dematerialization of objects such as gems and animals, raps and taps, the appearance of flashes or balls of light, and the actual materialization of a spirit being (seen as the highest manifestation of physical mediumship).[33]

Spiritualist literature provides two basic reasons for the rarity of physical phenomena over the past fifty years. First, when Spiritualism was new, people needed concrete, objective evidence of "Spirit's" presence; as more people began to accept the reality of spirit mediumship, the spirits began to manifest more in "mental mediumship," which provided a much needed sophistication of teaching and philosophy for the growing movement. Second, the mastery of physical mediumship is a long, arduous process that is unappealing to modern-day Spiritualists.[34] Both national Spiritualist sources and several camp mediums, however, have noted a resurgence of interest in physical phenomena during the 1990s. One medium interpreted this interest as a sign of the camp's growing confidence in itself and as a blessing that provided many people with physical proof of spirit communication in a way that mental mediumship could not quite match. "While it's much easier to sit down and communicate with spirit," according to Hines Bengtson, "you've never been hugged until you've been hugged by a table, until you've had that proof beyond what you could classify as your own imagination or your own thought process."

The certification given by the board of trustees comes in three classes. Class A certification allows mediums to give spirit messages in both public and private settings. Class B certification permits mediums to give messages only in private settings or in message circles—also known as séances. Class C certification recognizes physical mediumship skills "of an edifying nature." Some mediums receive camp certification through a transfer of certification or ordination rights from another Spiritualist organization. This transfer entails the granting, following board deliberations, of a provisional status during which the association can

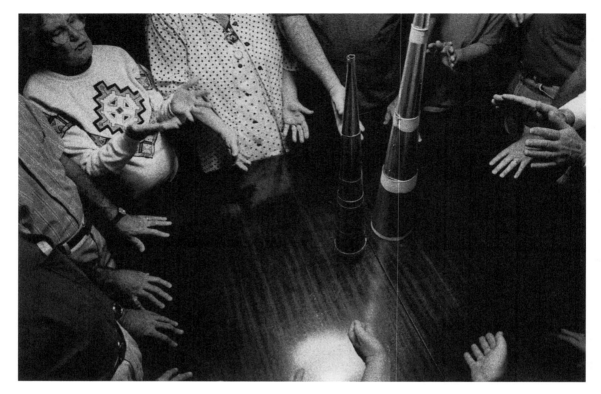

*Table-tipping at a private residence, 1997.*

observe a medium's work firsthand. After "several months to a year," the board, upon the reception of letters of recommendation from people who have observed the individual's work during the probationary period, may grant the medium permission to work permanently on camp grounds.[35] These rigorous certification steps make a great deal of sense, given the susceptibility of Spiritualism to fraud and other forms of unethical behavior as well as the camp's desire to protect the livelihoods of their established mediums.

Although spiritual healing has long been a facet of Spiritualism, the training of healers and the conducting of healing work has grown in importance in Cassadaga during the 1990s. For many members, healing ranks equal to teaching as the primary spiritual mission of the camp. The certification of healers is every bit as rigorous as that of mediums and follows the same basic steps. A student healer's curriculum contains many of the same classes as the mediumship curriculum, but it focuses on the ethical and legal dimensions of healing work and on the distinctive forms of Spiritualist healing. These include absent healing through mental prayer and the laying on of hands, or magnetic healing. In absent healing, students learn how to pray for people who are not physically present, but who can still be affected by a medium's healing intent and focus. As one medium explained, "The ill person doesn't actually have to know about it. Through spirit they can be healed."[36] Absent-healing treatments can be requested through a medium or by placing a person's name on a healing list in Colby Temple.

Magnetic healing is taught through what is termed "chair work." This training practicum consists of student mediums learning to channel forces of healing from the spirit world through their hands to a person sitting on a stool. As one medium described it, "I'm being intuitive in the sense that energy is coming through me and I pray that only that which is of God come forth. And you're radiating energy to the person, but it's coming through your hands. . . . We're working with the electromagnetic forces of their body, called the aura."[37] A student healer, Don Zanghi, spoke of magnetic healing in a similar discourse of energies and vibrations and emphasized a process of attunement and receptivity that is similar to that of mental mediumship: "I try to raise my personal psychic and spiritual energy level to raise the vibrations to open up to higher levels where the energy originates—that is, spirit guides, teachers, spirit healers, any beings in the higher realm that are of God—to work through me or give them permission to work through me. . . . My job is to just be the channel, not to worry about [whether] it happens or if it doesn't happen."

In special class exercises, Rev. Donna Bohrer said, students learn to feel a person's energy field and "see" with their hands. An observer of a healing session notices healers closing their eyes, rubbing their hands together, and then placing their hands on a person's shoulder, head, or any other part of the body they feel moved to contact. Medium Jim Watson spoke of making "passes" with his hands through the person's auric field and lingering at points in this field that felt "rough," or "cold," or "blocked." Spiritual healing by the laying on of hands is certainly not unique to Spiritualism. Aside from its pedigree in the New Testament miracles of Jesus and his disciples, the practice can be found in most Christian churches and in such alternative healing therapies as Reiki, polarity massage, and acupressure massage. Its popularity across traditions is a testament to the ever-present need in human societies for physical and spiritual healing.

As Watson explained the process, those who seek certification as camp healers must provide letters from six persons verifying positive physiological changes of specific chronic conditions as a result of a healing session. Once this evidence

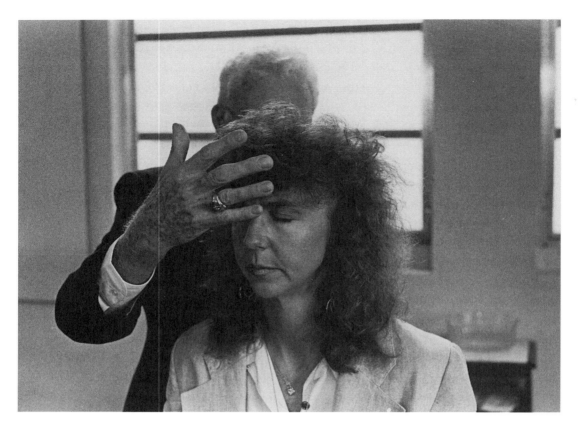

*Laying on of hands during healing meditation, Colby Memorial Temple, 1995.*

has been provided to the camp's board, a certificate is issued commissioning the person as a Spiritualist healer. Healers are admonished to inform themselves of the civil codes and local ordinances related to healing work and to conduct themselves in accord with these laws. Often the same person will seek certification as both a healer and a medium.[38]

Most of the mediums and healers I interviewed have a regular regimen of spiritual practices. Bohrer, for example, practices yoga and meditation to maintain bodily health and to increase her awareness of the spiritual energies around her. Her prayers are exercises in attunement with the divine being more than petitions or praise. Like other camp mediums, she burns incense and lights candles as aids to inner centering. Watson practices "constant prayer," which he explains as a continual remembrance of God's presence in his life, whether walking in nature, sitting in silence, or counseling a client. Hines Bengtson meditates each morning and practices a kind of retrospection each evening before going to sleep. She also blesses her food before meals to raise its vibration and engages in various attunements with the energies of natural phenomena. Her prayers are designed to keep her in constant communication with God and can include chanting the Sanskrit syllable "om" or Native American petitions such as "Keep me centered as I walk on the earth, heavenly spirit; keep my footsteps on the ground, though my songs reach to the sky; for these things I pray . . . and may I bring to the earth the love in my heart." During his morning meditations, medium William Deep burns candles and surrounds himself with religious icons and symbols to draw positive spiritual intelligences and forces.

Healing mediums speak of their special preparation for treatments. Steve Adkins, to take one example, asks that he be used as an instrument of intervention for the person before him and affirms three times that he is a "clear and open channel of light" who follows the "light of the Christ within." After giving permission for ministering spirits to work through him, he experiences various spirit presences who begin their work: "There are specific ones that I see that prepare the atmosphere, and then there are other ones that work specifically with the person. Sometimes it's a deceased loved one, and sometimes it's just a tremendous presence." Rev. Jerry Frederich prepares for a reading with a five-minute meditation. He then holds his client's hands or some item of theirs and silently prays, "In the name of Christ, in the name of the Almighty God I Am, let nothing come forth except that which is of God." He explains, "That just sort of sets the energy upwards, kind of gets me out of the way."

As is apparent from these examples, the figure of Jesus plays a prominent role in the spiritual lives of Cassadaga's members. As the camp's annual program states: "We consider him [Jesus] the greatest teacher and Medium the world has ever known, a God-man who knew and applied the Spiritual Law to a greater extent than any human soul who has ever lived, and we hold his name sacred in every way."[39] For many Cassadagans, Jesus is the ideal model of both mediumship and healing and the master who brought proof of eternal life. Unlike orthodox Christians, however, Spiritualists do not view Jesus as God incarnate, born of a virgin to be savior of the world. As Adkins expressed it, "I feel that Jesus Christ was the first one to bring across the Golden Rule in his part of the world, and he's the first one to base a religion totally on it. But to say that he was not a man is a mistake. Christ himself never states that he was born from a virgin anywhere in the Bible." For Eloise Page, Jesus was a highly developed man whose sense of oneness with God gave him tremendous gifts of inspiration, insight, sensitivity, and understanding. Drawing on esoteric traditions from the I AM Activity and Rosicrucianism, she also sees him as a high priest who was trained in the heavenly Order of Melchizedek for his teaching mission. Jerry

Frederich spoke for many camp members when he affirmed Jesus' sacred mission as a demonstrator of spiritual laws and a great prophet and teacher. He cautioned, however, that Jesus had said, "All these things that I have done, you shall do them greater," and that to see him as a god on a throne was to risk putting his gifts of mediumship and healing beyond the reach of ordinary human beings. For Frederich, all persons are children of God whose inheritance is to prophesy, teach, and heal. As Jim Watson expressed it, Jesus "was there to show, to demonstrate what everybody could do. Not what God could do necessarily, but what man could do. . . . He was a master teacher, a master healer who knew how to use the abilities that we all have. . . . He would heal the sick because he had that direct connection. And he would tell his disciples, 'That's all you have to do.'" This understanding of Jesus clearly reflects the camp's egalitarian ethic and its suspicion of gurus and charismatic leaders. Many of the people I interviewed found the camp's Christology to be a refreshing and empowering alternative to the view of Jesus offered in mainstream Christian churches.

A third level of professionalization at Cassadaga is ordination to the ministry. Ministerial credentials are given after a person has achieved certification as a medium or healer. The additional training, which usually takes two to four years, includes academic courses in comparative religion, metaphysics, parapsychology, the Bible, and comparative Spiritualism. Pastoral counseling units include addiction, crisis, grief, illness, and relationship counseling, as well as home, hospital, jail, and nursing home visitations. In the curriculum's professional and teaching component, units range from pastoral ethics, tax, finance, and legal issues, to teaching both large and small groups. Liturgical training covers such ceremonies as house blessings, healing services, marriages, memorial services, and naming services.[40] Of the twenty-four mediums listed in the 1996–97 *Annual Program,* thirteen were titled "Reverend," evidence that the ministerial step is an available option but one that is not chosen by roughly half of the camp's mediums. The training and education of ministers has been elaborated and refined during the 1990s, and camp leaders emphasize the high expectations, both moral and spiritual, that they place upon ordained mediums.

In summary, mediums and healers are the camp's primary spiritual functionaries. Both vocations require the traditional shaman's ability to function as an intermediary between the physical and spiritual worlds, because it is from the spirit realm that both the wise counsel of spirit beings and healing energies are believed to come. The training of mediums and healers is rigorous and comprehensive, reflecting both a desire to weed out the unscrupulous and the exploitative, and a need to limit the competition for clients among the camp's established professionals. Spiritual healers have long been a part of Spiritualism, but the popularity and importance of healing work at Cassadaga has increased during the 1990s. The camp affirms that spiritual healing occurs through an individual's self-healing ability, through the healer's ability to channel spiritual energies into the individual's body and mind by the laying on of hands, and through the work of spirits who, in response to prayer, carry God's healing energies to persons not present. At the same time, the camp makes it clear that spiritual healing should be seen as a *complement* to the work of traditional and alternative medical practitioners, and not as a *substitution*.[41] Although the medium, the healer, and the minister are individuals, none of their roles has meaning outside a community setting, wherein they can conduct their rituals and preside over various ceremonial events.

## Ritual and Community Life at Cassadaga

The Cassadaga Camp Meeting Association fosters a spiritually nurturing community life for its members through a variety of rituals, ceremonies, and annual events. For many residents, the camp's natural setting is itself a kind of holy ground that provides them a tranquil sanctuary from the harsh realities of the outside world and nurtures their spiritual unfoldment. In the camp's myth of origins, the medium George P. Colby was guided by his spirit guide Seneca to a site chosen by a "congress of spirits for a great spiritual center." Colby found the land "situated on high pine bluffs, overlooking a chain of silvery lakes," and was given to understand that the "resinous breath of the pines" and nearby spring would heal him of incipient consumption and poor health. When two of the camp's founders, mediums Emma J. Huff and Marion Skidmore, first saw the site, Skidmore is reported to have exclaimed, "This is the spot for the camp ground. It is lovely, and the spirit of the place seems right."[42] The association reinforces this tradition of Cassadaga as a sacred space by scheduling a yearly round of rituals and celebrations. These events are designed to facilitate encounters with the spiritual world and to strengthen the bonds of community feeling in the camp.

The tradition of Sunday church services dates back to the earliest days of the community. Until the late 1980s, these services began at 2:30 in the afternoon and often lasted until 4:00. In contemporary times, Sunday services are preceded by an adult Sunday school in the Andrew Jackson Davis building. This opportunity to learn about Spiritualist religion and philosophy lasts from 9:45 to 10:15 in the morning and is held from October to May, the camp's busiest season.

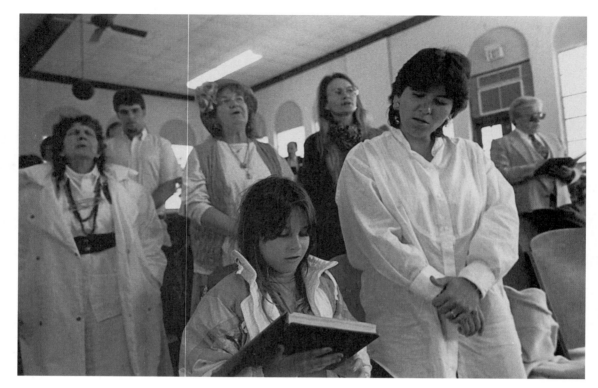

*Singing during Sunday church service, Colby Memorial Temple, 1995.*

Private healing services are available in the Caesar Forman Healing Center, a small gazebo-shaped structure in front of Colby Memorial Temple, Sunday mornings from 10:00 until 10:30. A healer waits in the center for visitors, who enter and sit on a stool while she conducts her laying on of hands and auric "passes." Children can attend Lyceum Sunday School for Juniors at the temple for forty-five minutes on Sunday mornings from October through May. The various Sunday morning classes allow the camp to better educate its members and to attract visitors who are interested in Spiritualist philosophy and practice. They also enable the camp's teachers to polish their skills in presenting their beliefs to a wider audience. This practice becomes valuable when, as often occurs, they are asked to teach classes on Spiritualism in other venues around the country. The healing services signal both members and visitors that Cassadaga's mission includes not only teaching but also healing those in need.[43]

Sunday morning worship begins at 10:30 in Colby Temple, a nondescript square-shaped building with no steeple, whose large opaque windows can be opened to allow in fresh breezes off Spirit Pond. The temple's interior resembles an aging auditorium, with rows of wood-slatted pews that slope downward before an elevated stage area. Upon the stage is an organ, an American flag, a row of armchairs for the presiding speakers and mediums, and a large lectern. During the mid-1990s the walls around the sanctuary were covered with framed pictures of religious figures such as Jesus, the Buddha, Mother Teresa of Calcutta, Krishna, Paramahansa Yogananda, and Yogananda's guru, Sri Yukteswar. At the center of the sanctuary hung a large oil painting of the cosmos that evoked a sense of Spirit's omnipresence in the universe. By 1998, the pictures had disappeared from the walls, likely a result of a change of leadership. Along the walls at the rear of the temple are tables with hymnals and leaflets, wooden benches, and between four and eight stools for the worship service's healing segment. A cross section of people is usually present for the weekly services, but the preponderance of participants are white middle-aged women, most of whom are not mediums. Often these women come in groups of two and three, and sometimes they bring their adolescent or young adult children. The number of male-female couples is usually small, and the overall attendance ranges from about thirty people to as many as two hundred during the camp's high season. The atmosphere is casual and informal, and dress styles range from blue jeans and T-shirts to jackets, dresses, skirts, and blouses.

The services, which are conducted on a year-round basis, begin with the lighting of three candles set in a candelabra on a table in front of the stage. The candles symbolize the union of body, mind, and spirit to which members aspire. Following an opening greeting by the officiant, congregants rise and sing from a book of conventional Protestant and Spiritualist hymns. A visitor is likely to hear anything from "In the Garden" to "Amazing Grace" and "For the Beauty of the Earth" led by a talented song leader and a competent organist. After affirming the camp's nondogmatic orientation, the officiant then asks the congregation to read the Declaration of Principles, which amounts to a credo for many Spiritualists. Its nine points affirm the central beliefs of Spiritualism and include the survival of personal identity after death, the possibility of spirit communication, the ethics of the Golden Rule, the moral responsibility of the individual, the ever-present opportunity for self-reformation, and the reality of prophecy and healing as "Divine attributes proven through Mediumship."[44]

The service then moves into its second phase, a guided meditation and healing ceremony. All who wish to avail themselves of a healing treatment are encouraged to walk to the rear of the temple and to sit on one of the wooden stools lined up along the back walkway. Typically, between ten and twenty attendees will receive treatments from certified healers during the next twenty minutes, while others in the congregation are asked to close their eyes and to follow a guided meditation led by one of the platform mediums. These meditations often begin with a request to "release anxiety and dis-ease" and to breathe in love, joy, hope, and light. Soft meditative music with inspirational themes plays softly in the background. In the meditations I attended the congregants were led on a long inner journey through beautiful natural settings. At a certain point those gathered met a spirit guide and received an important message. The guided visualization exercise usually lasts between ten and twenty minutes, depending upon the number of people desiring a healing treatment. There next follow another inspirational hymn and the introduction of a guest speaker. The speaker, who is often a Spiritualist from another city or region, gives a ten- to twenty-minute message, after which the offering plate is passed and camp announcements are made.

When the announcements are completed, the service enters its third and final phase, the transmission of spirit messages from the platform. This phase has long been a hallmark of Spiritualist services and purports to provide a demonstration of spirit communication. It thus not only offers messages of guidance and consolation to congregants, but also reinforces the core beliefs of Spiritualists with regard to survival of the personality after physical death and the possibility of empirically verifiable contact with those in the spirit realm. The platform medium typically asks a person sitting in the temple whether they can "come to them" or "enter their vibration." When assent is given, usually with a nod, the medium begins to transmit spirit messages that can last anywhere from thirty seconds to five minutes. These communications usually include at least two of the following themes: (1) greetings and encouragement from a departed relative; (2) interpretation by the spirits of events in the recent past, usually of a problematic nature; (3) diagnosis of present conditions; (4) prophecies of future trends and events. Platform mediums are skilled at reading the body language of the person to whom they are giving messages and at eliciting feedback that lets them know whether the messages are striking a chord. The more nods and smiles they observe, the longer the reading tends to last. The less confirmatory body language they elicit, the shorter the reading becomes. When the message portion of the service is over, the worship concludes with a benediction from the officiant and a closing hymn.

Elements of this worship service would be familiar to congregants in most mainstream Christian churches. The order of the service—an opening greeting and prayer, a singing of hymns, a declaration of belief, a sermon, a collection,

more hymns, and a closing benediction and song—parallels many Protestant denominational liturgies. Public healings are certainly familiar to participants at Pentecostal and charismatic services, and a sermon or message during the middle of a service is standard in most Christian churches. What is missing from and what is added to Spiritualist services from this generic framework, however, uncovers unique elements of Cassadaga's religious system. First, there are no crosses or other religious icons present in the temple, a clear indication that these services are not about the worship of Christ or the saints in any conventional understanding.[45] Second, there are no Bibles present and no Bible reading or interpretation of passages, absences that accurately reflect Spiritualism's preference for experiential contact with the spirit through meditation, healing treatments, and spirit messages over Scripture study. Third, there is no baptismal or eucharistic ceremony in these services, an indication of Spiritualism's rejection of the orthodox Christian doctrines of original sin and the eucharistic Atonement of Christ. Finally, the mundane, this-worldly assistance given, both in the healing treatments and in the personal advice delivered during the message portion of the service, discloses the empirical, practical ethos of the camp's religious system. Attendees at these services seem more interested in physical and spiritual empowerment in the present than in eternal salvation or damnation in the future.

Following the worship service, congregants walk to the Andrew Jackson Davis building, where light refreshments are served. At half past noon, the camp holds a one-hour message service that is open to the public. During this service several mediums "work together to bring short messages to as many people as they can reach in that hour."[46] This longstanding event often attracts curious visitors who have not attended the morning worship service. It also provides a forum wherein student mediums can refine their mediumistic gifts and offers a smooth segue between the formal church service and the private readings that generate hard income for camp mediums.

The week's other regular event is the Wednesday All-Message Service, which begins with a healing segment in the gazebo at seven in the evening, followed by the service itself thirty minutes later in Colby Temple. This service can be viewed as a Spiritualist variant on the Methodist, Presbyterian, and Baptist Wednesday evening Bible study and prayer meeting. It is designed to provide continuity of spiritual practice and guidance for church members during the week and to furnish platform reading experience to student mediums. The service follows a similar format to the Sunday worship service, with the lighting of the three candles, a welcome and invocation, a guided meditation, and an invitation to walk to the rear of the temple for an individual healing treatment. After a few brief announcements, the platform mediums begin bringing through messages from the spirit world to the assembled audience. There is no lecture or sermon, and everyone in attendance is offered a reading. Certified camp mediums and their students take turns performing from the platform, and the payoffs are not only the immediate service and counseling provided the attendees but also the opportunity for the mediums to attract subsequent private readings. Related to the Wednesday message services are Mediums' Night, a traditional camp event held the first Monday of each month in the Davis building, and Student Mini-Reading Days, which are held early Saturday afternoons and feature mediums-in-training. Both events offer the public fifteen-minute mini-readings and, like the Sunday and Wednesday services, allow mediums to hone their skills, attract new clients, and earn a small remuneration for their efforts. These events also reinforce the camp's distinctive focus on spirit communication and the empirical demonstration of human immortality.[47]

Several further rituals punctuate the camp's annual calendar at regular intervals and reinforce Cassadaga's teaching and healing mission. On one Friday evening during most months the camp holds a Candlelight Healing Service in Colby Temple. This unique ceremony takes place in a soft atmosphere of meditative music and candlelight. The service begins with a recitation of the camp's official "Prayer for Spiritual Healing":

> I ask the Great Unseen Healing Force
> To remove all obstructions
> From my mind and body
> And to restore me to perfect health
> I ask this in all sincerity and honesty,
>     and I will do my part.
> I ask this Great Unseen Healing Force
> To help both present and absent ones
> Who are in need of help
>     and to restore them to perfect health.
> I put my trust in the love and power of God.[48]

Following this invocation, congregants are given a small candle by an attendant and asked to go to a table to the right of the stage, where they light the candle at a larger taper and set it in a holder. Participants then move to an area in front of the stage and sit on open healing benches. As inspirational music plays in the background, camp healers give treatments with "passes" and laying on of hands

*Candlelight Healing Service, Colby Memorial Temple, 1995.*

that may last from three to twenty minutes, depending upon the number of attendees. In the camp's annual program, the person being healed is admonished to "A. Anticipate being healed. B. Believe in the Power of God Within to heal. C. Relax, let go and let God; the balance between body, mind and spirit brings healing."[49] These directions reflect the camp's understanding of God as an immanent intelligence and energy with which a person can come into harmony through a hopeful frame of mind and a relaxed surrender of fear and doubt. Following the treatment, participants rise, retrieve their candles from the table, and return to their seats.[50]

While the individual healing treatments are taking place, at the service I attended the rest of the congregation was taken through a guided meditation whose purpose was to "reinforce healing for family, community, and world" and to call down a "symphony of healing" from "healing angels." The congregation was led to a large coliseum surrounded by white megaliths. Each person saw himself/herself on a table over which hovered a white pyramid of light. This pyramid slowly descended onto the person's head and transmitted a healing energy. Throughout the meditation, a female singer periodically intoned inspirational songs accompanied by gentle notes on a keyboard. There were about twenty-three people in attendance, of whom seventeen were women and three were camp healers (two men and one woman). Several interviewees claimed that during the 1990s the number of participants in these ceremonies had been gradually increasing from year to year.[51]

Festive celebrations called Gala Days are held periodically between September and May each year. These events are designed to draw visitors and their families to Cassadaga and to reinforce the bonds of community among longtime members. They typically last from midmorning to late afternoon and feature craft booths; an old-fashioned bazaar; minireadings by mediums; children's entertainment such as storytelling, cake walks, and fishing booths; lectures on subjects ranging from hypnotism to physical mediumship; a picnic; and ceremonies derived from Native American traditions such as the medicine wheel and the sacred-pipe ritual. Gala Days hearken back to an earlier period in Cassadaga's history, when the camp offered cultural and social activities such as dances, concerts, plays, and dramatic readings during its busy winter season. In addition to this festival, the camp also regularly celebrates the Fourth of July, Easter Sunday (with a sunrise service), Halloween, and Earth Day with covered-dish dinners, picnics, and lectures.[52] Several camp leaders, including Steve Adkins, stressed the importance of these events in providing a sense of meaning and belonging for congregants who had no desire to become mediums or healers but were searching for a supportive and open-ended spiritual community.

The camp renews its bonds with past generations by celebrating founder George Colby's birthday each year in mid-January. In 1994 this birthday included a special lecture by pastor Janie Waidelich (now Henderson), who for a Sunday temple service dressed in period costume and dramatized Cassadaga's early history.[53] Other events of this genre include March celebrations of the anniversary of modern Spiritualism, "Pioneers of Cassadaga" observances, celebrations of Spiritualist pioneer Andrew Jackson Davis's birthday in August, and memorial ceremonies for "Camp members who have passed over to the Higher Side of Life." During a memorial ceremony the names of these members are read to "commemorate their existence and continuing service."[54] These events are reminders for the community that the human personality survives death and that the spirits of the departed continue to play an important role in the camp as guides and protectors.

In addition to these rituals and ceremonies, the community affirms its educational mission by offering classes, workshops, and seminars on Spiritualism and related topics throughout the year. A sampling of these educational offerings between 1993 and 1998 includes "Energy Alignment," "Phases of Mediumship," "Introduction to Madame Blavatsky and 'The Secret Doctrine,'" "Relationships: Here and Hereafter," "The Possible You," "Psychometry," "Automatic Writing Class," "Healing Angels and the Aura," "Rainbow Shamanism," "Auric Dimensions" (a Reiki class), "Yogananda," "Receiving Spirit Communication: A Séance," "An Evening of British Mediumship," "Psychic Slide Presentation & Skotography Workshop," and "Tools for Transformation." As these titles clearly indicate, the camp, in addition to classes in traditional Spiritualism, is tailoring its educational offerings to themes of increasing popularity across American culture, including self-help therapies, alternative healing, esoteric sciences, interpersonal relationships, angelology, and the development of psychic and spiritual potentials.

## Toward a New Age Therapeutic Community

The Spiritualist worldview at Cassadaga has undergone a subtle transformation over the past thirty years, as the counterculture generation of the 1960s has gradually begun to view the camp as a congenial environment for their eclectic spiritual explorations. As detailed in studies such as Wade Clark Roof's *A Generation of Seekers*, many of the baby-boom generation have developed a religious style that pays little attention to conventional denominational boundaries, that freely explores spiritual paths outside the religious mainstream, that values "spirituality" but remains ambivalent toward "religion," that crafts an idiosyncratic spirituality from a variety of traditional practices and beliefs, that is deeply concerned with self-empowerment and inner transformation, and that longs for an open-ended yet fulfilling sense of spiritual community.[55] Much of what Cassadaga offers is congruent with this generational style, especially its tolerant and respectful view of non-Spiritualist teachings, its relaxed and caring communal ethos, its focus on spiritual healing, self-empowerment, and self-transformation, and the eclectic content of its workshops, seminars, and classes. The influx of baby boomers into the camp's ranks is therefore comprehensible and even predictable.

Other scholarly observers of contemporary American religion have conceptualized the spiritual style identified by Roof as a kind of broad religious movement that they term New Age religion.[56] This religion has seven main characteristics: (1) a belief that humanity is on the verge of a radical spiritual transformation, which will entail a growing awareness of the interconnectedness of the human and natural orders; (2) an eclectic embrace of a wide array of spiritual beliefs and practices, and the proclivity to design one's own spiritual path using elements from many traditions; (3) an adoption of an ethic of self-healing and self-empowerment, including the embrace of alternative healing therapies; (4) a desire to reconcile the insights of religion and science in a higher synthesis that enhances the human condition both spiritually and materially; (5) a belief in the progressive evolution of humanity, both here and in the hereafter; (6) a belief in the possibility of revelatory communication between human "channels" and spirit intelligences such as angels; (7) a mistrust of conventional structures of religious authority.[57]

Because the Spiritualism of Cassadaga shares elements of all these characteristics, it is easy to see how the New Age style has gradually settled into the camp's complex and diverse religious ecology. Examples of this style include the profusion of alternative healing classes available during the 1990s, the many self-help and self-empowerment workshops that punctuate the annual calendar, the inclusion in Sunday and Wednesday evening services of a guided meditation using visual imagery and soft ambient music, the invocation in ritual settings of angels as both healers and messengers, the Native American medicine wheel and pipe ceremonies held regularly on camp grounds, the bookstore's profusion of New Age–related books, tapes, and paraphernalia (especially in comparison to its items for sale on Spiritualism proper), the camp's increasing emphasis on spiritual healing ceremonies, and the eclectic attitude toward non-Spiritualist beliefs and practices found among the town's certified mediums. In spite of this evidence of New Age influence, however, the camp is engaged in an ongoing struggle to differentiate its religious system from both New Age religion in general and from the alternative forms of Spiritualism that surround the camp proper. This struggle can be understood as an attempt by camp members to retain a distinctive religious identity that remains loyal to and founded in the traditional Spiritualism of its past while at the same time remaining open to further refinement and elaboration—particularly if these refinements and elaborations can help mediums better serve their clients and attract new members.

Evidence of the association's efforts at self-definition abound. The annual program, for instance, typically includes a letter of greeting and introduction to the camp by the current president. In 1994, this letter emphasized the camp's continuity with its past by highlighting the centennial celebration that began that year. This continuity was reinforced by an expression of pride in the camp's

*Native American Full Moon Ceremony, Seneca Park, 1994.*

listing in the National Register of Historical Places. One had only to "stroll around the Camp to feel as if they have been transported back in time." In the rhetoric of classic Spiritualist apologetics, the president affirmed that people were drawn to Cassadaga because they sought "a religion that is not born of fear and speaks only of a loving God."[58] The following year's introductory letter promoted the many opportunities to learn about Spiritualism available in the camp. In addition to the All-Message Service during which a "different medium each week demonstrates the continuity of life," there were Sunday Services during which speakers imparted inspiring guidance and healers channeled healing. In a nod to New Age sensibilities, the letter also emphasized the important role that spiritual healing played in the camp's religion and the availability of healing treatments both before and during the Sunday and Wednesday temple services.[59] In the 1996–97 program, then-president Barbara Joy Hines Bengtson stressed the camp's status as "the southern haven for Spiritualists and all those seeking understanding of, and solace from, God's gift of Eternal Life." She asserted that the camp's mission was to "philosophize, to worship, to practice and polish the gifts of mediumship, to live in the fellowship of kindred spirits and to share it [God's love] with all those who come seeking." Shifting to a more New Age mode of discourse, Hines Bengtson welcomed visitors to "stroll the camp grounds, commune with nature, pray, and meditate." She affirmed Jesus as "the Christ of this age," and claimed that all who lived under God's laws would come to desire greater understanding of "truth through higher consciousness."[60]

Another example of identity maintenance appears on County Road 4139. Just before the camp entrance, signs tell visitors that camp-certified mediums and healers are located only on the right side of the road. In an interview with the *Daytona Beach News-Journal* published November 13, 1993, under the headline "Soul Survivors," the Reverend Marie Lilla explained that camp mediums were not the same as the psychic readers outside the camp's boundaries: "We don't allow palm readers or tarot card readers or crystal balls here. It's all based on mental mediumship." Camp medium Fran Ellison elaborated, "I guess you'd call it (tarot cards and the like) somewhat of a crutch. You certainly wouldn't say they're not valid. It's just that you don't need them. You're working with different energies with those things, and a medium is communicating with spirit." In an August 19, 1993, *Orlando Sentinel* article, "A Gathering Place for Spiritualists," former camp president Janie Waidelich (now Henderson) tried to distinguish between the camp's religious identity and that of the businesses at its periphery: "Cassadaga attracts people who want to kind of pull on our reputation. You have to understand that we are a Spiritualist community and a religious community. I don't know much about the people across the street. Some might be good mediums, but I don't know them. Some do tarot cards and palmistry, none of which are part of our religion. We don't need such tools to practice it." Implying that palm reading smacked of fortune-telling, Waidelich declared that the camp's mediums were not fortune tellers, witches, or gypsies, and added, "That's not what we're all about."

The same article included the comments of Rev. June Bowermaster, the owner of the Purple Rose Metaphysical Stuff store across the street from the camp. Although Bowermaster lived within the camp's boundaries, she had been forbidden by association leaders to conduct her psychic readings on camp property. In her defense, she stated that her psychic readings were giving people what they really wanted, a sense of future trends and developments in their lives. Traditional Spiritualism, in her view, seemed no longer relevant for most people: "A lot of people don't want to hear anything from beyond the grave anymore. Everybody's so wrapped up in the economy, their health and their loved ones, that they don't care what Uncle Harry has to say any more." Perhaps a growing recognition by camp leaders of this statement's validity lies behind some of the long-term trends that can be observed in the community. For example, the traditional public séances of the first two generations at Cassadaga have largely disappeared. Séances, if they occur at all, happen in private settings and are by invitation only. The spirit materializations, trumpet manifestations, and other physical phenomena ubiquitous during the 1930s and 1940s have also largely fallen out of favor—although on occasion a small group of camp mediums renews their personal interest in such evidentiary phenomena. In addition, many of the messages communicated during Mediums' Days, All-Message Services, and Sunday worship services tend toward personal, professional, and business advice and prediction, rather than consoling greetings or metaphysical lessons from loved ones in the spirit world.

The gradual changes at Cassadaga have, not surprisingly, fostered simmering tensions within the camp. As medium Donna Bohrer reflected, "I would like everybody to feel comfortable in our church and I don't care from what religious background they come. I think that's the direction we need to be going in, and it's swinging away from when I first moved here—it was more Christian based than it is now, and my perception of it is that it swung from being Christian to more nondenominational. . . . Right now it seems that there is an effort to get the pendulum to swing back and to become more Christian and more patriarchal. . . . I've been involved in battles to decide whether or not it is appropriate for the women to be ushers . . . but I really think that if you don't allow it to grow and change, it stagnates and dies, and a lot of Spiritualist churches are dying because they are not reaching out. They are not attracting new members."

Current camp president, Steve Adkins, observed that the camp tended to reflect the religious backgrounds of its leadership: "If you were here ten years ago, the church's motif was all Christ—a big picture of Christ in the middle of the church . . . and this came because the older-term people all were closely aligned with Christian religions, whereas most of the people my age have come from no religious conviction of any kind for a long time when they come here. . . . If you look at the motif of the church now, it's predominantly yogic and Eastern philosophy and that's because the people that are in the church are into yogic and Eastern philosophy. They're not really professing traditional Spiritualism." Adkins also candidly acknowledged that the distinction between psychic readings and spirit mediumship was primarily a means of separating the camp's identity from that of the other Spiritualist churches and divining services in the township. Proof of this contention, he said, could be found in the annual programs, in which camp-certified mediums advertised themselves as both "psychic and spiritual counselors," "mediums and psychic artists," and "minister, psychic, and astrologer."[61] As if to reestablish some semblance of distinctive religious identity, however, Adkins continued: "The true theological slant of Spiritualism is no religious dogma, no religious creed, and we don't borrow from other religions as some have said. We are our own guided religion through direct spirit communication."

Former president Hines Bengtson is very aware of the New Age direction toward which the association appears to be tending. On the one hand, she is ambivalent about the public's perception of the camp as New Age, since that designation usually connotes a kind of inauthentic, trendy, and self-involved form of spirituality. On the other hand, however, Hines Bengtson openly acknowledges many of the millennialist beliefs that are the hallmark of New Age thought: "The fact of the matter is, that in three or four more years we are coming into a new age. And it's not just another one thousand years, it is an age per se—the dawning of the Age of Aquarius—we're still birthing and coming into that age, and part of the great wonder of Spiritualism is that if it rings true, we're free to look at it, to talk about it." Church member Don Zanghi agrees and asserts that in the dawning new age, long-term electronic communication with the dead will be open and available to everyone. For Hines Bengtson, the New Age's use of stones, crystals, and astrology is perfectly appropriate, for these practices help people understand "that every particle of creation has the life of God, of creation in it. . . . It's all about energy and we're coming to . . . recognize the energy in everything and how it can serve us and be used to serve others." When she discusses the camp's overall mission, Hines Bengtson enthusiastically uses the discourse of New Age planetary "light centers." "I believe that we're coming into an understanding of our higher purpose rather than just individual communication—but rather healing of people, not only one-on-one but in a greater concept and also as an anchor of light for the planet."

In summary, it appears that a generational shift is occurring at Cassadaga and that the short-term outcome of this shift is a move away from traditional Spiritualism—particularly public séances, material mediumship, and a Christian-influenced "church" style—and a move toward the open, eclectic, experimental, interfaith, millennial, and therapeutic spiritual ethos of New Age religion. The difficulty this presents falls out into two dimensions. First, the older residents—those who were socialized into an earlier version of Spiritualism—feel that they must struggle to protect their community from an indiscriminate acceptance of beliefs and practices that seem peripheral to Spiritualism's core identity and purpose—regardless of how popular such beliefs and practices have become. They understand the need for the camp to maintain a stable and coherent religious identity in a culture characterized by weak denominational loyalties and multiple religious identities. Second, members of the younger generation at Cassadaga desire to expand the conception of spirituality at the camp, so that it includes such practices as yoga, meditation, alternative healing therapies, and Native American medicine wheels and pipe ceremonies, and such beliefs as reincarnation, a coming planetary spiritual transformation, and the interconnectedness of all religious paths. For the younger generation of mediums, this transformation of traditional Spiritualism seems vital to the community's long-term viability in the postmodern religious marketplace. The changes in a New Age direction incorporate beliefs and practices that have been part of younger members' personal spiritual journeys and thus are greatly valued. The challenge that lies ahead for the community will be to balance a need for continuity with the past with the need to remain flexible and thus relevant in a rapidly changing religious ecology.

THE RELIGIOUS SYSTEM at Cassadaga is best understood in organic terms—that is, as a dynamic, developing set of beliefs and practices that must adapt itself to larger cultural forces and trends in order to survive. Over the past thirty years, the camp has become a haven for baby boomers whose search for a fulfilling and nurturing spiritual community has led them outside the conventional parameters of religious activity in America. The seeker metaphor has a special salience in this context, for many of the camp members I interviewed admitted that Spiritualism would most likely be a way station for them on a long spiritual journey. As Jerry Frederich put it, "I would say [that Spiritualism is] a way station because life is always evolving. Light is always expanding and it may take different forms." Other paths were beginning to draw Donna Bohrer's attention: "I'm interested in a lot of different things, particularly Eastern philosophies. Buddhism really resonates with me. I would like to stay with Spiritualism, but if this becomes a community where things become restricted then I'll go somewhere else for what I feel that I'll need." This view was shared by camp president Steve Adkins, who believes that Spiritualism at Cassadaga has certain limits that he would probably outgrow. "Spiritualism doesn't allow me to express my full set of beliefs, but it is the broadest expression that I can be allowed now. I feel I will move beyond the actual religion of Spiritualism itself—not as evolved to where I am higher than that but I will evolve beyond the bounds of Spiritualism—I can feel it now. I can feel the investigations that I'm doing moving beyond what is acceptable around here."

The baby boomers who have settled at the camp have brought with them a

New Age religious style that has affected every aspect of the community's life. From past-life regressions to neoshamanic trance states, and from yoga to the invocation of angels at candlelight healing services, an integration of diverse beliefs and practices has changed the face of Spiritualism at Cassadaga. As the older generation relinquishes its leadership role, the genteel, Christian-centered religion of séances and material mediumship is transmogrifying into a therapeutic community that exists to heal the sick, to counsel the confused, to comfort the bereaved, to empower the weak, and to teach the truth of personal immortality to a restless generation of spiritual seekers. The camp retains its continual interest in the scientific demonstration of spiritual truth, but now gives its members the opportunity to take an active role in their own healing process and to develop their inner spiritual gifts. Nor should Cassadaga be seen as unique in this regard. Spiritualist communities around the world are struggling to assimilate compatible elements of the New Age spiritual style so that they can remain vital and relevant to the needs of contemporary spiritual seekers. Indeed, the gradual transformation of Cassadaga's Spiritualism in the direction of New Age religion may very well represent the future of most Spiritualist churches both in the United States and abroad.[62]

To the extent that the camp can retain an authentic continuity with the core beliefs and practices of its colorful past while adapting itself to the exigencies of the postmodern spiritual marketplace, it should grow and prosper well into the next millennium. Part of this growth will likely entail an expanding array of spiritual traditions that will be incorporated into the community's annual round of rituals and events. In the end, the perennial human desire to communicate with the spirits of the dead and to receive their blessing and guidance will ensure Cassadaga a place in the larger tapestry of American religious life.

# Notes

1. Southern Cassadaga Spiritualist Camp Meeting Association (SCSCMA), *1996–97 Annual Program,* 2.

2. Vince Owens, interview by author, Cassadaga, Fla., May 14, 1998. Subsequent quotations or information in the text attributed to Owens are taken from this interview.

3. "The Nine Principles," May 29, 1992, 1. Photocopy.

4. Ibid.; SCSCMA, *1996–97 Annual Program,* 34.

5. Jerry Frederich, interview by author, Cassadaga, Fla., January 8, 1997. Subsequent quotations or information in the text attributed to Frederich are taken from this interview.

6. Eloise Page, interview by author, Cassadaga, Fla., January 10, 1997. Subsequent quotations or information in the text attributed to Page are taken from this interview.

7. Steve Adkins, interview by author, Cassadaga, Fla., July 24, 1996. Subsequent quotations or information in the text attributed to Adkins are taken from this interview.

8. Donna Bohrer, interview by author, Cassadaga, Fla., July 24, 1996. Subsequent quotations or information in the text attributed to Bohrer are taken from this interview.

9. Jim Watson, interview by author, Cassadaga, Fla., January 5, 1997. Subsequent quotations or information in the text attributed to Watson are taken from this interview. Some camp ministers invoke "Mother-Father God" in their public prayers. This bi-gendered invocation of the divine reflects the strong ethos of gender equality typical of the camp and of Spiritualism in general. Such invocations also suggest an infinite being indescribable in such limited terms as "father" or "mother."

10. "Lessons on Spiritualism," SCSCMA teaching material, n.d., 23–26.

11. Ibid., 28–29.

12. "Lessons on Spiritualism," n.d., 149–50.

13. Steve Hermann, sermon transcript, Cassadaga, Fla., March 9, 1997.

14. Steve Adkins, interview by author, July 24, 1996. William Deep, interview by author, Cassadaga, Fla., July 20, 1996. Subsequent quotations or information in the text attributed to Deep are taken from this interview.

15. "Frequently Asked Questions about Spiritualism" (cited May 19, 1998), http://www.webt.com/jloffredo/spfaq.htm; Internet (hereinafter, FAQs).

16. "Nine Principles," 3.

17. "Lessons on Spiritualism," 32–33.

18. Hermann, sermon transcript, March 9, 1997.

19. Barbara Joy Hines Bengtson, interview by author, Cassadaga, Fla., July 15, 1996. Subsequent quotations or information in the text attributed to Hines Bengtson are taken from this interview.

20. Fred Jordan, "What Is Spiritualism?" (International General Assembly of Spiritualists, n.p.) (booklet).

21. SCSCMA, *1994–95 Annual Program,* 26–29.

22. SCSCMA, *1995–96 Annual Program,* 27–30, *1996–97 Annual Program,* 27–30.

23. See, for example, Braude, *Radical Spirits;* Wessinger, *Women's Leadership in Marginal Religions;* and Carroll, *Spiritualism.*

24. FAQs.

25. See Anne Barclay Morgan's chapter in this volume for an elaboration of Eloise Page's path of mediumship.

26. Adkins interview; FAQs; Bohrer interview.

27. FAQs.

28. Hines Bengtson and Adkins interviews.

29. SCSCMA, "Steps to Certification as a Medium or Healer through the Southern Cassadaga Spiritualist Camp Meeting Association," Cassadaga, Fla., 1997.

30. Don Zanghi, interview by author, DeLand, Fla., July 18, 1996. Subsequent quotations or information in the text attributed to Zanghi are taken from this interview.

31. Frederich and Watson interviews.

32. SCSCMA, "Steps to Certification."

33. Simeon Stefanidakis, "Phenomenal Mediumship: A Look at Physical Manifestations" (cited May 19, 1998), http://www.fst.org/physmed/htm; Internet.

34. Ibid.

35. SCSCMA, "Steps to Certification."

36. Martha Foster, "Cassadaga—Florida's Spiritualist Camp," *Palm Beach Life,* January 1975, pp. 34, 35, 70–73.

37. Frederich and Watson interviews.

38. SCSCMA, "Steps to Certification."

39. SCSCMA, *1995–96 Annual Program,* 16.

40. SCSCMA, "Educational Curriculum/Requirements for Healer-Medium-Minister," February 28, 1997.

41. SCSCMA, *1996–97 Annual Program,* 11.

42. Federal Writers' Workshop Project, "Lake Helen's Southern Cassadaga's Spiritualist Camp," February 1, 1939, 1–8.

43. SCSCMA, *1996–97 Annual Program,* 9.

44. Ibid., 7.

45. It is worth noting that at the U.C.S.S. Spiritual Center in nearby Orange City, Florida, a much more Christ-centered flavor is apparent during the service. For example, the small chapel displays seven conventional framed pictures of Jesus, as well as a picture of the Virgin Mary and a large stained-glass cross. In addition, the opening statement of principles includes this creed: "We as Christian Spiritualists recognize God the infinite intelligence as our Father and Jesus Christ of Nazareth, the Divine Son of God, as the greatest teacher, medium, and standard bearer of truth the world has ever known." The first statement of principle for SCSCMA is simply: "We believe in Infinite Intelligence." The Christ-centered emphasis at the Orange City Spiritualist church clearly shows how Cassadaga's religious system distinguishes itself from the smaller Christian Spiritualist movement.

46. SCSCMA, "Colby Memorial Temple: Information for the Newcomer," 1996.

47. SCSCMA leaflets advertising "Student Mini-Reading Days," January 1998, March 1998, and "Mediums' Nights," March 1996, December 1996. In collection of Phillip Charles Lucas.

48. SCSCMA, *1995–96 Annual Program,* 14.

49. Ibid.

50. This advice for receiving healing reflects Spiritualism's status as a "harmonial religion," in Sydney Mead's classic formulation. Harmonial religions (among which are Christian Science and New Thought) teach that God is a positive healing force with which one must harmonize through proper thinking and living if one is to expect conditions of health and prosperity in one's life. See also Davis, *The Harmonial Philosophy*.

51. SCSCMA leaflet advertising "Candlelight Healing Services," May 1998.

52. SCSCMA *Annual Program* for 1994–95, 1995–96, 1996–97; SCSCMA leaflet advertising "Gala Day," May 9, 1998.

53. SCSCMA, church schedule, January 1994.

54. SCSCMA, church schedule, May 1998.

55. Roof, *Generation of Seekers*, 241–62.

56. See, for example, Heelas, *The New Age Movement*; Hanegraaff, *New Age Religion*; Lucas, *Odyssey of a New Religion*; and Lucas, "The New Age Movement and the Pentecostal/Charismatic Revival."

57. Ibid., 192.

58. SCSCMA, *1994 Annual Program*, 1.

59. SCSCMA, *1995–96 Annual Program*, 3.

60. SCSCMA. *1996–97 Annual Program*, 3.

61. SCSCMA, *1994 Annual Program*, 26–29.

62. Deep interview.

# "No Palaces among Us"

## *Cassadaga's Historic Architecture, 1895–1945*

S I D N E Y   P.   J O H N S T O N

"THIS CAMP," reported the *Volusia County Record* in 1909, "was organized in 1895 and has grown steadily ever since . . . and while we have no palaces among us, there are over fifty houses inside the grounds and near twenty outside. They are all good comfortable houses." Those words from the pen of Alice Spencer, corresponding secretary of the Southern Cassadaga Spiritualist Camp Meeting Association (SCSCMA), impart the simplicity and beauty of the historic architecture of Florida's Spiritualist retreat. Gently rolling pinelands, tranquil lakes, and narrow streets and alleys lined with historic cottages characterize this quiet, persistent religious community with its distinctive architectural heritage. Set in a town plan, Cassadaga's architecture has furnished Spiritualists with a worship center and a meeting hall as well as apartments, homes, administrative offices, and passive recreation sites over the past century. The collection of century-old wood-frame dwellings blends sensitively with several monumental masonry public buildings to contribute charm and ambiance.[1]

The town beckons architectural historians to investigate its social history through its architecture, which reflects the culture of mainstream American middle-class residents who happened to be Spiritualists. The early residents fashioned traditional Victorian homes, largely for seasonal residential use, with some interior spaces adapted to accommodate readings, séances, and other religious activities. That is to say, most dwellings were built from conventional house plans with various rooms later set aside or modified for Spiritualist rituals and practices.

This chapter compares the buildings of Cassadaga with those forms attributed by architectural historians to specific regions of the country; in the process, the text and the glossary at the end of the chapter will help clarify traditions carried into the Florida frontier by residents and builders. In addition, the built fabric of the community relates to culture, one of building a closely knit community within a town plan predicated on Spiritualist ideology. The buildings of Cassadaga display architectural influences that place the community within national contexts of popular culture and building trends. Relationships emerge among the town's economy, social organization, and religious context and the buildings and environments that resulted.

Anthony King suggests in *The Bungalow: The Production of a Social Culture* (1995)—and Dolores Hayden, in *Seven American Utopias: The Architecture of Communitarian Socialism* (1976), concurs—that the "social production of the built environment" is linked to "the way in which particular kinds of economy . . . and the ideologies with which they are associated, first give rise to distinctive institutions and activities, which in turn become embodied in urban and architectural forms." Construed as a corporate enterprise, Cassadaga's development embodied this historic process—a social pattern evolved into an institution, its activities based on the religious ideology King called "an economy of religion." That is, residents managed their resources to enhance spiritual awareness and progress. Development of the camp, guided by leaders in the national Spiritualist movement, combined religious needs with contemporary town planning ideals from the larger society and culture.[2]

Cassadaga's architecture reflects the personalities and forces behind the founding of the community. The town's historic buildings and green spaces, largely developed between 1895 and 1945 and listed in the National Register of Historic Places in 1991, primarily reflect the social and religious customs of the Victorian and Progressive eras. Some of Cassadaga's earliest settlers and founders—Emma Huff, Marion Skidmore, and A. B. Gaston, among others— also played instrumental roles in the development of the national Spiritualist retreat at Lily Dale Assembly in western New York. These early Cassadagans undoubtedly also participated in assemblies at nearby Chautauqua Institution, some sixteen miles southwest of Lily Dale on Lake Chautauqua. The organizers applied their collective impressions and experiences from establishing communities in the Northeast to the undeveloped Florida landscape. With their guidance and that of other like-minded newcomers, Cassadaga, the smallest of the three assembly grounds, emerged as a vibrant community of cottages and public buildings. The continuities and contrasts of the built environments of Cassadaga, Chautauqua, and Lily Dale furnish a backdrop and context for gleaning insights about Cassadaga's historic architecture.

Set in planned landscape designs, Chautauqua Institution and Lily Dale each have a distinctive architectural presence along the shores of lakes in Chautauqua County, New York. Organized in 1874, Chautauqua Institution, a planned community of some two hundred acres, drew people of various creeds from throughout the country to participate in annual programs. Lewis Miller, an architect and founder, helped design the town plan and constructed a seasonal cottage, now a National Historic Landmark. Paul Peltz, architect of the Library of Congress, designed the institution's Hall of Christ, and another renowned architect, Albert Kelsey, its Hall of Philosophy. By the early 1920s, the Chautauqua grounds had expanded to 331 acres sprinkled with nearly a thousand dwellings, a hospital, a bell tower, a gymnasium, public edifices, and parks and passive recreation sites. Many buildings displayed formal architectural influences, and by 1921 the institution's real estate holdings amounted to $1,250,000, including a waterworks, electricity plant, sewage system, and docks extending into Lake Chautauqua.[3]

Smaller in size and narrower in mission than neighboring Chautauqua Institution, Lily Dale Assembly was organized by the National Spiritualist Association in 1879 and incorporated in 1893. By the third decade of the twentieth century, the sixty-seven-acre site contained several hundred cottages, two hotels, the Octagon Building, an auditorium, and the Marion Skidmore Library. Infrastructure included electric service generated from a facility at Niagara Falls, a waterworks, and a telephone exchange. Rather close-packed cottages, primarily wood frame and two stories with wood shingle and clapboard exterior wall fabrics, lent the community an intimacy that contrasted to the larger amphitheaters, hotels, parks, and sacred architecture scattered throughout the grounds. Fox Cottage, the birthplace of modern Spiritualism, had been relocated to Lily Dale in 1916 from its original site in nearby Hydesville, New York. The architecture of both Chautauqua and Lily Dale displayed a blend of stylistic influences. Chautauqua, especially, intrigued contemporary architects. Frances Booth and James Cook of the American Institute of Architecture commented that the early twentieth-century landscape contained "a veritable museum of a great variety of architectural styles."[4]

The buildings of Cassadaga create an unusual ambiance and intimate sense of place that contrasts with that of these larger antecedent sites, mainly because they include relatively few examples of formally executed architecture. The community developed differently because of several factors. First, both Chautauqua and Lily Dale had been under way for almost two decades before Cassadaga was organized, and the town grew only moderately after World War I. Second, the economic and social forces that impacted the Florida Spiritualist retreat originated from a smaller pool of wealthy residents than that enjoyed by the western New York assembly grounds. In the 1920s, when Chautauqua Institution contained 1,000 dwellings and Lily Dale nearly 250 buildings, Cassadaga contained fewer than 75 buildings. An additional 25 homes stood on the periphery of the property. Although the SCSCMA occasionally relied upon the professional services of an architect to execute the design of sacred architecture and public buildings, most residents did not. Instead, carpenters assembled houses using plans developed with owners or derived from guidebooks. While few cottages displayed a formal architectural style, many included elaborate ornamentation in the form of decorative fascia, spindles, turned posts, and other trappings of Victorian architecture. Yet, tied to similar social and belief systems and guided in its development by some of the same founding personalities, Cassadaga reflected the northern assembly grounds in its narrow streets, alleys, and intimate linking of buildings. Its architecture thus becomes a lens through which to view building types transplanted largely from the Northeast and Midwest by the community's founders and residents.

Laid out in February 1895 on the heels of the incorporation of the SCSCMA, the town's first plan covered sixty acres of rolling terrain. Anchored at the southeast corner by Lake Colby, the plan allowed for some 250 building lots. Louis Redmond Ord, a civil engineer whose training and career remain undocumented, prepared the design at the behest of the camp's board of directors and completed the physical marking of streets, blocks, and lots in late 1896.[5]

In 1875 George Colby, Cassadaga's founder, had filed a homestead claim for the land on which the camp developed. A 1898 document claims that Colby's Indian spirit guide, Seneca, directed him to central Florida from Eau Claire, Wisconsin. Urged on by his spirit guide, Colby "followed a footpath . . . through the deep forest." He found "high bluffs, the lakes, the lay of the land, everything . . . exactly as it had been described by the spirit Seneca before leaving Wisconsin." On this rolling terrain, reminiscent of his boyhood home in western New York, Colby encouraged his fellow Spiritualists to develop a winter retreat.[6]

Ord's town plan took advantage of the natural features of virtually untouched back country. Only George Colby's dwelling and a few scattered homesteads interrupted an otherwise pristine landscape. Grand Avenue, the formal entrance into the camp, cut diagonally across the landscape, set back deeply from Lake Colby. Several small parks appeared in low-lying areas along the shore of the lake. Relatively short streets intersected Grand Avenue, and Chauncey Street ran along a high ridge near the western boundary. The parks would provide relief from the urban setting filled with houses that Ord envisioned. His plan called for irregularly shaped building lots near the parks, which fronted Lake Colby to form a large common measuring several acres. Residents named streets for native flora, landscape features, several founding members of the association, and former U.S. presidents Grover Cleveland and Abraham Lincoln.[7]

The association reserved sites along the eastern and northern fringe of the camp for public and sacred architecture. The construction of these wood-frame buildings on prominent sites overlooking Lake Colby and on some of the highest ground in the community presaged future development. The projects included an apartment house, auditorium, library, pavilion, and combination store/bazaar. Those structures, among the first to appear in Cassadaga, came in a variety of sizes and shapes with modest details that mirrored northeastern architectural forms.[8]

For the auditorium, the most notable of the early buildings, the association selected a site on the northwest shore of Lake Colby. The building, designed as a meeting hall and venue for worship ceremonies, exhibited octagonal styling, an exotic architectural form that enjoyed a renaissance in the early nineteenth century. Its exterior was finished with clapboards, its octagonal roof had a gable extension projecting from the rear elevation to enclose a stage, and it admitted natural light through large double-hung sash windows. With its completion in 1897 the building became a social center of the community, conveying a sense of permanency to Cassadaga. The auditorium's location and form revealed the significance the association's directors attached to its sacred architecture. Its site encouraged the camp to develop near Lake Colby and the eastern boundary of the grounds. The directors chose the octagonal form in part because it made the community's premier religious building unique. The simple, utilitarian, and well-proportioned lines of the building, sited, designed, and built by Tampa architect C. E. Parcell, prompted the editors of the *Volusia County Record* to comment that "it should serve as a model for other camps to follow." An octagonal entrance kiosk at the north end of Marion Street and a polygonal bandstand overlooking Lake Colby, both built about 1900, contributed to the character of the built environment in Cassadaga. These structures conveyed a familiar sense of place for visitors, many of whom had become accustomed to similar architec-

890 Lake Helen, Fla.
Entrance Camp Cassadaga.

CASSADAGA

*Original camp entrance, ticket kiosk, and Cassadaga Hotel, c. 1910. Courtesy of the
Florida State Archives.*

ture on the grounds of Chautauqua Institution and Lily Dale (see page 101).[9]

Circular and octagonal construction had been popular in America since the late colonial and federal periods, generally appearing in the form of octagonal wings and extensions on otherwise conventional houses. The style emerged in its grandest scale in sacred architecture with Circular Church in Charleston, South Carolina; Monumental Church in Richmond, Virginia; and Old Round Church in Richmond, Vermont. Thomas Jefferson's summer home, Poplar Forest, completed in 1819, is the earliest residential example of the style. Renowned architect Robert Mills has received credit for introducing the form in America. His break from the Wren-Gibbs colonial church plan contributed to a rebirth of the style during the 1840s. Orson Squire Fowler, a prominent Fishkill, New York, phrenologist with a penchant for combining fanciful superstition and scientific fact in his published works, popularized octagon architecture in house construction with *A Home for All: The Gravel Wall and Octagon Mode of Building*. In this book, Fowler argued that circular and octagonal architectural forms reflected natural shapes. These basic designs, Fowler said, would enclose more floor pace per linear foot of exterior wall than did more conventional rectangular or square plans, thereby reducing building costs and heat loss through walls.[10]

With nine editions published between 1848 and 1857, Fowler's book created substantial interest in the style, which in addition to its curious shape displayed polygonal or domed roofs, often pierced with belvederes or cupolas and exterior walls encircled by verandas. Fowler encouraged builders to use concrete in the construction of dwellings and to install novel features such as gravity water systems, central heating and ventilation systems, and indoor bathrooms. Fashionable examples appeared in Iowa, Minnesota, and New York, but few in the South. The style's popularity stalled as the romantic tradition gained architectural favor. Practical problems with interior room arrangements—quirky triangular spaces, pantries and closets with large windows, and parlors, living rooms, and bedrooms with a single exposure—also limited its acceptance. The largest concentrations of octagon houses appeared in New York, Massachusetts, and Wisconsin, with only a few thousand built by the 1870s.[11]

Use of the form diminished after the Civil War, although professionals in the building trades occasionally used octagon configurations. California's impressive Santa Cruz County Hall of Records, the Octagon Building at Lily Dale Assembly Grounds, and the four-thousand-seat Stuart Auditorium built in 1913 by the Southern Methodists at Lake Junaluska in western North Carolina today seem conspicuous for their octagonal forms. Yet to the Spiritualist faithful on annual southern pilgrimages, the octagon style introduced to the Florida back

*Harmony Hall, frame vernacular, built 1897.*

country by Cassadaga's founders became a tangible reminder of the Lily Dale summer retreat in New York.[12]

The directors financed the construction of an apartment house, library, pavilion, and combination store/bazaar north of the auditorium along Marion and Stevens Streets—simple rectangular forms with gable roofs. Harmony Hall, a two-story apartment house on Stevens Street, was completed in 1897 (see photo above). Its name drew both upon the Spiritualist belief in establishing harmonious relations and upon the early eighteenth-century town of Harmony in Chautauqua County. Its side-facing gable roof, tiered verandas extending across the front and rear elevations, and symmetrically placed windows distinguished it as a popular colonial New England type perfected by Pennsylvania Germans and adapted to other regions of the eastern seaboard. The building originally contained sixteen rooms, each twelve feet by fourteen feet, furnished with a bed, chairs, a rocker, a table, and a lamp. In its centrally located kitchen, renters could prepare their meals.[13]

The library, pavilion, and combination store/bazaar, all built in the late 1890s, lay northeast of Harmony Hall. About 1905, the directors combined the functions of the three buildings under one roof in a single large pavilion that stood north of Harmony Hall on Stevens Street (see photo on p. 104). Measuring some sixty feet square, the building housed a meeting hall and library with a small store at its south end. By 1910, the library had been named for Marion Skidmore, a familiar name for patrons of the Lily Dale Assembly. Later, the association

*Andrew Jackson Davis Hall, frame vernacular, built c. 1905.*

renamed the building Andrew Jackson Davis Hall to honor the achievements of
the prominent nineteenth-century Spiritualist leader.[14]

The Cassadaga Hotel, the largest project of the period, was developed by
private investors C. H. and Lucy Gregory of Chautauqua County, New York.
Completed in 1895, the building rose three and one-half stories. Easily the tallest
and largest edifice in the camp, the building occupied one of the highest sites in
Cassadaga at the head of Marion Street and consequently assumed a monumental appearance. The main body, protected by a front-facing gable roof, faced
east; there a one-story porch opened onto the Marion Street camp entrance.
Rear appendages projecting at various angles contained side porches, a kitchen,
and a dining facility. Within several years, a three-and-one-half-story rear addition provided more rooms, a large dining room, and a small portico to accommodate patrons entering from Stevens Street. Later, the Gregorys conveyed the
building to the Cassadaga Hotel Company, which was incorporated in 1914 by
Jean Campbell, Mary McDonnell, Joseph Slater, and several others. The ram-
bling structure easily ranked as the largest building in the settlement, eventually
containing some twenty thousand square feet of interior floor space.[15]

Brigham Hall, completed in 1897 on Stevens Street (see p. 105), was a private
project financed by brothers Hubbard H. and Fred Brigham along with their
respective wives, Sarah and Kate, all from Fitchburg, Massachusetts, and early
visitors and supporters of the camp. Located across the street from Harmony
Hall, the new apartment building contained eighteen small rooms with tiered

*Brigham Hall, built 1897.*

porches projecting from the front and rear elevations. The Brighams also built a seasonal cottage adjacent to the apartment building on Marion Street. The cottage and apartment building both had front-facing gable roofs, drop siding, and front porches. Gable dormers and corbeled brick chimneys projected from the roofs. Hubbard Brigham, a physician, died several years after their completion, and Fred and Kate Brigham sold their interest in the properties to Sarah Brigham. In 1910, Sarah sold the Marion Street house to Julia E. Vogt of Newark, New Jersey, and in 1912, following Sarah's death, the heirs deeded the apartment building to Frank and Mary Phelps of Fitchburg. The following year the Phelps sold Brigham Hall to the association.[16]

The board of directors, prohibited by charter from selling association property, established long-term land leases with prospective home owners—residents owned the dwelling they constructed, but not the property on which it stood. The agreement, adapted from a similar system used by the directors of the Lily Dale Assembly in New York, was codified by the SCSCMA into a standard lease about 1897, a legal instrument used with few variations for several decades. It banned barns and stipulated that a lessee should construct a "good frame building, of the assessable value of not less than $200 within two years . . . and said buildings to have brick chimneys." Annual leases ranged between five and eight dollars, and failure to pay could result in the association's assuming ownership of the buildings on the property. Besides prohibiting the sale and distribution of tobacco, alcohol, and other items, the association cautioned lessees to "observe and keep the regulations of said Board of Trustees concerning water closets and privies."[17]

The association used the lease to help insure that Cassadaga would become neither a town of hastily built shacks nor a permanent tent community. Assessable values of the period fell significantly below market value, and a "good frame building" assessed at $200 might have cost nearly $1,000 to construct. The *Florida Agriculturist*, a popular farm journal published in nearby DeLand between 1878 and 1907, in 1894 and 1895 advised those building homes in rural areas:

> All wood houses in this country are built upon block or brick piers, and should be at least two feet above the ground so that the foundation can be easily repaired. That also gives a free circulation under the house. Twenty by thirty feet, with sixteen feet studding is a good size, and there should be sixteen windows, four on each side and ends. There should be no mortising in the frame, but everything nailed together, a regular balloon frame. The frame should be well braced with a square roof. The house should be covered with novelty siding.
>
> [Bedrooms] should never be on the lower floor of a southern house. All the partitions in such a house can be made of ceiling, and should be ceiled overhead, in the chambers to keep out the heat and soot, [for] most every one burns pine wood. Porches need not be deep, as six feet gives a very good porch. Such a house ought to be built here for $250, but location as to facilities for obtaining materials would add to or decrease the cost.[18]

The first wave of development in Cassadaga, largely complete by 1899, placed most of the buildings at the northeast corner and along the eastern boundary of the camp, where founder George P. Colby located his home. Built in about 1895, the cottage displayed a steeply pitched cross-gable roof with an incised first-story porch, a second-story balcony opening along the front, and board-and-batten exterior wall siding. A utilitarian design, this boxlike form scattered throughout the Northeast and Midwest became especially popular with speculators and humble households. Colby's use of it for his Cassadaga home (which burned down several decades ago), and for a second cottage of similar scale and design built about 1926 and still standing in New Smyrna Beach, offers evidence of an early Volusia County settler relying on a northern architectural type to create a sense of place in two southern locales that he called home.[19]

Several cottages appeared along Marion and Stevens Streets. O. L. and Edella Concannon of Kansas City, Missouri, built a house at 1164 Marion Street about 1895. Two lots down from the Concannons, James D. Palmer of Hillsdale, Michigan, built a residence at 1160 Marion Street about 1897, and J. D. White moved into a new cottage at 1180 Stevens Street about 1898. But apart from the collection of public buildings and some scattered residences, construction generally languished during the first five years of Cassadaga's existence. Consequently, Ord's plan for the village, while viewed as creative in concept and sensitive to the landscape, was scrapped by the directors, for they believed it reserved too much of the association's prime real estate for green space and provided too few building lots along the lake shore. To avoid losing momentum gained during the initial meetings and to encourage prospective residents and visitors to build, the directors abandoned the original plan in 1901, cashiering the picturesque for the practical, a move that opened nearly forty new lots in previously designated park or public spaces. Curving Grand Avenue with its broad entrance and meandering connectors yielded to an unimaginative grid pattern. Palmetto and Pine Streets and curvilinear Park Avenue were eliminated. The association jettisoned the street named for former president Grover Cleveland and created a new avenue named for recently assassinated president William McKinley. Marion and Stevens Streets retained their names and alignments. The latter, named for Anna Stevens of Michigan, a wealthy winter resident and benefactor of founder George P. Colby, became the primary entrance. New streets named for contemporary directors and prominent settlers included Bond, Clark, and Palmer. Seneca Street memorialized Colby's spirit guide. The public green space, reduced to the area south of Seneca and east of Stevens, encircled Lake Colby, with a small park immediately north of the auditorium. The revised plan provided many new building sites but furnished little practical guidance for placing buildings based on their proposed function. Apparently, the directors believed that most subsequent development would come in the form of cottages and dwellings, with few buildings serving commercial, public, or sacred functions.[20]

Cassadaga's evolutionary town plan incorporates the social influences wrought by the 1893 World's Columbian Exposition in Chicago and the dynamic tension of the city beautiful and city practical movements. Developed by some of the country's leading architects, the exposition introduced city planning to Americans on a large scale. Its plan was prepared by Frederick Law Olmstead, whose creative works stressed the importance of converting a featureless terrain into a pastoral landscape. Olmstead designed Central Park in Manhattan and the Boston park system, which won national acclaim for offering residents of those cities escape from hectic city life without traveling to the country. The fair, built on land filled along the wetlands of Lake Michigan, featured a fully planned and unified collection of public and residential buildings, popularly referred to as the "White City." Thousands of people viewed the alternative to their drab and overcrowded cities. Its acclaim redirected the architectural tastes of the nation, and a subsequent redesign of Washington, D.C., prompted the organization of local chapters of the city beautiful movement, which sought to produce clean, well-planned towns and cities with divided boulevards, curvilinear streets, and irregularly shaped building lots. The cohesive blending of new platting techniques provided attractive vistas of public buildings and monuments and a seemingly peaceful and healthy urban environment. City beautiful opponents, often dubbed the "city practical," argued against the empty aesthetics, grand effects for the well-to-do, and general impracticality of the grandiose scheme. In the wake of the Chicago Exposition, Olmstead's plan and the supporting buildings yielded to more practical plans for Chicago's Jackson Park and surrounding industrial and residential developments.[21]

The struggle to develop better plans for urban American landscapes, defined in part by the push and pull of the city beautiful and city practical proponents, occurred in Dallas, Denver, Kansas City, Seattle, and other large cities. They experienced varying degrees of success in their attempts to incorporate parks, curvilinear streets, and an orderly plan of growth into the redesign of business districts and neighborhoods targeted for redevelopment. In Florida, several small towns, such as Auburndale, Fellsmere, and Sebring, were organized in the opening decades of the twentieth century using city beautiful principles. City planners and developers also adopted some of those principles in well-established cities, such as Jacksonville, Miami, and Tampa, where well-planned subdivisions, improved transportation systems, and passive recreation sites were developed. Although the rich texture of city beautiful ideals were all too often abandoned by municipal governments, the movement left an enduring legacy of many cleaner and more attractive communities. Cassadaga's landscape reflected aspects of both the city beautiful and the city practical movements that helped transform much of America's urban environment during the early twentieth century.[22]

The new design of Cassadaga helped spur house construction. Nine cottages were assembled in 1904 alone. Two years later, the association had leased about two dozen lots, and new cottages lined the streets of the camp, with the heaviest concentrations along Marion and Stevens Streets. In 1909 the *DeLand Daily News* reported, "The sound of the saw and hammer is a part of the amusement of [Cassadaga], for it tells its story of growth and improvement." Responding to the growth, the association replatted its property west of Chauncey Street into more spacious lots and opened an elliptical public green space, Horse Shoe

Park, in a shallow depression beyond the intersection of Seneca and Chauncey Streets. Although the association discouraged temporary quarters, occasional visitors, such as Edwin Bullock of Onset, Massachusetts, and Crescent City, Florida, were permitted to set up tents for brief periods along the Chauncey Street ridge and in Horse Shoe Park.[23]

The association funded various infrastructural improvements to make town life more comfortable. Roads were graded and finished with pine straw, and eventually paved with brick and lined with gas lamps. Acetylene, stored in tanks in a small building on McKinley Street, was piped underground along the main streets. In 1903, the association drilled its first deep well, and water was "conveyed to the cottages by a fine system of water works." A second deep well, drilled in 1905 by the developers of the Stevens subdivision outside the camp, was acquired by the SCSCMA in 1909, and by 1913 the directors had established a third well. Electric motors pumped water from the wells to a thirty-thousand-gallon tank on Prospect Hill west of Chauncey Street. The gravity-based system was supported by a windmill and gasoline engine to insure sufficient pressure to cottages, public buildings, and fire hydrants. Claud Tingley, professor of chemistry at Stetson University in DeLand, analyzed the water and found it "very pure and suitable for domestic use."[24]

By 1915, approximately sixty cottages and dwellings stood on the association's property (see p. 110). Newcomers developing seasonal cottages and year-round homes at Cassadaga during the period included A. A. Butler of Brecksville, Ohio; J. C. Collins of Louisville, Kentucky; William Critchley of Portsmouth, New Hampshire; Mary E. Gammon of Onset, Massachusetts; E. E. Hopkins of Beaver Dam, Wisconsin; Julian I. Mills, of Raleigh, North Carolina; A. K. Skeels of Cleveland, Ohio; physician G. N. Hilligoss of Cincinnati, Ohio; and Arthur J. Underhill of Canton, Ohio. Several early residents, such as August Norman, a photographer from Chesterfield, Indiana, also owned cottages in Lily Dale and traveled between the communities with the seasons. Mary Thatcher visited Cassadaga in 1896 and was among the first to develop a dwelling overlooking Lake Colby. About 1906 she built a large house on Stevens Street, where she accommodated guests through the 1920s. Each summer she returned to her cottage in Lily Dale. Early Cassadaga cottages built for J. Clegg Wright of Amelia, Ohio; publisher H. A. Buddington of Lake Pleasant, Massachusetts; and Melvin J. Holt of Woodstock, Vermont were later lost to fire or demolition. Association members Abby Pettengill and Emma Huff, both of whom owned cottages in Lily Dale, developed a hotel in Cassadaga around 1896 that was demolished fifteen years later.[25]

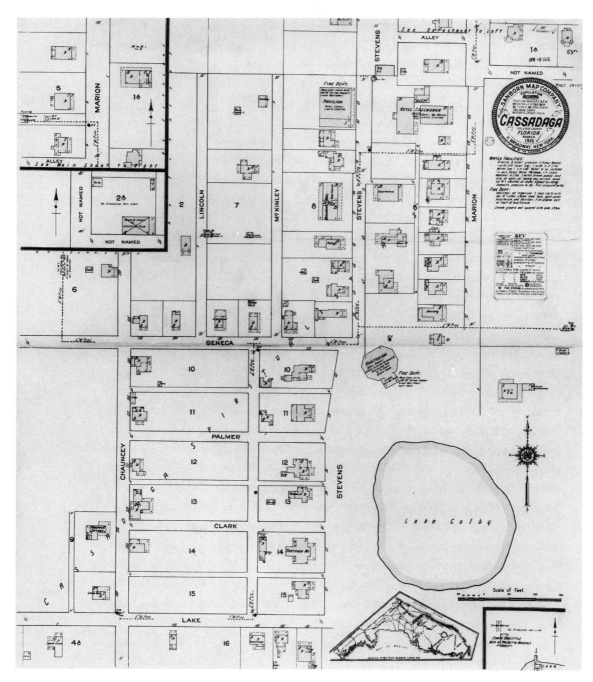

*Sanborn Company map indicating development of the Spiritualist community by March 1915. Although the auditorium and hotel were later replaced, relatively little other new construction occurred on the association's grounds during the Florida land boom of the 1920s. Courtesy Map and Imagery Library, University of Florida.*

Seeking a more traditional form of property ownership, some prospective home owners purchased real estate outside the association's grounds, where they built seasonal residences. Most of those dwellings sprinkled the northern edge of the camp's property. A community located farther north at the intersection of Webster and Marion Streets became known as the Vermont Settlement, apparently in recognition of the transplanted summer homes of seasonal residents from the Green Mountain State. Nearly fifteen new residences appeared in Cassadaga during the Florida land boom of the 1920s. Although construction declined during the Great Depression, about five new cottages appeared during the 1930s, and by the end of World War II some seventy-five dwellings occupied the grounds of the association.[26]

The vast majority were constructed from plans worked out on the site by a home owner and carpenter. That is, they were derived from folk or vernacular building traditions to suit the needs of the owners. The term "vernacular" refers not to inferior or mundane architecture but to a building form associated with a particular era and region of the country (as opposed to a particular genre of formal architecture). Specifically, according to the *Oxford English Dictionary*, it refers to vernacular architecture as "native or peculiar to a particular country or locality . . . concerned with ordinary domestic and functional buildings rather than the essentially monumental." "For many," asserts University of Florida professor of architecture Ronald Haase, "the word applies to things of the distant past, dead and gone and interesting only as seen through the dusty perspective of history." But referring to "the native language or dialect of a particular region or place," Haase believes, "gives life and energy and contemporary qualities to all things vernacular." Indeed, Florida's wood-frame vernacular architecture, perhaps more in that state than in other regions of the country, represented a broad swath of forms wrought by migrations of tourists and settlers whose ideas of house forms and regional building techniques differed significantly from the typical Florida "cracker" house, as portrayed by Haase. Still, Haase's study, *Classic Cracker: Florida's Wood-Frame Vernacular Architecture* (1989), overlooks many of the state's native dwellings, especially those outside the localized dogtrot, Georgian, and single-pen traditions of the rural South.[27]

*Common Houses in America's Small Towns,* an exhaustive architectural-geographical treatise published in 1989, compares the distribution of twenty-six primary vernacular house types in specific culture regions of the eastern United States. Its authors argue that vernacular houses are too "readily taken for granted in the American landscape," while "buildings of 'grand design' built to impress either the populace with the power and good taste of the patron, or the peer group," often receive undue attention. Vernacular dwellings, writes social historian Gwendolyn Wright, were embraced by many mid-nineteenth-century Americans as the "ideal home [for] an independent homestead, attractive enough to encourage family pride yet unpretentious and economical." Later in the Victorian era, according to Wright, "a picturesque site plan and natural building materials evoke[d] a return to nature, to a lost innocence and an earlier stability."[28]

Some of Cassadaga's homes were undoubtedly derived from or influenced by architectural guidebooks and popular magazines. Many popular vernacular building forms of the antebellum period, often modified and distilled by regional adaptations, were commonly used by builders during the late nineteenth and early twentieth centuries. Some descended from rural farm traditions of the eighteenth century, others from late-nineteenth-century urban conventions. A blending of influences tended to blur regional distinctions, and some traditional geographical forms became relatively common throughout America, changing over time to meet the needs of owners and occupants. Yet other forms retained a remarkable purity and authenticity to their respective regional heritage. Against this backdrop of provincial architectural adaptation, some indigenous construction techniques gained widespread application following the Civil War through the use of architectural guidebooks, such as Calvert Vaux's *Villa and Cottage Architecture: The Style-Book of the Hudson River School,* which helped enhance America's appreciation for fashionable dwellings and made affordable "the luxury of good architecture." Within several years the building market was flooded with guidebooks, such as those published by architects George E. Woodward, Edward Thompson, and Charles and George Palliser. Through those publications architects and builders encouraged prospective owners to develop a dwelling as a self-conscious extension of their way of life. Elevations, floor plans, paint samples, perspective views, and sample contracts for use with architects and builders helped home owners visualize a home and thread their way through the intricacies of design and construction. Although many dwellings pictured in those pages defied architectural classification, the publications nevertheless promoted good architecture. In 1895, *Ladies' Home Journal* began offering house plans, in the words of its editor Edward Bok, to make "the small-house architecture of America better." The magazine featured the works of such renowned architects such as Ralph Adams Cram, William Lightfoot Price, and Frank Lloyd Wright. Popular magazines of the early twentieth century helped regional architecture evolve into more universal applications.[29]

But most of the plans for Cassadaga's homes developed through an organic on-site process between home owner and builder, who translated the sum of their collective experience of buildings into a new home based around an old form. Most carpenters employed the balloon framing technique to assemble dwellings, a method of construction introduced in Chicago in the 1830s that rapidly replaced the age-old, time-consuming post-and-beam system of mortise-and-tenon joinery. In general, the dwellings of Cassadaga resemble the common vernacular cottage and house forms of the Northeast and the upper Midwest, specifically but not surprisingly Michigan, New York, Ohio, Pennsylvania, and Wisconsin. Relatively few conventional southern regional archetypes were built on the association's grounds. Dedicated to an economy of scale, most of Cassadaga's early home builders eschewed the pretentious for the vernacular. By 1915, at the end of its second decade of development, the community's ambiance evoked a rural settlement, with independent homesteads set in a distinctive, quaint town plan. The dwellings blended upper Ohio River Valley and northeastern architecture, giving seasonal residents and winter visitors a familiar sense of place and a home visually and culturally linked to their permanent residences hundreds of miles away.[30]

Other cultural traditions made Cassadaga distinctive. Some residents named their cottages, hanging a sign from the porch or posting it on a fence. Such labels were part of America's popular culture during the Progressive Era. Mountain retreats and seaside cottages often displayed fanciful names such as Idlewyld or Suitsus, names of native flora, or the name of the home state of the seasonal resident. Names assigned to cottages in Cassadaga during the 1910s and 1920s included Blue Bell Cottage, Forestside, Grand View, Loma Vista, Magnolia, Peekboo, and Prospect Cottage, reflecting the aspirations of residents as well as the cottages' physical locations and surrounding vegetation. Even some pathways were assigned names. Orange Lane, a picturesque alley connecting the hotel and auditorium, ran along the rear property lines of the rows of houses facing Marion and Stevens Streets (see p. 114).[31]

The association's grounds currently contain fifty-six historic buildings—three are public or commercial, and the remainder are residences that may include a room for readings. Nearly all of the dwellings have a slender profile consisting of a front-facing gable roof with front and rear porches, a design well suited to the narrow streets and lots created by the association. The overall pattern of architectural forms reflects the substantial presence of northeastern and upper midwestern building traditions, some of which are seldom seen elsewhere in the South—not surprising in light of the evidence that, with few exceptions, the original owners of Cassadaga's houses came from the northern half of the country.[32]

*Orange Lane, a pathway that connected the Cassadaga Hotel and the auditorium, in the distance, c. 1912. The view is from the third story of the hotel, with Brigham Hall rising at the right and the auditorium in the distance. Author's collection.*

Cassadaga's most common dwelling type, the irregularly massed vernacular house, combines what architectural historian Wilbur Peat describes as "masses or blocks of different sizes in an informal way." The form symbolized a trend toward informality and resisted the symmetry of traditional dwelling design. The upright-and-wing, the earliest form of irregularly massed dwelling to evolve, originated in upstate New York and spread across the upper Midwest. Representing nearly one-third of the dwellings built in small towns in the region during the late nineteenth century, the form became the most popular type of dwelling in Cassadaga. Other common house forms in the camp display more formal lines, with few of the "breaks, jogs, and angles" promoted by George Garnsey, a prominent builder-architect of the 1880s.[33]

One of the best-preserved upright-and-wing models stands on Stevens Street. Built for Mary Gammon, a winter resident from Onset, Massachusetts, the residence has a traditional form with a two-story, front-facing gable projecting toward the street and a one-and-one-half-story cross-gable extension, or wing, protruding at a right angle from the north elevation (see page 115). Contrasting arrangements of square-cut and fish-scale wood shingles protect the exterior walls. Windows appear asymmetrical and consist of both sash and casement types. A shed wall dormer interrupts the smooth slope of the wing extension, and a veranda extends across the facade, supported by turned posts and decorative brackets. Issues of the *Boston Globe* dating from 1902 were found decaying in the walls during rehabilitation nearly fifteen years ago, a discovery that suggests a date of construction for the cottage.[34]

A large house, historically named Grand View, rises at a prominent location at the intersection of Lake and Chauncey Streets. Facing east, the house once offered a view of Lake Colby, a vista now obscured by vegetation. Built about 1905 for Frederick Mack of Windsor, Connecticut, the two-story house has a veranda extending across the front facade and north elevation, and drop siding serves as the exterior wall fabric. A pair of symmetrically placed double-hung sash windows open on the second-story facade to provide adequate ventilation. The dwelling rests on buff brick piers, and a chimney with alternating red and white tiers of sandstone brick pierces the roof.

Another irregularly massed cottage on Stevens Street was built about 1905 for A. B. Gaston, a winter resident from Cochranton, Pennsylvania, and later of Meadville, New York. In 1892, Gaston established the *Cassadagan,* a monthly magazine published in Lily Dale, where he maintained another seasonal cottage. Two decades later Gaston served as vice-president of the SCSCMA and as secretary of the Cassadaga Hotel Company. Wall dormers interrupt the cottage's

*Gammon Cottage, frame vernacular, built c. 1902.*

front-facing gable roof and rear cross-gable extension. The dormers lend a sense of height to the dwelling's decidedly horizontal profile. Double-hung sash windows with four panes provide natural interior lighting. Although composite asbestos shingles cover the original wood exterior wall fabric and a porte cochere of relatively recent construction projects from the north elevation, the dwelling retains much of its original character.[35]

A cottage on Stevens Street, completed about 1898 for J. D. White of Lake George, New York, retains much of its original ornamentation. In a front-facing gable, reminiscent of single-pile designs, variegated wood shingles cover the gable end and a waved wall surface shields the lintel of the central window on the second-story facade. The first-story facade, essentially a polygonal bay with canted wall surfaces, was protected by a veranda adorned with milled posts and jigsaw-cut brackets.

Double-pile dwellings, that is, houses two or more rooms deep with two rooms across the front, account for another significant number of Cassadaga homes. Renaissance concepts of symmetry, carried from England to America during the colonial period, led to rooms of equal depth and the use of gable roofs. Double-pile houses gained their widest distribution along the Atlantic seaboard, with heavy concentrations in New England and the southern seaboard regions. The style spread throughout Pennsylvania and was closely associated with western New York. The gable-front variant facing the street with a slender profile was well suited for the narrow lots of urban cities and of Cassadaga. Although this type of dwelling remained less common in southern towns than in the North, builders' plan books and catalogs helped the type gain national acceptance in the early twentieth century.[36]

The association made use of traditional double-pile conventions in the construction of Harmony Hall. Its side-facing gable roof was pierced by evenly spaced interior chimneys, and the central hall and double-hung sash windows extended the symmetry. The board-and-batten exterior wall fabric contrasted with the horizontal wood sidings in predominant use throughout the community. Brigham Hall illustrates the gable-front double-pile form better than any other building in the camp. Rising two and one-half stories, the building exhibits a rectangular plan with a front-facing gable roof. A tiered porch protects a symmetrical facade. Turned posts, balustrades, and a first-story pent roof with brackets lend the apartment building much of its charm. Dormers protrude from the roof, and wood drop siding covers the exterior walls. Simple in form, with central halls accommodating a stairwell, these apartment buildings have offered rooms to visiting Spiritualists for a century.[37]

Single-pile dwellings, "the starting point for developments which eventually led to the diminution of vernacular characteristics in domestic architecture," are another common building type in Cassadaga. Traditionally serving lower- and middle-income people, the form included I-houses and dog-trot, hall-and-parlor, saddlebag, and gable-front cottages. The single-pile dwelling was inexpensive to build and easily adapted as an affordable seasonal cottage. A residence located on Lake Street, built about 1899, displays conventional I-house features. A side-facing gable roof pierced by a brick chimney is surfaced with metal crimp panels. Board-and-batten walls contrast with the predominate clapboard and drop-siding exterior wall fabrics found elsewhere in the community. One-story front and rear porches project from the main body of the house.[38]

Several dwellings from the bungalow tradition contribute to the community's character. The bungalow was a popular residential building design in Florida during the first three decades of the twentieth century. (The name derives from the Bengalese "bangla" or "banggolo," an indigenous peasant hut whose form was adapted by the British in India during the eighteenth and nineteenth centuries.) The California Mid-Winter Exposition of 1894 influenced the emerging bungalow form, which matured into a popular dwelling type about 1910. The exposition emphasized the interplay of angles and planes. An extensive display of structural members became an integral component of the style. Gustav Stickley, the foremost proponent of this building form, experimented with a variety of textures and materials applied to rectilinear plans. Stickley believed that the character of a bungalow should be "so natural and unaffected that it seems to sink into and blend with any landscape." He urged builders to use local construction materials and to construct bungalows "planned and built to meet simple needs in the simplest and most direct way." Although no Stickley homes were built in Cassadaga, many home owners applied his principles in the construction of their dwellings.[39]

Publications like Stickley's *Craftsman* furnished plans for relatively inexpensive models. William Comstock's *Bungalows, Camps, and Mountain Homes* appeared in 1908, offering floor plans and tips for building a picturesque retreat buried deep in the woods, by a lake, or near a seashore. *House and Garden* and other magazines ran articles about economical use of space, interior decoration, landscaping, and the pursuit of nature in the suburbs. Scaled-down versions flooded Florida during the early twentieth century. A bungalow was typically a one-or one-and-one-half-story dwelling with a low-pitched gable roof with wide unenclosed eaves. Exposed roof rafters and knee braces mounted under the gable ends provided depth and texture. The porch, a dominant architectural feature of the style, extended across the facade, with the roof supported by tapered square columns that either extended to ground level or rested on brick or stone piers. A variety of wood sidings, native stones, and brick, often arranged in interesting combinations, served as the exterior wall fabrics.[40]

Ray B. Sherman, a contractor and future SCSCMA president, built a house on Lake Street about 1922 (below). Typical of modest bungalows going up throughout the United States during the 1920s, it displayed a side-facing gable roof pierced by a shed dormer to provide additional space and natural lighting in the half story. A porch incised in the primary roof extended across the facade, and a square bay with a shed roof protruded at the east elevation. Sherman arrived in Cassadaga in 1904 with his parents, Joel and Mary. His father had practiced dentistry in Willoughby, Ohio, for some twenty years before moving to Florida in 1890 to assist in the local Bond Lumber Company's operation. He relocated to Cassadaga in 1904, the same period that Eber W. Bond began his lumber and brick companies in nearby Lake Helen. Loma Vista, as the Shermans called their home on Lake Street, was completed in the upright-and-wing tradition in 1909. During the 1920s, Ray Sherman developed several buildings in Lake Helen, including a two-story apartment house on Garden Street.[41]

A smaller version of the bungalow form, at 1222 Bond Street, was completed about 1928. The cottage was owned by George Pierce, a retired physician, and

*Sherman Cottage, bungalow style, built c. 1922.*

*Norman Cottage, colonial
revival style, built c. 1906.*

his wife, Anna, who occupied it as a winter home, spending summers in Middle-
ton, New York. Contrasting wood shingles and simulated log veneer lent the
cottage a distinctive appearance.[42]

One dwelling displays the influences of the colonial revival style. Located at
1164 Stevens Street, the house (above) was completed about 1906 for August
Norman, a Chesterfield, Indiana, photographer who also maintained a home in
Lily Dale. It has a front-facing gable roof with a closing pent roof along the eave
line. A polygonal bay projects from the northeast corner of the second story and
another bay at the south elevation. A veranda with round columns sweeps across
the facade and north elevation.

Colonial revival emerged as a dominant style of American residential architecture during the first half of the twentieth century, marking a rebirth of interest
in the early English and Dutch houses of the Atlantic seaboard. The Georgian
and Adam styles were the backbone of the revival, which also drew upon
postmedieval English and Dutch colonial. The style was introduced at the Philadelphia Exposition of 1876, when the centennial of the Declaration of Independence sparked renewed interest in the architecture of the colonial period. Many
of the buildings designed for the exposition were based on historically significant
colonial designs. Publicity of the exposition coincided with efforts by national

organizations to preserve Virginia's Mount Vernon and Old South Church in Boston. About the same time, a series of articles on eighteenth-century American architecture appeared in both the *American Architect* and *Harper's*. The publicity helped popularize the colonial revival style throughout the country, although its vogue in Florida was eclipsed by the bungalow and Mediterranean revival styles. The typical colonial revival house was an eclectic mixture of several colonial designs. Identifying characteristics included gable, hip, or gambrel roofs, often pierced by dormers, and an accentuated door, normally with a classical surround. Simple entry porches or large verandas protected the entrance.

In addition to displaying the influence of the colonial revival style, the former Norman house resembled dwellings developed from "ready-to-assemble" house kits of the early twentieth century. Although undocumented, it is plausible that several of Cassadaga's houses, including the former Norman and Sherman houses, were ordered by mail or built using plans featured in an architectural magazine or journal. Between 1895 and 1940, Sears, Roebuck and Company, along with Alladin Homes, Gordon Van Tine, Hodgson Company, Montgomery Ward, and others, sold house kits, a side effect of which was to help spread new architectural styles. The Alladin Company, organized about 1905 in Bay City, Michigan, advertised a Readi-Cut House that could be assembled in one day. In 1918 alone Alladin Company sold 2,800 kits, and by 1925 Sears, Roebuck had sold more than 30,000. Most companies offered varying degrees of services and materials. A full line of lath, plaster, paint, and precut wood products were available, with consumers advised to secure their masonry products from a local distributor. Frank Lloyd Wright's "Fireproof House for $5,000," a carefully crafted partly prefabricated dwelling offered by the Richard Brothers of Milwaukee, appeared in *Ladies' Home Journal* in 1907. By 1910, the market was flooded with architectural plans and building kits that closely mirrored contemporary architectural trends. While colonial revival persisted as a popular design with those companies, styles such as bungalow, mission, Queen Anne, and Tudor revival were also available.[43]

Part of the distinctive milieu of Cassadaga derives from dwellings built of materials harvested from Volusia County soils and manufactured by companies organized by Eber W. Bond, a native Ohioan of entrepreneurial talent. In the 1860s, Bond established a wagon factory in Willoughby, Ohio, where he served several terms as the town's mayor. A decade later he moved to Michigan and organized a lumber company. In 1881, intrigued with the South's yellow pine industry and seeking a warmer climate, he relocated to west Volusia County and built a railroad from the St. Johns River east to DeLand.[44]

In 1903, Eber established businesses in Lake Helen, in part because of the town's superior rail connections with both the Florida East Coast Railway and Atlantic Coast Line Railroad and in part because of its close proximity to the Spiritualist camp. He incorporated E. W. Bond Company and Bond Sandstone Brick Company, each with a capital stock of $100,000. At Lake Helen he installed the company's general office, an extensive sawmill operation, and in September 1904 a brick factory, one of the few in Volusia County. The operations, among the largest of their type in Florida, were featured in trade journals of regional distribution, such as *Southern Lumber Journal* and *Logging*.[45]

The Bond family had developed Spiritualist leanings during their days in Ohio and Michigan. That interest was rekindled in the 1890s. Frank Bond, son of Eber and an active supporter of the Cassadaga community, belonged to the SCSCMA and served on the board of trustees until his death in 1906. Eber Bond had served as an officer in the National Spiritualist Association and continued his activities as president of the SCSCMA. The Bonds' close ties to Spiritualism did not prevent them from resorting to the legal system to resolve disputes with the association. In an 1899 case, the circuit court awarded the Bonds $1,660 for the SCSCMA's default in payment for materials used in the construction of a building. Respected for their business acumen, the Bonds maintained good relations with Cassadaga's residents and board members. About 1903, Eber Bond built a cottage on a prominent site at 1175 Stevens Street overlooking the park and auditorium (see p. 122).[46]

By then, Bond was an influential supplier of lumber and bricks throughout Florida.[47] Landmark buildings constructed with Bond bricks included the Clarendon Hotel in Daytona Beach, Espanol Hospital in Tampa, Palatka City Hall, and St. Anastasia's Convent, Rectory, and School in Ft. Pierce. In Volusia County, Bond bricks built the Codrington Building, Fountain Building, Lake Helen's railroad station and school, the Landis & Fish Building, Volusia County Bank, and Stetson University's Sampson Hall, Conrad Hall, and Cummings Gymnasium. Bond bricks also supported the chimneys and foundations of many Volusia County dwellings, including most of those in Cassadaga dating after 1904. Many local dwellings also displayed clapboard and drop siding, decorative fish-scale, diamond-shape, and rectangular shingles, jigsaw-cut ornamental details, and interior door and window moldings and flooring harvested from Volusia County's forests by Bond's company.[48]

Architect John P. Mace of nearby Lake Helen also impacted Cassadaga's architecture and physical development. He worked for twenty years as an architect and builder in Ohio before moving to Lake Helen in 1885, and by 1889

*Left to right: The E. W. Bond Cottage beyond the white wooden fence of Colby Park; the Concannon Cottage and Spencer Cottage; in the foreground, a corner of the auditorium appears, far right. c. 1910. Author's collection.*

Jacksonville's *Florida Times-Union* could comment in an article on that town that "Queen Anne cottages designed by Mace, the Ohio architect, and roomy verandahed dwellings vie with each other in beauty. They are painted in delicate and pretty shades—grays, drabs, and cream[s]—with gables, towers, balconies, and other features in keeping with their style." Inferential architectural evidence, based on comparisons between residences documented as Mace designs in Lake Helen and dwellings with similar massing and detailing in Cassadaga, suggest Mace designed several late-nineteenth and early-twentieth-century cottages in the assembly grounds. Beyond several fashionable residences in Lake Helen, his notable achievements in that town included Blake Memorial and First Congregational churches and Hopkins Hall. He also designed the 1889 Volusia County Courthouse, and DeLand Hall and Stetson Hall on the Stetson University campus.[49]

Replacing dilapidated buildings played a role in Cassadaga's architectural evolution, as, for example, in the early 1920s, when the association was confronted with an auditorium rendered unserviceable by insect infestation and humidity. The directors commissioned Tampa architect B. Clayton Bonfoey to design a new worship center. Using a rectangular plan, he sited the building at an oblique angle to the intersection of Seneca and Stevens streets. The octagonal auditorium was demolished in 1923, and construction began on the new building in July of that year. In the mission style, a revival form that gained popularity in the 1890s and flourished in Florida during the 1920s, the building was constructed with Bond sandstone bricks. The *DeLand Daily News* reported: "The building is fire proof, built of brick with the front faced with a white cement. It took energy, courage and a lot of money to put it into operation and completion which is due to Mr. Joseph Slater, Sr., as president of the Spiritualist association." Property owners were encouraged to "keep pace, clean up, paint and put the commons and streets in perfect order which will have a tendency to show harmony and cooperation."[50]

Dedicated as Colby Memorial Temple, the building introduced a new style of architecture into the community while preserving the historic central location for Cassadaga's sacred architecture (see below). Visually distinguished from neighboring buildings by its size and materials, the building displayed a symmetrical rhythm, textured with stucco, horizontal belt courses, buttresses terminating in capped urn finials, and arched window and attic piercings. A cast sunflower medallion, date plate, and tripartite statuary niche adorned the central shaped parapet, from which tapered off straight parapet walls finished with staged coping. The sunflower design on the parapet represented a sacred symbol of Spiritualism. As believers understand it, "the sunflower turns its face to the light of the sun, [as] Spiritualism turns the face of humanity to the Light of Truth."[51] The interior of the building was austere, devoid of either an entrance hall leading to the central part of the church or the sacristy spaces common in

*Colby Memorial Temple, mission revival style, built 1923.*

conventional Catholic and Protestant houses of worship during the early twentieth century.

Bonfoey's connections to and prior contacts with Cassadaga and Spiritualism remain undocumented. A native of Connecticut and one of Florida's prominent architects, Bonfoey followed in the footsteps of his father, a Hartford contractor. He worked for his father as a teen before studying building design and construction at Hillyer Institute in the early 1890s. He superintended numerous projects in Hartford until 1903, when he left the city for Tampa and became the second architect to register with the Florida State Board of Architecture. Between 1907 and 1917 Bonfoey associated with M. Leo Elliott, an architect who also gained prominence in Tampa. Bonfoey & Elliott designed some of Tampa's most notable structures, including Tampa City Hall, Centro Asturiano and Circolo Club clubhouses, and the Fuller, McElmurrary, and Watrous houses. Some eight hundred projects throughout Florida have been attributed to Bonfoey, but Colby Memorial Temple is the only one in Volusia County. Earl Johnson, a Tampa contractor, supervised the construction of the temple, which was assembled using sandstone bricks and lumber from the Bond company.[52]

Located west of the temple, at 1214 Stevens Street, a two-and-one-half-story masonry building destined to be the largest dwelling on the association's grounds, the Snipes house was developed in an American foresquare form with restrained influences of the Italian Renaissance style (see below). Completed in

*Snipes House, Italian Renaissance style, built 1927.*

1927, it replaced a wood-frame structure built about 1903 for Josephine DeBartholemew. Symmetrical in appearance, the house was built with textured concrete blocks. The hip roof was pierced by dormers and a hooded brick chimney. A porch with square brick columns supporting a hip roof extended across the facade. Construction was financed by Joseph and Charlotte Snipes, who bought the 1903 house and leased the property from the association in 1917.[53]

Besides demolition, fire transformed the landscape of Cassadaga. Small fires had periodically destroyed or damaged cottages, but none compared with the conflagration on December 26, 1926, that consumed the Cassadaga Hotel, the Reid Williams house, Herbert Hollely's store and post office, and the camp entrance gates. Longtime resident C. H. Wetherell collapsed from a heart attack in the process of protecting his home from the flames. The blaze was a defining moment in the history of the camp and inspired resident Harriet Bowers to write a poem, "The Fire at Cassadaga," published in the *DeLand Daily News*, December 28, 1926.

T'was the night after Christmas,
    the camp was at rest,
The people enjoying the sleep
    of the blest,
When in tones full of fright,
    out on the night air,
Someone was calling
    "The Hotel's on fire!"
The glare in the sky,
    and a loud crackling noise,
Soon called to the street
    the men and the boys.
And work as they would,
    no headway could make,
Though they did their best
    for everyone's sake.
Streams of water,
    ladder units though they may be
Were a help, in a way,
    to the Community.
But the fire it kept spreading
    to nearby domains,

Till three other buildings
    were caught by the flames:
The Post office, store, and
    a cottage, too,
And the Postmaster's home
    have gone from our view.
The fire desiccation
    which lays all around
Causes sadness to all on
    our happy Camp Ground.
But time is a healer
    for all ills below,
And we have no control
    over nature, we know.
Nor water, nor fire
    can we ever control
So each incident
    is a part of the whole.
Old Mother Nature will
    show that all's well,
And Cassadaga will still have
    a story to tell.

The loss, estimated at $50,000 and attributed to faulty wiring, provided the hotel company and association directors with an opportunity to put a new face on the camp. A rebuilding campaign was initiated by outgoing president Slater, who made a special trip by train from Columbus, Ohio, to donate $1,000 to the effort. Contributions reached $8,000 in March 1927, and eventually benefactors donated $22,135. A bond issue netted an additional $29,400. The directors insisted on a fireproof building and in May commissioned architect William J. Carpenter to design it. New foundations were laid in the summer of 1927, but funding shortfalls forestalled construction. Additional mortgages totaling nearly $60,000 insured completion of the first phase of the project, facing Cassadaga Road, which opened in December 1927. The second unit, extending along Stevens Street, opened in November 1928 (see photo on p. 127).[54]

Carpenter worked closely with the directors to design the new building. Their choice of mission architecture for the Cassadaga Hotel transformed the entrance of the camp and linked it to the temple farther south on Stevens Street. Monumental in form and presence, the hotel facade was reoriented to the north, rather than repeating the east/west axis of the original building. The building was protected by a cross-hip roof adorned by a central shaped parapet. A one-story central block, embraced by projecting cross-hip extensions and containing the front entrance, vestibule, and a second-story balcony, softened the fortresslike appearance of the front facade. A one-story veranda welcomed patrons and shaded visitors along the west elevation. Textured stucco on the exterior walls contrasted with the foundation of rusticated cast block. Arrangements of French doors and double-hung sash and fixed windows helped illuminate the hotel's interior. After the building was completed, a flagpole was installed at the west elevation. The N. N. Jacobs Lumber Company of DeLand restored the entrance gates on Stevens Street, donating brick columns finished with stucco and embellished with urns and a drinking fountain sconce. Mrs. Palmer Mensink, proprietor of Mensink & Makarius, a Daytona Beach jewelry and novelty shop, furnished ornamental plants and supervised their installation. In addition to her Daytona Beach home, Mensink occupied a seasonal cottage in Cassadaga.[55]

The temple and hotel, the largest construction projects undertaken in the history of the association, stood out from the community's preponderant wood-frame architecture, lending a significant 1920s character to a setting otherwise cast in strong Victorian lines. Building construction tapered off in the late 1920s, following the collapse of the land boom and onset of the Great Depression. Most subsequent dwellings were modest in size and detailing, and relatively few were

*Cassadaga Hotel, mission revival style, built between 1927 and 1928. Courtesy of the West Volusia Historical Society.*

constructed before the latter half of the 1930s. Moreover, only a few buildings were constructed during the 1940s and 1950s. While the character of many large American cities was transformed by urban renewal programs of the 1960s and 1970s, resulting in extensive demolition of older buildings, Cassadaga remained largely intact.

The architecture of Cassadaga reflects the mobile nature of the Spiritualist culture. Most houses were built as seasonal cottages occupied for several months each year, their residents migrating between Cassadaga and their native homes on annual pilgrimages. Bills of sale, lease assignments, and newspaper chatterbox columns reveal another dimension of the socially mobile character of the winter retreat culture. Homes frequently changed hands, as residents regularly moved into and out of the religious center. O. L. Concannon's Marion Street house, built about 1895, was barely two years old before he conveyed it to architect C. E. Parcell. Subsequent owners before 1918 included C. E. Francis, Laura G. Fixen, and Kate Lawber. In 1905, Eber Bond sold his Stevens Street cottage, then about two years old, to Mary Hardenburg. A. J. and Emma Underhill of Canton, Ohio, sold their home on Chauncey Street, built about 1912, to George Moon of Canton in 1916. Between 1916 and 1930 no fewer than four people owned and made use of a dwelling on Chauncey Street. W. E. and Elizabeth Greenwood sold Prospect Cottage, their circa 1906 home on Chauncey Street, to Bettie Shofner in 1918, and Hiram Clark sold the cottage he had built about 1910 on Chauncey Street, to Evangelina Bach of Lily Dale in 1916. Ray Babcock of Syracuse, New York, occupied several houses in Cassadaga before constructing a new dwelling in the Vermont settlement in the 1920s. By contrast, some residents owned their homes for long periods. The Sherman houses on Lake Street were maintained by family members for several decades. Longtime resident Herbert Hollely owned dwellings on Lincoln and McKinley Streets for many years, leasing out the former to seasonal visitors.[56]

The owners of Cassadaga's houses took pride in the homes they designed, built, and lived in. Although many were modest cottages of perhaps only five hundred square feet of interior floor space, several were much larger and all originally reflected the pride of the first owner in a cherished seasonal home in Florida. Many of Cassadaga's historic dwellings still stand, displaying their original materials fabricated at a local lumber mill and brick factory whose saws and kilns fell silent nearly six decades ago. Other cottages have not survived.

The death of a dream ended, in some caes, in fire, in others with demolition after insects and humidity rendered a house unlivable. Not as dramatic but no less insidious have been the effects of alterations and modifications. Most small cottages built in Cassadaga between 1895 and 1915 had experienced several changes in ownership by the 1950s and by then had become a maintenance challenge. Daunted by the prospects of scraping and repainting, and persuaded by a new "maintenance free" material, some subsequent home owners installed asbestos panels and vinyl or aluminum siding over the original wood boards of their houses. Too often, knee braces mounted under the eaves, jigsaw-cut designs on fascia, and other decorative features were removed or covered during the renovation. Clipped window sills and lintels too often left small openings through which insects and small varmints could gain access into interior spaces. Porches enclosed with glass or plywood diminished the original harmony and texture of some dwellings. Much of the character and charm of Cassadaga's homes disappeared in a process often termed "remuddling" in the historic preservation community. Although Cassadaga escaped the effects of urban renewal, the success of effective siding salespeople has eroded some of the town's distinctive atmosphere.

YET CASSADAGA still defines a small part of the historic built environment of Volusia County, conveying the influence of a northern urban community in the central Florida landscape and retaining much of its Victorian-era character. Between 1895 and 1945, Cassadaga's Spiritualists gradually changed a segment of Volusia County's frontier environment into a permanent community. The names of streets and avenues and building forms, such as the octagonal auditorium and the double-pile character of Harmony Hall, connected the Florida Spiritualist culture to its religious roots in New York. Still, Cassadaga's "good comfortable houses," described in 1909 by Alice Spencer, embodied traditional vernacular or folk forms. Never palaces, the buildings of Cassadaga conveyed more about mainstream American culture and popular architecture at the turn of the century than about Spiritualism. Yet the architecture of the camp also helped define Cassadaga as a Spiritualist center, the largest and oldest of its kind in the South.

The association directors consistently hired professional architects to design buildings for public use and sacred architecture. The SCSCMA's primary social mission, to "provide for . . . assemblies and meetings for literary, scientific, philosophical, moral, and religious instruction," was worked out, in part, through its built environment. Creative in their vision, the directors adapted the design of the landscape to insure the economic viability of the community, and in the process insured beauty through a creative organic process with integral relationships between public and private architecture. The resulting intimacy of buildings and site expressed the integration of religion and retreat, built fabric and natural landscape.

## Notes

1. *Volusia County Record,* January 15, 1909.
2. Quote from King, *The Bungalow,* 4–5.
3. Downs and Hedley, *History of Chautauqua County,* 1:324–35; Conover, *Houses in Western New York;* American Association for State and Local History, *National Register of Historic Places.* 509.
4. Withey and Withey, *Biographical Dictionary of American Architects (Deceased),* 135; Works Progress Administration, *New York,* 439; Gould, *The Chautauqua Movement;* Downs and Hedley, *History of Chautauqua County,* 1:422–24; Booth and Cook, "Chautauqua Institution Historic District, National Register of Historic Places Nomination," ms., p. 1, 1973. National Register of Historic Places, Washington, D.C.
5. Map Book 2, p. 70, Volusia County Courthouse, DeLand, Florida; *Volusia County Record,* June 20, 1896.
6. Federal Writers' Workshop Project, "Southern Cassadaga Spiritualist Camp," 1–2. The Federal Writer' Workshop Project reounted this story from interviews with older residents and by researching newspapers of the 1890s.
7. Plat Book 2, p. 70, Volusia County Courthouse.

8. *Volusia County Record,* December 14, 1895, December 5, 1896, March 13, April 3, November 6, 1897.

9. Deed Book 44, p. 3–5, Miscellaneous Book J, p. 519, Volusia County Courthouse; *Volusia County Record,* June 20, 1896, March 13, April 3, 1897, October 21, 1905.

10. Whiffen, *American Architecture Since 1780,* 83–86; Blumenson, *Identifying American Architecture,* 49; McAlester and McAlester, *American Houses,* 235; Roth, *Concise History of American Architecture,* 122; Kennedy, *American Churches,* 242–43; *Dictionary of American Biography,* s.v. "Orson Squire Fowler," 6:565–66.

11. McAlester and McAlester, *American Houses,* 235; Maddex, *Master Builders,* 52–55.

12. Whiffen, *American Architecture since 1780,* 83–86; Blumenson, *Identifying American Architecture,* 49; Kennedy, *American Churches,* 272; Lasley, *Names and Places,* 11. Frank Lloyd Wright's Annunciation Greek Orthodox Church in Wauwatosa, Wisconsin (1959), represents an adaptation of circular sacred architecture with roots in Constantinople and the Byzantine empire. Wright disavowed the association, writing, "It is never necessary to cling slavishly to a tradition. The spirit of religion is all that will live because it is all that is really significant as life changes and emerges."

13. *Volusia County Record,* December 5, 1896; Southern Cassadaga Spiritualist Camp Meeting Association, *Nineteenth Annual Convention* (1913) (hereinafter *Nineteenth Annual Convention*).

14. *Volusia County Record,* October 21, 1905, November 25, 1910; *Fire Insurance Map of Cassadaga, Volusia County, Florida* (1915), 1 (hereinafter *Fire Insurance Map,* 1915).

15. *Volusia County Record,* December 14, 1895, December 5, 1896; *DeLand Daily News,* December 27, 1926, November 6, 1928; Deed Book 27, pp. 13–15, Record of Incorporations Book 2, pp. 392–95, Volusia County Courthouse.

16. Miscellaneous Book K, p. 329, Miscellaneous Book L, pp. 228–31, Quit Claim Book 4, p. 91, Volusia County Courthouse; *Volusia County Record,* March 27, April 3, 1897; *DeLand News,* November 14, 1910.

17. *Volusia County Record,* February 27, 1904; for sample leases see Miscellaneous Book K, pp. 379–86, 473, 637–40, and Miscellaneous Book L, pp. 28, 90, 109, 215, Deed Book 204, p. 386, Deed Book 205, pp. 299–301, Volusia County Courthouse.

18. *Florida Agriculturist,* November 14, 1894, January 30, 1895.

19. Jakle et al., *Common Houses,* 138–40; Deed Book 184, p. 303, Tax rolls, 1925–1926, Volusia County Courthouse.

20. Miscellaneous Book J, p. 519, Deed Book 44, p. 3–5, Plat Book 2, p. 70, Volusia County Courthouse; Wilson, "Plan of the Camp Grounds."

21. Reps, *Urban America,* 349, 501–2; Scott, *American City Planning since 1890,* 1–2; Wright, *Building the Dream,* 176; Atterbury, "Model Towns in America," 26; O'Neill, *The Progressive Years;* Link, *Woodrow Wilson;* Gannon, *Florida.*

22. Wilson, *The City Beautiful Movement;* Robinson, "New Dreams for Cities"; Reps, *Urban America,* 502, 505. The clerks of court at Highlands County (Sebring), Indian River County (Fellsmere), and Polk County (Auburndale) maintain copies of town plans within which the aforementioned towns and cities developed.

23. *DeLand Daily News,* January 22, 1909, *DeLand News,* February 16, 1916; Map Book 4, p. 57, Deed Book 211, pp. 472–74, Volusia County Courthouse.

24. *Volusia County Record,* February 27, 1904, October 21, 1905; Deed Book 51, p. 437, Volusia County Courthouse; *Fire Insurance Map,* 1; *Nineteenth Annual Convention.*

25. *DeLand News,* November 14, 1910, January 19, 1916; *DeLand Daily News,* December 23, 1921, April 1, April 22, 1927; *DeLand Sun News,* October 1, 1931; Miscellaneous Book K, pp. 366, 532, Miscellaneous Book L, pp. 28, 90, 109, 221, Deed Book 79, pp. 212–215, Deed Book 44, pp. 95–98, Volusia County Courthouse; *Nineteenth Annual Convention.*

26. *DeLand Daily News,* December 23, 1921; *Nineteenth Annual Convention; Fire Insurance Map,* 1.

27. Haase, *Classic Cracker,* 11; Jakle et al., *Common Houses,* 67–69.

28. Jakle et al., *Common Houses,* ix, 2; Wright, *Building the Dream,* 73, 96; *Fire Insurance Map,* 1. On America's wood-frame dwellings, see also Cummings, *Framed Houses;* Kimball, *Domestic Architecture;* Kelly, *Early Domestic Architecture;* Peat, *Indiana Houses;* Mattson, "Gable Front House"; Pillsburg and Kardus, *Folk Architecture.*

29. Vaux, *Villa and Cottage Architecture,* 26–27; Palliser and Palliser, *Palliser's American Cottage Homes;* Woodward and Thompson, *Woodward's National Architect;* Haase, *Classic Cracker,* 11; Ferraro, *"Ladies' Home Journal* Houses."

30. Jakle et al., *Common Houses,* 140–41, 143–44, 163–64; *Volusia County Record,* February 27, 1904; *DeLand Daily News,* December 23, 1921; *Fire Insurance Map,* 1915, 1; *Fire Insurance Map of Cassadaga, Volusia County, Florida* (1925), 1 (hereinafter *Fire Insurance Map, 1925*).

31. *Volusia County Record,* February 27, 1904; *DeLand Daily News,* December 23, 1921; *Fire Insurance Map,* 1915, 1; *Fire Insurance Map,* 1925, 1.

32. Wilbur Peat, quoted in Jakle et al., *Common Houses,* 153. See 140–44 and 153–69 for further descriptions of the vernacular house. Based on the classifications developed by Jakle, Bastian, and Meyer, the dwellings of Cassadaga fall into the following categories: irregularly massed (21), double pile (8), and single pile (16). Subsets within each category include camelback, composite, cross plan, L-plan, T-plan, and upright-and-wing for irregularly massed; cube and front-facing gable for double pile; and front-facing and side-facing gables and I-house forms in the single-pile classification. Other stylistic influences found in small numbers, some crafted by professionally trained architects and others from plan books, consist of bungalow, colonial revival, and Italian Renaissance.

33. Ibid.; McMurry, *Families and Farmhouses,* 32.

34. Jakle et al., *Common Houses,* 157–60; *DeLand Daily News,* December 12, 1923.

35. Downs and Hedley, *History of Chautauqua County,* 1:425; *Nineteenth Annual Convention;* Tax rolls, 1910–15, Volusia County Courthouse.

36. Jakle et al., *Common Houses,* 126–27, 133, 143–44, 213.

37. *Volusia County Record,* March 27, 1897.

38. Jakle et al., *Common Houses,* 106–7, 124–25.

39. King, *The Bungalow,* 17–18

40. Ibid.; Alladin Company, *Alladin Homes "Built in a Day" Catalog No. 29, 1917* (Bay City, Mich.: Alladin Co., 1917); Baker, *American House Styles,* 114–15; Whiffen and Koeper, *American Architecture,* 316; McAlester and McAlester, *American Houses,* 453–63.

41. *DeLand Daily News,* July 18, 1923, January 9, February 1, 1924; C. L. Coy, *DeLand City Directory* (Tampa: Coy, 1934), 269; *Fire Insurance Map,* 1915, 1.

42. Tax rolls, 1927–29, Volusia County Courthouse; Coy, *1934 DeLand City Directory,* 269.

43. Stevenson and Jandl, *Houses By Mail,* 19–35; Alladin Company, *Alladin Homes,* 2–13.

44. Rerick, *Memoirs of Florida,* 2:438–39; *Florida Agriculturist,* January 1, 1898; DeLand, *Story of DeLand;* Record of Incorporations Book 1, pp. 12–13, Judgment Book 2, p. 125, Volusia County Courthouse; *Volusia County Record,* December 5, 1896, August 8, 13, 29, 1913; *New Smyrna Observer,* March 7, 1936.

45. Rerick, *Florida,* 2: 438–439; *Florida Agriculturist,* January 1, 1898; Hebel, "Florida's Bonds: Men Who Made Lumber History," 24–25; "The E.W. Bond Company Mill," *Logging* 5 (August 1917), 247–263; "The E.W. Bond Company Mill," *Logging* 5 (September 1917), 266–291.

46. Rerick, *Memoirs of Florida,* 2:438–39; *Florida Agriculturist,* January 1, 1898; Judgment Book 2, p. 125, Volusia County Courthouse.

47. Rerick, *Memoirs of Florida,* 2:438–39; *Florida Agriculturist,* January 1, 1898; Hebel, "Florida's Bonds"; "E. W. Bond Company Mill."

48. 1903 and 1904 tax rolls, Volusia County Courthouse; *Florida Agriculturist,* January 17, 1906; *Volusia County Record,* November 25, 1905, December 18, 1914; Hebel, "Florida's Bonds," 24–25; *Florida Times-Union,* August 2, 8, 1899; "E. W. Bond Company Mill," 274, 279, 291.

49. *The (DeLand) Supplement,* June 13, 20, 1888; Florida Agriculturist Job Shop, *DeLand: A Famous Resort* (DeLand: Florida Agriculturist, 1888), 44, 69; *Florida Times-Union,* April 7, 1889, December 29, 1897, February 12, 1901; Gold, *History of Volusia County,* 415; Record of Incorporations, Book 2, p. 199, Volusia County Courthouse; *Volusia County Record,* May 6, 1893, January 16, 1914; *DeLand News,* March 11, 1910; *Life in Florida,* April 6, 1889; *Florida Agriculturist,* January 1, 1898.

50. *DeLand Daily News,* July 5, December 26, 1923, January 15, 17, 1924.

51. National Spiritualist Association of Churches of the United States of America *Yearbook* (1998).

52. *DeLand Daily News,* July 5, September 5, December 12, 26, 1923, January 6, 15, 17, 1924; Moore, *Men of the South,* 281; *Bartow Courier-Informant,* November 6, 1913, September 17, 1914; *Winter Haven Chief,* March 24, May 8, June 3, 17, 21, October 12, 29, December 21, 1925, January 14, November 30, 1926; Grismer, *Tampa,* 384–85. Bonfoey prepared the plans for Tampa's Strand Theater, Stovall Professional Building, Leiman-Wilson House, the Roosevelt School in Tampa Heights, and the Hinson House, identified by some architectural historians as the most elegant second Renaissance revival residence in Tampa. Bonfoey also designed Arcadia Elementary School, the public library, and John Swearingen House in Bartow, the DeSoto County Courthouse in Arcadia, and the Broadway Arcade, Lake Region Hotel, Postal Arcade, Runkle Building, and St. Joseph's Catholic Church in Winter Haven.

53. *DeLand Daily News,* March 10, April 1, 1927; Deed Book 205, pp. 299–301, Deed Book 225, p. 388, Volusia County Courthouse.

54. Mortgage Book 89, 1–3, 341–344, Mortgage Book 90, 152–161, Volusia County

Courthouse; *DeLand Daily News*, March 16, 19, May 2, 1927, January 4, November 6, December 26, 1928. Carpenter established his main office in St. Petersburg shortly after World War I and organized a branch office in DeLand several years later. In the 1930s he relocated to Daytona Beach. A member of the American Institute of Architects, he designed St. Petersburg's YMCA and the Espiritu Santo Hotel in Safety Harbor. During the mid-1920s he prepared the plans for several of DeLand's landmarks and developed a lucrative practice designing schools throughout Volusia County. Minute Book 4, pp. 493, 545, 557, Minute Book 5, pp. 1, 37, 217, 221, 257, 279, 291, 437, Volusia County School Board, DeLand, Florida; *DeLand News*, August 25, 1920; *DeLand Daily News,* January 21, May 13, August 24, 1921, January 14, 1924, November 23, 1925, June 2, 1926; R. L. Polk, *Daytona Beach City Directory* (Jacksonville: R. L. Polk Co., 1935), 77.

55. *DeLand Daily News*, November 6, 21, December 26, 1928, January 4, 23, 1929; Deed Book 231, pp. 204–6, Volusia County Courthouse.

56. Tax rolls, 1899–1903, 1917–35, Miscellaneous Book J, p. 519, Deed Book 79, p. 212, Deed Book 85, p. 479, Deed Book 193, p. 527, Volusia County Courthouse; *DeLand News*, December 6, 1923; *DeLand Sun News*, February 1, 1928; Coy, *1934 DeLand City Directory,* 266.

# Glossary of Architectural Terms

ARCHITRAVE: The lower part of a classical entablature, which rests directly on the capital of a column. Also, molding around a window or door.

BALLOON FRAMING: A type of lightweight building construction that employs two-inch boards of varying widths, generally fastened by nails at right angles to each other, to produce a basketlike frame that forms the skeletal system for a building. Balloon framing, introduced in the 1840s, remains the prevalent method for constructing wood buildings.

BARGEBOARD: A decorative board that hangs from the projecting end of a gable.

BAY: One unit of a building that consists of a series of similar units, commonly the number of window and door openings per floor or the number of spaces between columns and piers.

BELT COURSE: Also known as "string course." A horizontal molded band across the facade or around the walls of a building.

BRACKET: A support element under eaves, shelves, or overhangs, often more decorative than functional.

CASEMENT WINDOW: A window with the sash hung vertically and opening inward or outward.

COPING: A protective cap, top, or cover of a wall, parapet, pilaster, or chimney, often of stone, terra-cotta, concrete, metal, or wood. Commonly sloped to shed water to protect masonry below from moisture intrusion.

CORNICE: Projecting ornamental molding along the top of a building or wall.

DORMER: A structure projecting from or cutting through a sloping roof. Usually housing a window or ventilating louvers.

DORMER WINDOW: A window used for lighting the space in a roof in the same plane as the wall (wall dormer) or projecting from the slope of the roof (roof dormer).

DOUBLE-HUNG SASH WINDOW: A window with two sashes, one above the other, arranged to slide vertically past each other.

EAVE: The projecting overhang at the lower edge of a roof.

ENTABLATURE: In classical architecture, the part of a structure between the column capital and the roof or pediment. An entablature is comprised of an architrave, frieze, and cornice.

FACADE: The face or front elevation of a building.

FASCIA: A flat molding or face with a vertical surface and little projection.

FENESTRATION: The arrangement and design of windows in a building.

FINIAL: An ornament that terminates the point of a gable, pinnacle, spire, or other point of relative height.

FRIEZE: The middle horizontal member of a classical entablature, above the architrave and below the cornice. Also, a decorative band in a belt course, or near the top of a wall below the cornice.

GABLE ROOF: A double-pitched roof with pitches at opposite but equal angles meeting at the roof's ridge.

GAMBREL ROOF: A ridged roof with two slopes on each side, the lower slope having a steeper pitch.

HIP ROOF: A roof with four uniformly pitched sides.

LATH: A narrow, thin strip of wood or metal used as a base for plaster or stucco.

LATTICE: A network of diagonally interlocking lath or other material used as screening.

LIGHT: A window or opening in a wall that admits light; also, a pane of glass.

LINTEL: The horizontal beam over a door or window.

LOUVER: A door or window with fixed or movable slanted slats.

MASONRY: Stone, block, brick, or hollow-tile work used in wall construction.

MASSING: The combining of several masses to form a building volume.

MODILLION: An ornamental bracket used in series under a cornice.

MOLDING: A continuous decorative band that is either carved into or applied to a surface.

MULLION: A vertical member separating windows, doors, or panels set in a series.

MUNTIN: a member separating and supporting panes of glass in a sash or door.

ORIEL: A variant of a bay window that projects from a wall surface either from an upper floor, or without supporting foundation piers on a lower floor.

PARAPET: A low, solid protective wall or railing along the edge of a roof or balcony, usually used to obscure and surround a flat or built-up roof.

PATERA: A flat, round, or oval disk or medallion in relief.

PEDIMENT: A wide, low-pitched gable end of the roof; also the triangular crowning element used over doors and windows.

PILASTER: An engaged shallow pier or pillar attached to a wall, often with a capital and base.

POLYGONAL BAY: A small projection from a wall surface displaying three or more sides with obtuse angles.

PORTE COCHERE: A large covered entrance porch through which a vehicle can pass.

QUATREFOIL: A four-lobed pattern divided by cusps, or tracery arcs.

QUOIN: Units of stone, brick, or wood used to accentuate the corners of a building.

SASH: A frame in which the panes of glass in a window or door are set.

SHED ROOF: A single-pitched roof, usually protecting a porch and attached to a main structure.

SIDELIGHT: A framed area of fixed glass along the side of a door or window opening.

SIDING: Building material used for surfacing a frame building.

SOFFIT: The exposed underface of an overhead component of a building structure.

SPINDLE: A turned-wood element used in stair railings and porch trim.

STUCCO: A type of masonry plasterwork used for surfacing exterior or interior walls.

TERRA-COTTA: A fine-grained, brownish-red, fired clay used for roof tiles and decorations.

TRANSOM WINDOW: A small window, movable or fixed, over a door or another window.

# FIVE

# Keepers of the Veil

## *Life Stories of Cassadaga's Senior Residents*

### ANN JEROME CROCE
### AND PAUL JEROME CROCE

IN 1997 AND 1998, we interviewed some of Cassadaga's more prominent and long-term residents, gathering their life stories, returning to each several times for more information and clarification. We chose them for their individual characteristics and for the contributions they have made to Cassadaga, but also for the picture that, collectively, they represent of the community. Because Spiritualism allows for a range of personal interpretations and beliefs, each person who speaks in this chapter conveys a different aspect of it.[1]

Cassadaga is a community of people who value their individualism and respect that of others, but who also share a common purpose, vision, and way of life. Some might be considered "different" or even "quirky" by mainstream standards, and in some cases it has taken considerable courage—or more accurately, they might say, considerable prompting by Spirit—to follow the path that led them to Cassadaga. All had other lives, other careers, and other religions before they came to Spiritualism and to Cassadaga, and each brings the legacy of these experiences to this community and to its expression of Spiritualism. Family background, professional training, religious experiences, forms of service to the world—each of these factors enters into the particular contribution every one of them makes; each impacts, however subtly, the ways in which these people help shape Cassadaga's religion and way of life.

## When Spirit Takes You Over: Gladys Reid

Gladys Reid lives in an apartment in a multidwelling house that was none too spacious to begin with. Her home is what might in a more modern building be marketed as an "efficiency." Outside the door is a patio overflowing with potted plants in various stages of bloom. In a semicircle on the patio are some chairs and a little table; this is part of her living space, welcoming plants and animals as well as the people who find their way here. The kitchen door is open, and visitors jingle a set of sleigh bells to announce their arrival. There is a sense of home here, with the plants hanging inside louvered windows and the breeze that somehow finds its way through even on this hot afternoon in Florida's June.

Gladys answers the door, a bit stooped; "I have a bad back," she explains as she seats herself on the sofa in the main room. There are two toy stuffed animals, cats, on the chair next to the bed; most other surfaces are covered with books of all kinds, from romance novels to mysteries, nature books to spiritual reading. Decorating the walls are a familiar rendition of Jesus at the garden door, some floral pictures, and several images of Native Americans, including the centerpiece over the sofa, a large muscular warrior rendered in paint on black velvet.[2]

Gladys does indeed have a bad back; it is painful for her even to change her position while sitting. "My vertebrae are crumbling," she says, more cheerfully than one might expect. Complications of osteoporosis have made it difficult for her to talk for long without inducing a cough that doubles her over in pain. The cough passes as quickly as it arrived, however, and immediately she is herself again: smooth healthy cheeks, bright blue eyes with as much life and mischief in them as a child's, and a smile like the sun after a storm.

Gladys is known for her abilities as a healer. When she arrived in Cassadaga in 1973, healing was not a visible part of the camp's activities. She initiated the healing component that is now an integral part of Sunday services in Colby Memorial Temple, and until her back prevented her, she offered healings in the Caesar Forman Healing Center before each worship service. Gladys's influence is clear when one visits Cassadaga today: from the Reverend Harry Fogle Healing Park to the monthly candlelight healing services in the temple, healing has become a mainstay in Cassadaga's activities and ministry.

Gladys grew up in Massachusetts, and she still has the accent to prove it. The youngest of six children, she worked hard on the family farm, where "it was a good life; we didn't have a lot to wear, but we had a lot to eat." From earliest childhood, Gladys helped tend the chickens, the cows, and the crops; "we all

*Gladys Reid, 1994.*

had our own work to do." Gladys wonders now if the active physical labor that began in childhood and characterized her whole life might have contributed to her current health problems, but her memories of the hard work are all positive. Indeed, she feels that farming has the potential to teach people valuable lessons and to provide resources that are lacking today. "Money is the root of all evil. If we'd just let people have a plot of land with a garden, maybe some chickens, the economy would be in much better shape." Religion was not a major force in the family's daily life, but on Sundays they rode by horse and wagon to the Congregational church in town. In snowstorms, when the horse could not make it through, they used the oxen. In those days, Gladys recalls, there was no salary for the church's minister. Instead, he was supported by his parishioners' most natural currency: "You gave the minister the excess from your farm."

Gladys herself did not have experiences with Spirit as a child. However, she had a legacy that she would learn of later. "I didn't know my mother was a Spiritualist until after she passed. My father told me. She was a life member of the [Spiritualist] church in Brockton." An uncle on her father's side, moreover, was gifted in levitation: "He could walk across the room and tables and chairs would fall all over the place." Now that Gladys is well acquainted with the workings of

Spirit, this element of her family background does not surprise her in the least.

Gladys's mother died when she was twelve, and when her father passed away sixteen years later, she and her brothers and sisters sold the farm. "I would like to have kept it," she says, "but it was too big to run it myself, and my brothers didn't want it." To support herself, she "did a little bit of everything," and then opened the beauty shop in Wareham that would be her focus until she moved to Cassadaga. Located among the mix of immigrant cultures in eastern Massachusetts, the beauty shop served a diverse clientele. "I loved to hear about the different ethnic groups, the different cultures. It got us away from people talking gossip," as is the stereotype of beauty shops. In many ways, the beauty shop was an education for Gladys. And it was there that she first became drawn to Spiritualism. "I had been searching" spiritually, and in 1960 two customers talked about their experiences with the nearby Spiritualist church. Gladys liked what they said, and her attendance at worship services led to further study in classes there.

Gladys was married for fifteen years; she and her husband had no children: "I didn't feel I was capable of bringing up a child the way they should be. If I followed my father's example, I'd be too severe. And besides, I was in my thirties when I married." Gladys's late husband was a strongly committed Catholic who had served as an altar boy and whose mother was "right from Ireland." As Gladys's own spiritual searching led her toward Spiritualism, their religious differences became clear. But, she laughs, it was never a problem. "He was a Democrat, I was a Republican. We got along fine." While Gladys worshipped in the Spiritualist church, her husband continued to attend Catholic mass, and the marriage remained peaceable.

Gladys was in her forties, "the prime of life," when she began to attend the church in Massachusetts, and in meditation "Spirit took me over a couple of times. It was wonderful, and I wanted to go over more, but they won't let you." She shakes her head with a smile. "I was taking classes, and I saw some of the most wonderful things. I never got that way again, in that vibration." But Gladys's own path was to lead in a different direction. "In class one night someone asked me what I was going to do. Without thinking, the first thing out of my mouth was, 'I'm going to be a healer.'" So, Gladys says, "I've been healing as long as I've been a Spiritualist."

Although her back now prevents her from performing healings, Gladys radiates contentment as she remembers her experiences as a healer. "I would go into Spirit, lose myself in Spirit; Spirit would take me over. It's a wonderful feeling to have Spirit take you over." In healing, she says, she was fully an instrument of

God. "How can I heal? Only God can." When asked how she herself came by the gift of healing, Gladys explains: "A healer is something you have to want to be. If you want it bad enough, Spirit will give it to you. I guess we all have it in us," but, she adds, it requires the interaction of individual desire and the presence of Spirit to activate it. Healing, she says, is evidence of God's love and benevolence toward us, and Gladys is grateful that God's love encompasses the healer as well as the healed.

Asked for memories of particular moments in her healing, Gladys muses, "It's hard to tell you anything about the healings," because, as with mediumship, "it's supposed to leave your mind once it's done." The rules of confidentiality accord with the workings of Spirit in this regard, because often Gladys would not remember what had happened during a healing, coming back to consciousness only after it was over. She does know, though, despite many successes, "I couldn't heal AIDS." She had two clients with AIDS, one of whom died; the other, who came from Canada, has fallen out of touch. Still, she wonders what might have happened if they had come to her earlier, since the disease was far advanced when she met them.

As "a God-given gift," healing is something that cannot effectively be taught; "it's not the same when it's from training," says Gladys. Mediumship, on the other hand, "requires training to know how to contact Spirit, how to interpret what they say and all." For this reason, Gladys says, perhaps it is more legitimate for a medium to charge money for a reading than it is for a healer to charge for a healing. "If you're a true Spiritualist, you don't accept money. [The gift of healing is] something God gives you, so how can you accept money for it?" Gladys is deeply interested in mediumship, but for her it was the path to finding her real gift: "I used to be a medium, but you can't do both; what do you do when you're in the middle of a reading and you see the person needs healing?" What she liked most about mediumship was "working with Spirit, they feeding you and you feeding them," and the synergy of medium and Spirit feeding the client as well. As with her experience of healing, Gladys says, "a good medium is one who gets out of the way. Spirit guides have a way of casting you aside, taking over so they have a clear field," and the medium's job is simply to let that process happen. Gladys remembers being disappointed in some clients' misunderstanding of mediumship: "Sometimes people came and wanted a fortune teller, they wanted to know if their husband was cheating or something. That's not Spiritualism." With healing, Gladys found, the misunderstandings were fewer, the motives purer and more accurate.

"People," such as scientists and skeptics, "say you can't communicate with

Spirit, but you can. When you die you take everything with you but your body, so why couldn't you communicate?" Everyone, Gladys says, can communicate with Spirit; "that's what meditation is for." This experience is not just exciting and enlightening but also useful: "Once you can contact Spirit it's a wonderful thing. They can guide you. I think that's what they mean by a guardian angel, just someone from Spirit who guides you." She explains, though, that not every piece of advice deserves to be followed. "Among spirits there are, like here, those you should listen to and those you shouldn't." This is not a problem, however, because instinctively "you just know the difference." Furthermore, even after death there is change: "When they cross over they have to learn to come back, same as we have to learn to contact them."

And indeed, for Gladys learning is one of the most important parts of life— not book learning, though books are an important source of inspiration for her, but the continual revelation that comes from living in an attitude of wonder. In mulling over her memories, she often becomes reflective and murmurs, "I wonder why." She sees her current illness as a lesson that has not yet revealed its full meaning, and she wonders about the irony of a healer having to endure such pain. Nevertheless, she has not gone to a healer; "I try to heal myself, to listen for my guidance. Spirit's helping me to get through this too." Life on this earth plane, she says, "is a school; we have to learn all the phases."

In childhood and now in advanced age, Gladys feels an affinity with animals. The animals on the farm were always a special interest of hers, the wild ones as well as the livestock. "I asked Spirit once why I love animals and birds so much. Spirit said my last life was on a farm but was snuffed out in the middle, and that's the only thing I know about my past lives." Now she loves to sit outside and watch the birds and the squirrels, who go about their business unaware of her presence. "Animals have wonderful healing powers, you know, to heal themselves. Instinct is from God," and, as humans become aware of the healing instinct in animals, they may be able to contact it in themselves as well. "There's a lot of life that's around us every day, and we don't see it" until we make the effort to look. In her current condition, Gladys knows, she has no choice but to look and to wonder, with the expectation that eventually, like the animals, she will achieve the clarity of understanding that expresses itself in God-given instinct.

"With Spirit," says Gladys, "all your needs are met." She laughs. "Your wants are something else again."

## Still Searching: The Reverend Tom Berkner

The Reverend Tom Berkner's office at Cassadaga is on the second floor of a well-tended house on a quiet side street. The stairs are on the outside of the building, scaffold style, and covered with a narrow sloping roof; the place has the feel of a beach house in summer. On the outside landing perched high above the ground, a handwritten note on the door announces that the bell is broken: "Knock loudly." Inside, the apartment is made up of rooms on two levels, with a step down to an enclosed porch. Used more as an office than as a dwelling, it is neat and clean, the furnishings solid and straightforward. There is a Bible within easy reach on a coffee table. Original landscape paintings on the walls demonstrate the versatility of this medium and healer: "I used to be able to do a few of these a year, but I don't seem to have time any more," he explains ruefully.[3]

Tom Berkner is associate pastor of the church at Cassadaga, and he feels strongly called to this kind of service, which he describes as "my heart's desire." Having been affiliated with Cassadaga for about thirty years, he has served as pastor and as director of the lyceum program, which he has helped to nurture into a thriving series of Sunday lessons.

Among the youngest of his parents' thirteen children, Tom lost his father before the age of three and was raised by his mother, who was Catholic. Growing up in their Pennsylvania town just outside of Pittsburgh, he was conscious of the family's Catholic identity even though their churchgoing was erratic. "Not every one of us were Catholic people, but we were brought up in that faith. I guess I've been in the Catholic church as many times as I could count on my fingers. I have ten fingers and that is just about all," he remarks dryly.

Perhaps the most decisive turning point in Tom's life occurred in his early adolescence, when one of his older brothers converted to Christian fundamentalism during a revival that was "like a brushfire burning right down the Ohio River Valley" and pressured the family to follow in his footsteps. "From there on it kind of snowballed." Their mother converted, as did most of Tom's siblings. Young Tom found himself attending a fundamentalist church. "I went to all the functions and participated in all the services and activities—even on Saturday evenings we used to go to a farmhouse several miles away from the town" for prayer meetings. But this religion never fully made sense to Tom. In services, "when they said come to the altar to be cleansed of your sins, I found myself going down every week. I started wondering why I felt I had to do this, if I was saved. Why do I have to go to the altar every time?" Tom did not press the issue with his family, but "I just didn't feel as comfortable as I would want to be with

the religion because it was so dogmatic and so strong with that idea of the Lord Jesus Christ as my savior." The family's new church sponsored a seminary education for the brother who had first converted; he remains a minister in a fundamentalist church, and one of Tom's dearest desires is the two of them might come to a reconciliation. He feels that their common calling to the ministry and their parallel commitment to the mysteries of healing, should be the basis for an understanding between them, but the fundamentalist branch of the family has never accepted Tom's Spiritualism.

Tom finished high school at the beginning of World War II and then enlisted in the navy. His service took him to Florida, where he was stationed for a time in Sanford, a short distance from Cassadaga. The connection was not yet to be made, however, and at the end of the war Tom left the navy and went to Florida State University on the GI Bill. Married now, he earned degrees in education because this was an interest of his wife's. The job market was tight when he finished school, so he spent several years "doing odd jobs, selling insurance, working on automobiles," and was employed by an Orlando funeral home whose owner was so impressed with Tom that he offered to send him to mortuary school. Tom had no interest in remaining in the funeral business, though, and soon he began a thirty-three-year career as a teacher and administrator in the Orange County schools.

It was Tom's second wife who was the catalyst for his introduction to Cassadaga. She said, "'I want to go to Cassadaga,' and I said, 'I don't want to go to Cassadaga.'" While living in the area during the war, he continues, "I had heard about this Cassadaga place and all that and I said, 'Nah, I don't want to go there,' and she said, '*We will go.*'" Her persistence paid off, and Tom received an excellent reading from the Reverend Wilbur Hull. "It taught me everything that one would want to know about himself." Tom was amazed and intrigued. The Reverend Hull suggested that he go to Ann Gehman's church in Orlando, where Tom found the kind of religion he had always wanted without knowing how to identify it. "There was just something so peaceful, so harmonious . . . Something told me that there was peace, that I did not have to run to God and say 'Forgive me' all those times. So that's where I met with Spiritualism," about twenty-eight years ago.

Tom's shift to Spiritualism, which led him into mediumship classes and then to ordination, has always rankled the fundamentalists among his siblings. "My brother kept saying, 'You know you've left Jesus Christ as your savior. You know

*The Reverend Tom Berkner, 1994.*

you're going to Hell,' and I responded, 'I'm not going to Hell.' He said, 'You are going to Hell.' I asked, 'Why are you so bitter about this? Do you know everything about Cassadaga? If you know then you might be able to say something about it.' He said, 'All I know is that you don't accept Jesus Christ as your savior.' I said that I don't accept him as my savior but I do accept him as my teacher, as my guide, as my counselor. But to say that he came here for me, to die on the cross? He did not die for that purpose. He died for the principles of his teachings." For Tom, a central attraction of Spiritualism was "the idea of not having to . . . confess my sins to a crucified God; knowing that there was more to life than that I'm a sinner; knowing that God is a loving God." It seems only logical to Tom: "Why would man have to be created to be destroyed? If he's going to throw me in Hell, how can he be a loving God?" Tom's experience with different religions has convinced him that "religion is not made by God, but by man. Everything man touches, there's going to be some deceit behind it. They may not know it's deceit, but it's there, even if only a little."

Spiritualism, however, has revealed to Tom some of God's truths, which are untouched by human duplicity. The logo on his business card reads "Love." Here and there around his office are reflections of the same notion: thumb-tacked to a wall, a photograph of a red rose on a black background, the word "love" in small letters printed above it; a greeting card with a cartoon bear, arms outstretched, offering a hug. "Not being egotistical," he explains, "but people say I'm about love. That's what God has given me." Surprisingly, this stolid man chokes up as he explains the insights that Spiritualism has ushered into his heart: "I am love. I'm a spiritual person, I am Spirit. God said, 'I'm in you, you're in me'; there's no separation between you and God. God is here, within." As a medium, what Tom hopes to give his clients in readings is "belief in yourself, that you are God, you are a creative person, you can create anything your heart desires." "Everything," he asserts, "was created in love and with love. There is no evil. There are unlearned, undeveloped spiritual people." Their actions may sometimes be destructive, but the only real problem in this world made of love is "lack of understanding."

For Tom as well as for those he observes around him, an ongoing challenge is "walking in the light that God has given me." In praying for people, he habitually prays for "the lamp unto their feet," that they will see their way clearly. "It's a challenge where people are not listening to themselves," he says, explaining specifically, that "if I'd been more attuned to myself, I'd have stayed in the navy." Since God is both within and around us, Tom feels, we need to connect with ourselves as well as with the Spirit outside us.

As a medium, Tom understands that "everybody *is* a medium, but they don't know what they can do. It has to be a goal of connecting that dimension of life with this dimension of life." Most people, he asserts, are more psychic than mediumistic, having insight into "the energies of another person" more easily than they can communicate with "the so-called dead." Even he himself, with all of his years of experience, sees "more the present and the past, not so much the future." When people press him, he explains, "I can't tell you what will happen in the future, but I can give you a prediction. Someone asks me, 'Am I going to get married?' I say, 'Do you want to get married?' If the answer is yes, Tom affirms the creative power of the human spirit: "'Then you will, if you have your mind set on it.'"

After nearly thirty years as a Spiritualist, Tom is "still in the process of searching. What is my purpose in life?" He has a special yearning that has not yet been satisfied. "I wish some day I can really be a motivator," he says, then corrects himself, noting that "nobody can motivate anybody; you can talk to them, but they have to motivate themselves. But I'd love to be something of that, like a young kid on a street corner preaching about Jesus Christ. I want to be an inspirational speaker off the top of my head. I'm still wanting Spirit to give me the guidance, to open up opportunities for me to do that." Tom waits for the chance, "not so people will know there's another religion, but that people will know themselves."


## Follow Your Hunches: The Reverend Jean and Nick Sourant

The Reverend Nick and Jean Sourant live in a two-story clapboard house in a sleepy back corner of Cassadaga. Set on one of the few hills in central Florida, their house exudes the kind of charm one expects from the residence of doting grandparents, or perhaps of the "little people" in the stories they might read to their grandchildren. Flowers and vines thrive in pots all around the house; wind chimes and stained glass decorate porches and windows. Inside, each little room has its own character: the cozy farmhouse kitchen; the living room with its comfortable sofas and rockers and its every surface displaying Jean's teddy bear collection in orderly array; Jean's sunny and hospitable consulting room decorated everywhere with Native American paintings and dolls; Nick's little office with its handsome antique roll-top desk and the supplies for a dozen interests, hobbies, and enthusiasms strewn around like the debris after a volcanic explosion. Wel-

coming, whole, and full of delightful quirks, the house expresses the essence of these two individuals and of the relationship they share.

Nick Sourant was not raised with a Spiritualist faith, although perhaps the mystical elements embedded in liturgically rich Russian Orthodoxy predisposed him to sympathy with the life of the spirit in this world. Certainly, his attraction to Spiritualism did not come from a rejection of his ancestral faith. Instead, Spiritualism came to him unannounced and as a complete surprise.[4]

When he was eleven, Nick and his sister developed strep throat, and in the ensuing fevers, his sister died. Nick vividly remembers his own worst moments of struggle with the disease. It was not only a physical trauma, but also a spiritual awakening because, as he remembers, "I had a near-death experience." He palpably felt his spirit rise out of his body and hover "in a corner of the room looking down at a body that the doctors were working on." It was so sudden that there was no time for fear or reflection.

Almost as soon as he looked down curiously and serenely on this medical crisis, the doctors said, "He's gone," and started to leave the room. With the vigor that would characterize his energy throughout his life, his spirit "snapped back into the body," and he began his slow recovery from the illness.

Once healed, he remembered his spiritual experience but hesitated to tell anyone about it. Finally he mentioned it to his grandfather, an Orthodox priest, who reeled back from the story and could only say: "Don't talk about it! . . . Get it out of your mind . . . Don't talk about it." Although this response made young Nick furious—and primed him for sympathy with spiritual experiences in general—he tried gamely to live within the expectations of his family's faith.

Even though he did not have another major spiritual experience for years, he did have frequent quiet reminders of his contact with another world. His sister stayed in touch after "passing to the spirit world. When something tickles my nose I know she is around."

Nick kept these experiences mostly to himself for years, but some dreams he had as a young adult stoked his curiosity. "My venturing led me to San Jose, California, where I began studying the ancient mystical order of Rosicrucians. That was really the beginning of my search for the meaning of life." The driving question for Nick is "Why are we here?" His answer stems from his belief in the "continuum of life" from the "span of life on this earth" to forces beyond us. This awareness forms the core of his Spiritualist belief that Spirit inhabits the body but is not confined by its material limits. Equally important for Nick is the con-

*The Reverend Nick Sourant, 1994.*

viction that Spirit also has a vital purpose to fulfill while housed in the physical world.

Nick worked as a mechanical engineer for most of his life. Engineering might seem an unlikely job choice for a person with childhood out-of-body experiences and a lifelong involvement with many different ways of exploring spirituality. But once again for Nick, the spiritual intruded into his naturalistic world: Sometimes at work "I would develop an understanding in the field without having the benefit of knowledge. . . . I found that if I would go through a tiny little meditative state, the answer would come to me." He learned from experience to trust his instinct, "and if I didn't interpret it, ninety-five percent of the time I would be right; but if I did interpret it, it would be lost."

Nick never felt antagonism for the scientific assumptions of engineering. Instead, he began to see that his spiritual awareness could build on his scientific knowledge and work. "Parapsychology is the extension of our perception," he notes. For example, just as our eyes can identify shapes on a card in front of our face, "my brother and I, although we are three thousand miles apart," can still identify each other's cards "ten out of twelve times" if we are "mentally sending" the information about the shapes. To Nick, the point is not that the laws of physics are wrong, but that they are "not totally correct, because the laws of physics as they have been taught say that energy only operates in the material realm."

No single dramatic incident convinced Jean Sourant of the reality of the spirit world. Instead, she says serenely, "I'm a natural medium—I've been this way all my life." For Jean, Spiritualism flowed out of daily experience, especially at first, during dreams. "When I was young, I did not know about mediumship or Cassadaga or anything." But even as a child, "I would have dreams of what I should do and what was going to happen and all."[5]

She was not raised with the strong imprint of any one religion. Her father, who died when Jean was still young, believed in spiritual healing. She was raised by her mother, who was a member of the Church of Christ, although "she almost never went to church." She did read the Bible faithfully, and she was very spiritually reflective. When young Jean "knew when it was going to rain" or "when to clean the house for unexpected guests," her mother "almost always paid attention." Now Jean is grateful for her mother's belief in her insights, knowing how easily skepticism can discourage children with gifts like hers.

As she grew up, Jean realized, "When I meditated long enough and regularly,

*The Reverend Jean Sourant, 1996.*

I could receive without being asleep." At those moments, "I am seeing into the future through dream state." For her, meditation is associated more with physical relaxation and mental focus than with anything conventionally religious, and she has found that her mediumship improves "when I am on vacation."

Jean had these experiences even during the thirty years of her marriage to an engineer who was an agnostic and "typical scientist." Her first husband was so busy that he was simply not around the family very much, "but I could always see him," she adds wistfully. She once called to warn him about an accident she foresaw, but he ignored it. He took to calling her "the witch." After the marriage dissolved, she met Nick through spiritual enrichment classes and through the Church of Awareness in Orlando, of which Nick was a leader. Throughout her adult life, Jean has been a teacher and a champion of early childhood education, and when she lived in Orlando she was one of the people who first brought Montessori education to central Florida.

Nick is proud of his wife's spiritual talents, observing with a twinkle in his eye, "She doesn't need a car phone." Jean is more matter-of-fact about her extrasensory experiences: "When I am totally in meditation state and totally relaxed, I will have dreams that will absolutely come true." And she is not just seeing visions. As she puts it, "I am clairvoyant, clairsentient, and clairaudient—I'm sensing a whole scene."

Prompting her proudly, Nick adds, "There's also clairsmelling." Jean smiles and muses, "Yes, the burned popcorn." Years ago, when Jean was with her good friend and fellow medium Connie at a movie, some girls made popcorn for them but burned it by accident. Sensing one girl's embarrassment, Connie said gamely, "Oh honey, don't worry about it. Just give that to me—I love burned popcorn." Of course, she hated the stuff, but between Connie and Jean, "it became a joke . . . [that] only she and I were in on . . . and that is how we communicated." Since Connie's death, she will "come through to me," Jean observes casually, and "when I want to know beyond a doubt that it is her, she will give me the smell of burned popcorn."

As in life, across the spirit planes Connie and Jean remain good friends who watch out for each other and carry on their mission to help others. For example, while the Sourants were on a cross-country trip to visit family, they were heading toward Santa Fe, New Mexico, when Connie said to Jean, "Go to Las Vegas." Jean did not know why, but she did smell the burned popcorn, and of course it was impossible to ignore Connie's advice. At first, it seemed unlikely that any good would come of the trip, since the hotels and even the parking lots were crowded to capacity. Then the positive coincidences began to happen: the Stardust had one free parking space, and the Golden Nugget, which required reservations six months in advance, received a cancellation by fax just as Jean went to the front desk—and "it was for one of the cheapest rooms!"

Meanwhile, one of Connie's clients was having some serious problems and wanted help. Before her death, Connie had told him, "When you need help, turn to Jean." Having been calling for days, the client was growing frustrated about not being able to reach Jean during her long road trip. By what some might call a coincidence, he was vacationing in Las Vegas at the time Connie detoured Jean there. As Jean was playing a slot machine, Nick's instincts told him to go walk around the crowded casino, and he bumped into the client, who was, of course, eager to see Jean. Just as the two men walked up to Jean's slot machine, "I got three white sevens!" It was a joyous token of their good fortune. The client chuckled that "when you get home, you'll find a lot of messages on your answering machine." Meeting in person was, of course, even better, and their conversation was indeed just what he needed. Connie knew that: "See, we never lose track of people even though we are in Spirit," Jean observes. To Nick, this was a lesson in "intuitions and instincts. . . . We always follow our hunches." Most people try to "make it happen," but much of Jean's and Nick's counseling is based on encouraging people's trust in Spirit, enabling them simply to "let it happen."

Because of this outlook, the Sourants have a personal policy of "not letting clients come more than twice a year—we're not a crutch for them; we're only here to help them help themselves," as Jean puts it. Nick boils this policy down to a philosophical maxim: "You cannot give to another that which he is not prepared to receive, nor can you take away from another what is not already yours." With this philosophy, the Sourants believe in letting experiences flow, since all incidents and coincidences have purposes whose meaning will become clear over time.

In Jean and Nick's approach to their vocation, spiritual experiences are not ends in themselves but are part of their mission to help people. The couple refers to helping others as their prime calling, with Spiritualism as a means to that end. Once they moved to Cassadaga, they were able to devote themselves more fully to helping others because, like many of the Cassadaga residents, they have "retire[d] into Spiritualism." To them, this is not just good fortune, but also the best approach to Spiritualism, which they believe should be "a way of life for nurturing the spiritual self," as Nick puts it. "You are not supposed to make your income totally from it." Healing is even more sacred than mediumship; as Jean says, "I do not accept a donation for healing because that is a God-given gift."

Jean speaks readily of helping a host of people, "from street people to profession-als—even shrinks!" In fact, many psychologists "have reached the point where they cannot get through" to their own clients, so "many refer their clients to me." Jean makes no claims to being a psychologist and she respects their work, but for tough psychological cases, "I get through to them psychically and into a differ-ent phase and then they open up so they [the psychologists] can help them." Jean eagerly notes, "When they open up to God force, they all find a great seren-ity." She says that "kids here know that if they get into trouble, they can come to this house and be safe." Perhaps because of the more pointed search for purpose in old age, Jean adds that "my special calling is with the elderly."

Like their fellow Spiritualists, the Sourants believe that Spirit can manifest itself in any religion. Jean has a special affinity for Native American artifacts and rituals, and Nick has worked with spiritual teachers from many religions. He reports learning from his evolution from Orthodoxy to Methodism to Presbyte-rianism to the Church of Awareness to his current Spiritualism; after all those stops on his religious quest, he harbors no antagonism toward any religion. Those that were part of his quest each had significant spiritual potential: "All religions are very valid for the people that are following them." Their potential grows from their spiritual origins. Jean notes, for example, that "everything we do has a root in the Bible." When people wonder about her ability to see people who are dead, she responds, "What do you think Mary Magdalene saw when Jesus appeared to her? She saw his spirit but not his physical body." Her belief that "many of the things in the Bible are the same things that can happen now" gives her both a reverence for the holy Christian Scriptures and an openness to the Spirit's "manifestations" in other times, other cultures, and other forms that orthodox religions fail to recognize.

The Sourants have a boundless faith in the power of human consciousness to reach higher states of awareness. But this power is not just the self's own waiting for release; instead it is the power of the self to connect with the power of the universe. An irony that is difficult for most Americans to accept is that this power comes from the humility of accepting one's status as a mere vehicle for broader powers. As Nick likes to say with a characteristic sparkle in his eye, human beings "are the floppy disks to the mainframe in the sky." More seriously, he clarifies, "We are not unique. We are one grain of sand in life, and at our best we can live our lives on a continuum with the life force." Although Jean and Nick Sourant are known for their outstanding work as mediums, they prefer to say that "we are all mediums."

## Just a Coach: The Reverend Jerry Frederich

Spiritualist, medium, and pastor, the Reverend Jerry Frederich feels he is following in his Mormon father's footsteps. Although he has not stayed within the fold of the Church of Latter-Day Saints, especially with its current "family values" traditionalism, he admires the original Mormon belief in the awesome presence of God in all things and in the ability of all Mormon men, as priests of the faith, to perform healing. One reflection of the continuing influence of his Mormon upbringing is that the most important model for Jerry's thinking about Spiritualism is Jesus. He feels that Jesus was a "way-shower and a healer—the greatest medium that ever walked the earth." Jerry finds support for his vocation in Jesus' promise to his followers: "You will have all these gifts and greater."[6]

Mormonism was not always a vital faith even for Jerry's father, who was an alcoholic until Jerry was in the eighth grade. The elder Frederich followed the twelve-step program of Alcoholics Anonymous (AA) starting when he was thirty, and since he never wavered, it gave the rest of his life great focus and energy. After that, while he remained at his job as a chef on the railroad, his true vocation was ministering informally through the AA movement. His energy and his attention to the power of the spirit always made the younger Frederich think of him as a Mormon who was "not in the mold of most Mormons." Now that Jerry serves as the church's pastor at Cassadaga, he likes to say,"Like father, like son: I also do not follow the party line."

Jerry's first brush with the unorthodox came at fourteen, when he had five out-of-body experiences. Watching a movie about Aboriginal medicine men solidified his sense that he was in touch with something profound and sacred, but still, he did not know what to make of these events, and he did not talk to anyone about them. When he was a teenager, he says with a laugh, his gifts could be "a way to scope out girls thirty miles away." He remembers, for instance, "soaring over the Chippewa River, not particularly to go visit the girl I had a crush on, but when I got near her house I thought I'd go visit. I saw her and her family at their home, feeding the chickens." He remembers one visionary experience after which his awareness ended at three in the afternoon, and he "stayed blank until eight that night," when he "came back to material consciousness in the middle of talking with my aunt and uncle in the kitchen." He realized that he has the ability to "leave the body just by thinking," but he did not pursue these gifts or their implications for years. "Something flashed in me, 'You're not supposed to do that, you'll get in trouble.' I wasn't frightened, I just knew other people wouldn't understand it. So I flicked the switch and blocked it out."

Later, early in his marriage, Jerry enjoyed "a time of great inner peace in my life" and began to allow his out-of-body experiences to come again. During this time, he noticed that he had developed a new habit when he was putting away clean dishes: He put the spoons in a particular pattern upright in a cup. His wife commented on it, and he shrugged that he didn't know why he was doing it, so he went back to the old way. The out-of-body experiences stopped abruptly. Twelve years later, his aunt, who had raised him for a substantial part of his childhood, came through to him while he was meditating and remained with him during his meditation for the next two months. At that time he realized that she had always kept her spoons upright in a cup, and he feels that she was helping his astral travel as well.

At midcareer, Jerry felt his life was "falling apart." His work as a tailor was proceeding well, but his marriage of fifteen years was in trouble, a situation made more difficult by his understanding of the Mormon belief in eternal marriage. "Although we tried to hold the marriage together by will power," Jerry observes with some sorrow softened by the years, "it was clearly breaking up." Moreover, he had terrible kidney stones that gave him very bad back pains. These were exacerbated by the emotional troubles: The stones were "the pain of the divorce solidified."

After some casual reading in Spiritualism, he decided to accompany a friend to a Mediums' Night at Cassadaga; "I just thought, 'Why not?'" After receiving a reading that was interesting but not earthshaking to him, Jerry entered into a conversation among some of the attendees and "someone mentioned natural law. I felt a quickening in my heart." Feeling led, Jerry soon returned to attend a lecture on natural law by Rev. Eloise Page. She spoke, "like Plato," with a seer's passion and clarity for the ultimate truth—and delivered the entire lecture without notes. He also attended unfoldment classes on meditation with Rev. Diane Davis, and he admired her suggestions about ways to cope with physical and emotional problems. He was intrigued, even if not totally convinced at first, but as he recalls energetically, these talks "sure beat the heck out of TV."

As his health worsened and the doctors talked of operations, he tried meditating as he had heard and read about. The meditation and Mormon healing cured what the doctors could not, and to their amazement, he avoided surgery. Given his sympathies with old-school Mormonism, Jerry himself was not particularly surprised, but now he was ready to take his longstanding admiration for Mor-

*The Reverend Jerry Frederich, 1994.*

mon traditions and his father's spirituality and apply them to his newfound faith in Spiritualism. He attended more and more classes and found that going to them "was the highlight of the week." He was still a little skeptical, so he decided to do a test. At a Christmas party for one of his classes, he poured the champagne liberally, hoping to see if, when under the influence, the Spiritualists let their guard down. When he discovered that, although they talked more, "they were not very different than when on stage" in the classes, he was convinced he wanted to pursue mediumship as his vocation. "That's when the training really started—now I was learning in order to pass it along to others, not just for myself." After six years of study, he became certified in 1985.

He had been working for eight years as a tailor in Daytona Beach. With jobs that included sewing the patches on the drivers' outfits at the Speedway, he had accumulated enough money to give him some career flexibility. He decided to quit his job and to cut his tailoring work down to three days a week to allow himself two days to serve as a medium. When he lost this more limited tailoring work soon after, he said to himself, "OK, I get the message," and turned to mediumship full-time. In 1987, he was ordained as a minister. For the next few years, he remained active at Cassadaga, especially through service as lyceum director, and he taught classes throughout Florida, from Jacksonville to St. Petersburg. His calling at Cassadaga expanded in 1997 when he was invited by camp president Barbara Joy Hines Bengtson to buy a house in town and to serve as associate pastor. Within a few months, the board of trustees of the community asked him to serve a three-year term as pastor.

Jerry thinks of his mediumship as a kind of counseling, but counseling that includes a spiritual dimension. He works with people, first, to make sure they are in "a cohesive frame of mind." He attends to "imbalances on all levels," mental, emotional, and spiritual. He is convinced that whatever help he provides is not directly his doing, for the clients must "feel the God-power for themselves—I am just the coach." "All people," he says, "are vehicles of Spirit."

Jerry does not set out to solve people's problems, but instead to use "the same process" of opening up their own powers for dealing with "health, friends, finance," or any other issue. The process is a matter of developing intuitiveness. He refers to his original profession when explaining how this grows. There is no one-size-fits-all answer, but instead each solution is tailored to the individual. There are "no problems, but only conditions that need attention"—and the solutions must grow from each person's own total self. Moreover, the particular problems can actually begin to solve themselves: "Set the attention on a goal, and let the universe arrange the details."

The problems emerge only as a result of our misusing our God-given free will. "Where you put your attention, that is your reality." "We are free to set up barriers" and free to "distort our relations" to that natural balance. The chief barrier we create is fear. Jerry maintains that "there is no such thing as a martyr." When people come to him with "oh, poor me" feelings, that is a sure sign that their fears have taken control of their life forces. Just as victims "bring it on themselves," so they can only achieve solutions by themselves. On their path, because of free will, they can, of course, create more problems. When people remain too rational, they are "not drawing on all their resources" and they are "cutting off access to their higher self." By contrast, Jerry tries through daily discipline to make himself an open vehicle for Spirit: "Prayer, meditation, affirmation, visualization—these are all different ways of using my free will to create a reality for myself or others."

Once people begin to figure out their path, he "does not have to stay with them," although he sees nothing wrong with an "occasional tune-up." Jerry has unflinching faith in people's ability to solve their problems, because "God does not make junk." His optimism stems from his picture of God as the "law of balance," and so he is convinced that in all of God's creation, "nature will correct itself because it cannot tolerate an imbalance."

Jerry provides a host of metaphors to describe the process of counseling and healing. When he talks with people, he does not always witness the results, nor does he expect acknowledgment from them, but he remains confident that he has "dropped a seed" that will grow—perhaps much later, and perhaps he will never hear about it. The connections he makes with people are like electricity. "In counseling, I'm a battery. I don't tell them what to do; I ask, 'Have you ever thought of doing it this way?' Then I watch what happens, how they construct their own experience, add their own creativity, and it's delightful to watch."

One of Jerry's favorite metaphors is the internet. "Our subconscious can get on the internet of the universe. We can go out and tap into something bigger. The internet is made up of contributions from people everywhere, and so is universal consciousness."

One very material gift has, he believes, changed the character of Cassadaga for the better. When he arrived in 1979, both the church and the fellowship building, Davis Hall, lacked air conditioning. There was little hope for raising enough money for the equipment, but it came through. First, a spiritual music group raised some unexpected seed money, and that set the idea in motion, giving people confidence that the money could be found. Donations started coming in, and people contributed time and materials to the project. With the cooling of the buildings, Cassadaga has been transformed from a winter resort to a community offering year-round services.

Other changes have brought improvement also. Jerry strongly supports the apprenticeship system, because it allows for the nurturing of people's talents right on site. Before this system, Cassadaga was "like a frontier outpost," and it was "difficult to get credentials," but now it has a steady stream of "home-grown healers and mediums."

Jerry firmly believes that recent changes, ranging from the air conditioning to the apprenticeship system, have made the community stronger. He does not worry about a decline in Spiritualism since earlier days. To the contrary, he is glad that since Cassadaga has become less of a retirement community, it has more young people and makes newcomers and curious visitors more welcome than ever before. In addition, the younger Spiritualists, he argues, are even more vital than the Spiritualists of previous generations, because they are more willing to "apply Spiritualism to their work life." He notes one example of a nurse in Tallahassee, a former student of his; she "plants seeds" in patients with her conversations, and she has "turned eight people around." Another former student has applied what she learned creatively, by developing the practice of teaching people to communicate with animals.

As the youngest of the Cassadaga residents interviewed for this chapter, Jerry offers a palpable enthusiasm about the future. He sees keenly the road ahead, and he is clearly excited about the new directions the community might take. In the next few years, for instance, he anticipates growth here, as the general population's interest in spiritual issues continues to rise. The opening of the learning center will further expand the community's outreach. The energy of newcomers will invigorate the community, he feels, and the addition of their perspectives on Spiritualism will provide new ways for its good works to heal and uplift the world. Referring at once to past, present, and future, Jerry observes, "Cassadaga is very blessed."

## No Long Faces: The Reverend Lillian Weigl

The Reverend Lillian Weigl answers the phone with a lilting, "This is Lollie." She greets the visitor on her comfortably furnished porch with a warm handshake and a penetrating eye. A great-grandmother, she has the capacious lap and the ready laugh of one who understands children and enjoys them deeply; she says that if she just sits still, the children come to her. Her voice, schooled by years of experience with nurturing and guiding people through moments of cri-

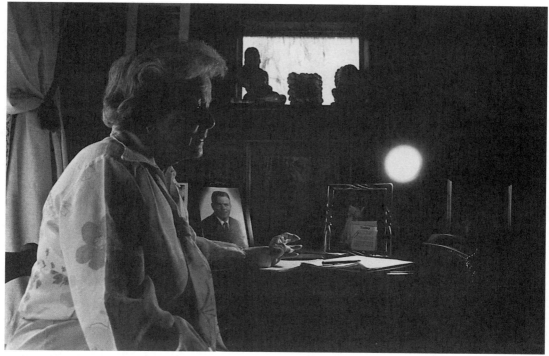

*The Reverend Lillian Weigl, 1994.*

sis large and small, is soft around the edges and firm at the core. In every interaction, it is clear that Lollie Weigl is a woman who has found her own way, a way
that has brought others much joy.

Born a tenth-generation evangelical German Lutheran in a small town in
Pennsylvania Dutch country, Lollie grew up with the church shaping every aspect of her life. At her birth, "they thought they were going to lose me for some
reason, so they sent for the pastor to sprinkle me." When the town needed a new
gymnasium, it was built as an addition to the church, so that even basketball was
enjoyed under the church's roof. Sundays began with the German Lutheran
service in the morning, followed by Sunday dinner, often with the pastor and his
wife as family guests. Sunday afternoons there was catechetical study, and after
supper was the evening service in English.[7]

At home the church's teachings were a daily part of family life. Lollie's
mother, a graduate of Boston Conservatory of Music and a trained registered
nurse, had blazed her own trail despite turn-of-the-century conventional expectations of her, perhaps leaving a legacy of example for her equally determined
daughter. For now, though, Lollie's home was devoutly Lutheran and encouraged only compliance with religious and social norms. While raising Lollie and

her two younger sisters, her mother served as the church organist for more than twenty-five years. By the age of fourteen, Lollie herself was teaching Sunday school; now she says with a laugh, "I have to take back all those words I spoke in those days."

Lollie remembers the pastor waxing eloquent in his sermons, transported by enthusiasm for what he was conveying to his flock. "We were all going to burn in Hell, we were all sinners, he'd say. But then later he'd be saying that God loves us. I wondered, then why would He throw us in Hell? I was a good girl, I did all my chores, I took care of my sisters, so why would He do that to me?" But as a child Lollie didn't voice the questions that ran through her mind; "I valued my scalp too much."

As a little girl Lollie did say things sometimes that got her into trouble, but she quickly learned to suppress them. Clairvoyant, clairaudient, and clairsentient from early on, she saw and heard things that were normal to her but that struck others as odd at best. "People from the other side would come to visit me, and I'd know things before they happened. My mother would say, 'Don't say that outside of this house,' and my dad said, 'There's no need to say it here either.'" Once, walking to school after a snowfall, Lollie and her sisters saw a woman dressed in a fur-trimmed green coat. Lollie remarked, "She's so pretty and blue," and the other children teased her about not knowing blue from green. But, Lollie explains with a smile, "I was looking at her aura." Although Lollie felt humiliated by the teasing she received as a child, she bears no malice anymore. With the understanding of one who has experienced the challenges of child rearing, she sums up her childhood: "Having children who have second sight isn't easy on families, if the child is the exception in the family."

Leaving home to marry at eighteen, Lollie was widowed by cancer four years later. She found herself the sole support of a two-year-old son, J.B.: "I felt helpless, but my German practicality kicked in. You can't sit here and mourn, I told myself; you have to do something for yourself and J.B." Soon she completed a degree in business with a specialty in hotel and restaurant management, launching a career that would eventually, through what some people might call coincidence, bear fruit at Cassadaga, when in a pinch she was enlisted to manage the hotel there. Two other marriages ended in divorce. Then Lollie found her life partner, John Weigl, with whom she celebrated her forty-fifth wedding anniversary in 1998.

John, she says, "is an exceptional man." Catholic by upbringing, he inherited the determination and persistence of his Austrian father and Hungarian mother. Like others whom Lollie feels need to be revered more for their contributions to the community, he is not a medium but helps to keep Cassadaga alive. He serves as the camp's association director, contributing organizational skills as well as practical help with individual residents' everyday needs. "We have a lot of very fine people here in this camp," says Lollie with gratitude.

John's mother became a major figure in Lollie's life. "I was fortunate in having one of Anna Weigl's sons love me," she says. While her own children looked on, those who had married into the family fought with each other over the privilege of Anna's visit to their home on holidays. Lollie recalls sitting with Anna at a family gathering many years ago. Looking around at Anna's fine crop of children and grandchildren, Lollie asked her which of them she loved the most. With a smile, Anna replied, "The one that needs me the most at the time."

Lollie and her own son were very close throughout his life: "We were *we*, not *I*." For instance, when John Weigl pressed his marriage proposal, Lollie called her son, then nineteen years old and in college, to ask his opinion. He thought about it, then called her back: "I think it'd be a good idea if we married Weigl." Lollie's shift into Spiritualism was the greatest strain on their relationship. At first, when she began attending classes in parapsychology and then naturally followed the path toward Spiritualism and mediumship, he "probably thought his mother was doing some goofy things and would never go public with them." When she was offered her papers for ordination to the title of reverend, he objected that she was going too far. Years later, as it became clear that mediumship would be a major part of her life, he "finally decided that I was doing less harm than good" and accepted his mother's new life.

The loss of her son to the effects of his smoking has been the most traumatic element in Lollie's life. Afterwards, she was ill for two years and finally received a diagnosis of depression from delayed grief. "I was saying, 'I'm a Spiritualist. I believe in life after death, so I don't have such grief,' but I didn't realize how much I just wanted to touch him, to hold him." It comforts Lollie that he appears now and then to mediums at Cassadaga, charging them, with characteristic humor, to "give the reverend mother his love."

Although Lollie's transition into mediumship was gradual, she remembers one significant turning point. Sitting with a group of women, a religious discussion group, "I said, 'I'm no longer a Christian. I'm a Spiritualist.' I just knew that there'd be a hole in the ceiling and I would be dead," she laughs, as those lingering effects of her conservative religious upbringing have long since worn off. After many years of study, she was offered her mediumship papers by the Universal Fellowship, a northern counterpart of the Southern Cassadaga Spiritualist Camp Meeting Association; she has since transferred them to Cassadaga. "I really didn't want my mediumship papers," she remembers. "I was gainfully employed in the hotel industry, doing a good job using my talents. But the organization became insistent and said to take them even if I didn't use them, so I did." A few years later, her ordination papers came the same way. After giving readings for friends on an informal basis, she gradually began taking on clients, and "the next thing I knew I was working."

"Spiritualism answered so many questions for me," Lollie says; "the transition into it was just natural." It put into perspective her questions about the religion of her upbringing: "Hellfire and damnation were invented by pagan Egyptian priests who were losing their congregation" and hoped to keep it by fear. "For years I lived with the idea that my close ones were my life. Spiritualism taught me that there were a lot of things that were my life." It gave her a more expansive universe and a more effective role in it. As a Spiritualist, Lollie feels both called and equipped to make a positive difference in the world. "I went from a religion of fear to a religion of love and hope. Here there's no one threatening me, and there's everyone encouraging me to do better, thanking me for what little I've been able to do."

"Spiritualism is my lifestyle. It was formed to help. It's about the simple act of giving" of oneself, one's money, one's physical resources, of whatever the situation requires. "The world is in such need of help, and it's so easy to help, and it becomes an automatic thing as a Spiritualist. The realization that I have received more than I've given makes it worth the effort to try harder all the time. . . . When I get to Heaven, someone will be waiting for me with their hand outstretched, saying, 'Lollie, would you help?'"

Young people concern Lollie especially keenly, and she gives them special attention whenever she can. She offers the example of a young woman who phoned the camp association in extreme distress about her house being haunted. Although Lollie recognized the call might be a hoax or the result of hallucinations from drugs or mental instability, she was drawn to try to help anyway. "I don't believe in evil; I've never seen evidence of it, though I've seen humans make mistakes. Our Creator wouldn't unleash evil things on us." Even though the woman in distress was not yet able to receive this comforting truth, Lollie still saw it as imperative to help her through her problem in a way that was appropriate for her: "If she's convinced that there's something paranormal in her house, we have to convince her that it's gone, for her own good." Helping people means meeting them where they are at a particular point in their lives and fulfilling their current needs. In as many forms as there are people, "healing is a big part of what we do."

Lollie Weigl's brand of Spiritualism is enlivened by a pantheon of personalities. She delights in telling stories about Spiritualists who have influenced and inspired her and about those who contributed to the strength of the Cassadaga community, where she has lived since 1970. Reverence for these people's contributions is a consistent theme in her account of Spiritualism; she is keenly aware of the colorful and generous figures who have blazed her path of faith before her. She speaks warmly, for instance, of the multilingual George Lamsa, author of the Lamsa Bible, a new translation that clarifies the sacred text from a Spiritualist perspective. Lollie is grateful for his scholarly contributions as well as the humor with which he spiced his serious teachings. Correcting the standard translation, "he said that the Bible doesn't say to turn the right cheek toward someone who hit you on the left but to turn *away* the right cheek; he said you could get punch-drunk being hit so many times."

Lollie's mediumship, too, benefits from the contributions of many people. She has several spirit guides who help to give her access to the spirit world. Dr. Marcus comes infrequently and usually assists in cases involving a family dispute. A German man, Heinrich, whom Lollie calls Henry, heralds his arrival with a scraping noise. There are two Native American guides as well. One, Blue Moon, remained nameless to Lollie for years until a frequent visitor to the camp drew her portrait and she identified herself to him. The other, Hannah, has an affinity for children and helps Lollie particularly in readings involving the loss of a child. Even in especially tragic situations, Hannah has reassured Lollie's clients that their children are happy and safe in the spirit world.

But Lollie's most consistent spirit guide is Jerry, who is legendary at Cassadaga for his faithfulness. He came to Lollie in meditation many years ago, before she was a Spiritualist. "I was meditating, and suddenly here in front of me was this man, broad shoulders, in buckskins. He said, 'Hi, my name is Jerry, and I'm going to be with you for a long time.' I said, 'Okay . . .'" Even during Lollie's two-year illness, when she was unable to call on him and did not conduct readings, Jerry remained. "A man with less patience would have thrown up his hands," she says with wonder. Jerry likes young people, and he especially likes "the pretty ladies," for whom he will dress up and with whom he flirts from the other side. "His comments are sometimes not repeatable," chuckles Lollie. Jerry's colorful personality is such a natural counterpart to Lollie's that "frequently I'm introduced as Lollie and her friend Jerry. I feel like Edgar Bergen and Charlie McCarthy, but I don't know which one is me."

Jerry does try to keep Lollie in line. "He's on me about losing weight," she admits. When Lollie goes too far in asking for information in readings, Jerry lets her know. Once when a client returned three times to ask for a prediction about a family member's time of death, Jerry finally answered, "The area of passing is not in my area, it is an area of God's, and it most certainly is not in yours." "So there," Lollie adds with a mischievous nod.

Reminiscing about her experiences in Spiritualism and mediumship, Lollie says, "You run into a lot of things where you say, 'This is too far-fetched, this couldn't be happening.'" It is happening, she knows, but her sense of wonder remains and fuels the stories she tells. Once, for instance, she witnessed a spiritual healing of a man who had suffered from an unexplained open sore on his leg since childhood. No doctors had been able to diagnose or to treat the wound. As she was preparing for the healing, Jerry told her to get a tin pan, and she produced an old medical basin from her attic. She put the basin under the man's leg. During the healing there was a loud clunking sound, and in the basin they found a large fang; the man explained that he had been bitten by a rattlesnake as a child, but that the doctors had been certain the wound was clean. His leg healed well afterward.

"Physical phenomena," Lollie goes on, "can be very amusing." Once she and a friend were practicing levitation with a three-legged table, and another medium, Abby Perry, came in. Lollie invited Abby to take a turn with the table, but Abby demurred: "You don't want me to do that." Finally Abby gave in to Lollie and her friend's insistence, and the table flew up into the air and landed upside down in her lap. "Abby said, 'I told you you didn't want me to do that.'"

Lollie remembers with personal affection a moment when she and her friend and fellow medium Mae Graves Ward were sitting together in the Weigls' house. "Mae asked me, 'Was your mother just a wee woman?' I said yes, she wasn't even five feet tall. 'And was your father a big man with black hair who loved the ladies?' Oh yes, I said. 'Well, your mother just came through saying, "Well, we weren't rich, but we were comfortable," and your dad is saying, "Oh my God, she's even crying poor mouth over here!"'"

"Spiritualism is not all that serious," says Lollie. "We don't go around with long faces." Certainly Rev. Lillian Weigl doesn't, nor does she tend to leave any in her wake. "I'm no Pollyanna," she clarifies, acknowledging the destructive power of human negativity and fear. But as a religion of love, she says, Spiritualism means optimism and security. "If I truly believe that Spirit is with us, I don't have to worry." Spiritualism is a matter of faith "in myself, my Creator, the people around me, those from the unseen side who care." And in Lollie's life, there are many of these.

*Christmas Candlelight Message Service, 1997.*

THESE LIFE STORIES span a tremendous amount of time and space. Taken together, they offer an especially human insight into the nature of Spiritualism through the ways in which it is expressed in individual lives. From Mormonism to Catholicism, from Amish country to Orlando before its massive growth through tourism, from engineering buildings to teaching and nurturing children, the experiences of their lives come together to enhance the Spiritualist tapestry at Cassadaga. Through the diversity, there are some clear common themes.

The religious traditions represented in the lives of these Spiritualists continue in certain ways to inform how they interpret Spiritualism. For Tom Berkner, for instance, Christianity is central, and the focus on Jesus is clear: Spiritualists "accept Jesus. We accept His teachings." Tom's discourse is sprinkled with biblical quotations that he uses to illustrate Spiritualist views, and he notes that "clairvoyance and Spirit are part of the Bible." Jerry Frederich interprets Jesus as an exemplar of the principles for which Spiritualism stands:

"Christ came here to prove the laws, to teach them," but the kind of service that Jesus exemplified can be manifested in a variety of places and is not confined to the Christian church. For Jean Sourant, Native American religion expresses compelling truths. Lollie Weigl explains, "We don't believe that Jesus Christ was the only son of God. Jesus said, 'Why call ye me good? There is but one that is good, and that is God.'" As these elders express it, Spiritualism is fundamentally ecumenical and recognizes valuable teachings in a wide variety of other religions. They are constantly reading and learning about other religions to further their quest to understand truth itself. Jerry notes that when "working with people" as a medium, "my mind shifts sometimes into their religious tradition, whatever it might be," even though he is unaware of it while it is happening. "My own background is Mormon, Christian, but any tradition can lead people to Spirit."

Another striking commonality among the people we interviewed is their self-effacing manner. Again and again, they insisted that the credit for what they accomplish as mediums, psychics, and healers is not their own but God's. They see themselves simply as luckier than most people, perhaps more aware than others of the gifts we all share. Jerry Frederich notes, "All people are vehicles of Spirit," with mediums being simply those who have developed this capacity further than most. The humility extends to other aspects of their self-concept, as Gladys Reid illustrates: Having been for some time the only certified healer in the community, she says, "I don't like to lecture or give interviews. I wouldn't when I was over at the Healing Temple. I figured I didn't know enough." Her parting words to the interviewer—"Don't say too much about me."

A sense of humor and even a sometimes childlike imagination accompany all of these people on their spiritual journey. Like boys with a new set of building toys, Nick and Jerry are both fascinated with the nearly science-fiction quality of computer age technologies. Lollie chuckles that she and Jean share "a weakness for gambling." These are personal characteristics, but their appearance among mediums seems especially significant: In each case, we see Spiritualists interested in aspects of daily life that have a dimension reaching beyond the everyday and the predictable. Nick and Jerry's optimism about the internet's possibility for human enlightenment, Jean and Lollie's interest in games of chance—both are examples of the Spiritualist awareness of the metaphysical operating through the physical. Even in their hobbies and enthusiasms, we see that these are extraordinary people leading ordinary lives.

Virtually everyone we interviewed described Spiritualism as "a way of life." This means that it is more than a religion, more than a moral code, more than a lens through which to view and make sense of one's experience, because it encompasses all of these. Moreover, it entwines them: The religious belief in life after death opens the possibility of communication between the earthly and the Spirit planes, which means that events on the earthly plane may be more than they seem at first glance. Interpreting daily experiences with a view to their eternal significances, these Spiritualists feel keenly the responsibility to behave according to a moral code that is acceptable both here and hereafter. Coming full circle, the religious belief in the immediate presence of Spirit makes it easy to live morally, because Spirit is always nearby to offer support when it is needed.

A strong part of the moral code that these Spiritualists feel called to uphold is the edict to give generously at every turn. She knows that the original text has it the other way around, but Lollie Weigl says, "To me it's 'As you receive, so shall ye give.'" Every one of the people in this chapter emphasizes that their abilities as psychics, mediums, and healers are a gift from God, entrusted to them with the understanding that they will disburse them to the world. In this light, it is clear that keeping their gifts to themselves would transgress the intentions of God, the original source of their abilities.

Similarly, the question of assigning a monetary value to their spiritual abilities is a very tricky one. While it has become standard practice among mediums to charge by the hour, Gladys Reid recalls that "we used to give readings and just read till Spirit stopped us," regardless of how long it took. Most of the people in this chapter have "retired into Spiritualism," as Jean Sourant puts it; they have the financial stability of a lifetime career behind them and perhaps can afford to donate their services when they are needed. However, they are also mindful that they are part of a community of mediums and that others might not be as lucky, so as a kind of gesture to citizenship, they do charge for their services. The inner conflict remains, though. As Lollie Weigl says, "If I have a woman who tells me she has four children and no job and her husband has run off, and I charge her, how have I helped her? I haven't—I've only added to her problems."

Money is a central concern as these longtime Cassadagans reflect on how things have changed in their community. Gladys Reid sums up the general sentiment: "The camp has gone too commercial." Objectively, the camp seems far from commercial: Mediums have their offices in their homes, marked only with handmade wooden signs; their advertising is limited to a rack of business cards in the bookstore; and a free telephone is available in a corner of the bookstore beside a dry-erase board listing the mediums available that day. But Lollie Weigl recalls warmly such figures as Mae Graves Ward, Mona Berry, and Gladys Custance, "the old-time Spiritualists. We were lucky; they were the ones we mixed with" while learning Spiritualism. They stood, she says, for "caring, faith—faith in what Spiritualism dictates." Nick Sourant remembers that "when we were coming into Spiritualism, we sat around our elders and listened to them and absorbed their knowledge. We took time and we sat, and we never looked at the clock." By contrast, he says, "the younger generation wants more instant gratification." In particular, "they want credentials."

Even so, these elders also have tremendous optimism about the future of their community. They all feel that the belief in the power of Spirit remains strong among the younger generation at Cassadaga, and as teachers, many of them have seen firsthand the vitality of those who follow in their footsteps. Much of the problem, perhaps, comes from the attention that Cassadaga has received in recent years from outside. Ironically, while the general public's increased interest in spiritual topics demonstrates the strength and the abiding relevance of Spiritualism, it also brings influences from the wider culture. Gladys Reid declares that "that New Age thing is spoiling the camp," and adds quizzically, "I haven't figured out *yet* what 'New Age' means." For Gladys and her generation, the insights of Spiritualism are far from new.

The sense of the interconnectedness of the everyday and the metaphysical is central to the way in which these Spiritualists live. Every moment, for them, is imbued with Spirit. They use the words "Spirit says" as comfortably as they might say, "My sister tells me." Indeed, one of the things that might strike a visitor most forcibly is the very ordinariness of their acquaintance with the spiritual realm. Far from the exoticism one might expect of those who converse with the dead, these are people around whom an air of comfortable domesticity hangs like the shawl on the back of an old porch rocker. For some, this may be because their clairvoyance and clairaudience have been with them since childhood; as Lollie Weigl says, "It was just normal to me" to see and hear people her family did not see. For others, such as Gladys Reid, the gifts were manifested later in life, and it was at first a revelation to experience what God had provided. For all of them, though, the continuous presence of Spirit is always the source of wonder and gratitude, a daily revelation of ultimates in the smallest details.

# Notes

1. The authors thank Stetson University students Suzanne Hartley and Leslie Coulter for their assistance with this chapter, and they extend warmest thanks to its subjects for sharing generously their time and themselves.

2. Gladys Reid, interview by Ann Jerome Croce, Cassadaga, Florida, June 10, 1998. Subsequent quotations or information in the text attributed to Reid are taken from this interview.

3. Tom Berkner, interview by Ann Jerome Croce, Cassadaga, Florida, June 18, 1998. Subsequent quotations or information in the text attributed to Berkner are taken from this interview and an interview by Suzanne Hartley, Cassadaga, Florida, October 21, 1997.

4. Nick Sourant, interview by Paul Jerome Croce and Suzanne Hartley, Cassadaga, Florida, October 8, 1997. Subsequent quotations or information in the text attributed to Nick Sourant are taken from this interview and an interview by the authors, Cassadaga, Florida, May 6, 1998.

5. Jean Sourant, interview by Paul Jerome Croce and Suzanne Hartley, Cassadaga, Florida, October 8, 1997. Subsequent quotations or information in the text attributed to Jean Sourant are taken from this interview and an interview by the authors, Cassadaga, Florida, May 6, 1998.

6. Jerry Frederich, interview by Leslie Coulter and Paul Jerome Croce, Cassadaga, Florida, February 26, 1998, and by the authors, Cassadaga, Florida, May 7, 1998. Subsequent quotations or information in the text attributed to Frederich are taken from these interviews.

7. Lollie Weigl, interview by Ann Jerome Croce, Cassadaga, Florida, May 28, 1998. Subsequent quotations or information in the text attributed to Weigl are taken from this interview and a second interview by Ann Jerome Croce, Cassadaga, Florida, June 19, 1998.

# SIX

# The Reverend Eloise Page

## Learning a New Language, a Student's Perspective

ANNE BARCLAY MORGAN

## Introduction

I HAVE BEEN STUDYING over the last ten years with one of Cassadaga's most prominent teachers, the Reverend Eloise Page, and so I am able to present an insider's perspective to complement the other chapters in this book that emphasize historical and analytical perspectives on the Cassadaga Spiritualist camp.[1] I am a firm believer in the possibility of spiritual growth. The life circumstances that led me to become one of Eloise's students fall into a pattern similar to those of many other people who have been drawn to study with her. Put simply, we were so drawn because of troubling events in our lives and because we were seeking deeper answers to life's challenges and conundrums. I hope that these descriptions of her life and teachings, as well as the annotated references at the end of the chapter, will encourage both scholars and the general public to explore her teachings in greater depth and provide enlightening new directions for the reader's own spiritual growth.

## Eloise's Life Pattern

Psychic mediums are not necessarily born with fully developed abilities or into families with a heritage enriched by such faculties. Eloise Page is a noteworthy example of a psychic medium whose difficult early life coupled with a devout faith spurred a search for spiritual understanding that led her to develop exceptional psychic faculties for serving others. Eloise is highly regarded by the Cassadaga community. As one of her many students, I, too, have been inspired by the "unfoldment" of her life and her teachings, which demonstrate the potential for our developing our own psychic abilities.[2]

Eloise Brown was born on October 15, 1910, in Muskegon, Michigan, the younger of two children. Her mother, Grace Spring, at the age of only fifteen had married William Brown, then twenty-seven, who worked in construction and had served in the Spanish-American War. Although Eloise inherited her black hair from her father, it was her mother's life pattern and temperament she would more closely follow. Her mother was restless, having had her first child, Russell Earl Brown, at sixteen and Eloise at nineteen. Although Grace sometimes received intuitive feelings about forthcoming events, these were neither discussed nor considered noteworthy. Her family, of a simple educational background, was not religious.

As a result of struggles in her youth and early adulthood, Eloise was guided by inner visions to pursue seventeen years of training in spiritual awareness and mediumship. In her forties, she embarked on a new life path. She has touched many people's lives in the intervening years with her psychic abilities and wisdom. Now in her late eighties, Eloise still gives readings both in person and by telephone and holds classes in her home.

Eloise Page's childhood was anything but idyllic. When she was five years old, her parents divorced. Her mother left the family, so her father placed Eloise with an unrelated elderly couple who wanted a child. This event became a fundamental trauma in her life. For the next year, Eloise felt deeply lonely. When she suffered lockjaw from an infected tooth, surgery was performed on her at home on the dining room table; she still has a scar. When her mother heard about the operation, she returned from Illinois and reconciled with her ex-husband. They remained together as a family until Eloise turned thirteen. Then her mother abandoned the family again. Her father rented a home in the country and asked his mother, who was from France, to come look after the household. (He later bought the home and remodeled the house.) Her grandmother was "very cold," Eloise relates. For eighth grade, Eloise asked whether she could attend private school, since she felt so shy in public school. Her request granted, she had to walk two and a half miles to catch the bus to the Catholic school. Her grandmother wouldn't allow her a snack after her daily walk home and locked the cupboards. Eloise complained to her father, but he sided with his mother. Eloise felt deeply hurt and perceived her father as indifferent to her well-being.

At thirteen, Eloise walked four and a half miles to her mother's home in Muskegon to explain to her mother in person that she could no longer live with her father. She stayed with her mother through high school. In her sophomore year, her mother married a successful real-estate agent, so they lived fairly comfortably for a while. Eloise went to mass every morning, excelled in her religion classes, and at fourteen converted to Catholicism. In her junior year, she received permission from her mother to attend Marywood College and Academy, a Catholic boarding school of the Dominican order in Grand Rapids, Michigan. In the summer, instead of going home, she spent six weeks in total silence and meditation with the nuns. At sixteen, craving the security that she never found in her family, Eloise applied to become a nun. The priest told her that she was too young; she needed to finish school, spend one year in the outer world, and then, if she still desired, come back to the convent. In her senior year, Eloise returned to school in Muskegon and lived with her mother. After Eloise's stepfather died, her mother started drinking heavily, leaving Eloise alone for days at a time while she went on binges.

Eloise was a straight-A student, but out of concern for her mother, she quit school at Christmas in her senior year and proposed traveling with her to Florida in the hope that a change of climate might benefit her mother. They found a place to stay on the Indian River around Melbourne. But here, too, Eloise's troubled mother left her daughter alone. She became romantically involved with a bootlegger whom she eventually married, and the threesome drove back to Michigan in Eloise's Ford roadster. A month after their return, her mother found her husband with another woman and made him leave.

Eloise started dating Clayton Christopher, whom she met at a Muskegon restaurant where she often had dinner. After one of the couple's visits to Clayton's family, an automobile driven by a young boy collided with Clayton's vehicle. The collision threw Eloise onto the hood, permanently damaging her spine. Despite their lack of money, on August 15, 1928, Eloise and Clayton married. The newlyweds went to live with Clayton's sister in Tucson, Arizona, where they ran a bakery and restaurant for the owners. Besides selling baked goods, candies, and cigarettes, and serving coffee and sandwiches, Eloise mopped the floors and cleaned the equipment at the end of each day. Her spouse delivered baked goods. Every day, Eloise turned all the money earned over to her husband and never paid attention to finances.

When Clayton began leaving home at midnight, she became suspicious. Questioned about his behavior, he replied, "We got married too young." After a fight one night, Eloise walked four miles into town to call her mother to request money. "I was so hurt and devastated," Eloise recalls. After sitting up all night waiting for an answer, she walked back and found that her husband had locked up everything, so she stayed with a neighbor for a few days. She consulted a lawyer, who told her that she had no rights according to Arizona law, for she had lived in Tucson only ten months. He kindly gave her sixty dollars, then reluctantly consented to take Eloise's dinner ring in exchange. She managed to rent a room and secured work caring for children. After some weeks, her mother sent Eloise enough money to pay for her trip home. Since her mother no longer had a house, Eloise, considerably disillusioned by her second attempt to find outer security, went to live again with her father, on the eve of the Great Depression.

By then, her French grandmother had left. Her father and brother hunted and fished for food, while Eloise tended the house and raised a vegetable garden on their five acres to supplement the game. Her father and brother shared the home—but not conversation—with her. Her father would say only, "You are just like your mother," implying that she had her mother's loose morals.

After the breakup of her marriage, Eloise vowed to God to abstain from dating for three years, during which she hoped to come to understand what had happened to her. It was a lonely period in her life, but it was also a time of great learning. She took long solitary walks to Big Black Valley about three miles from home, where she witnessed the beauty of nature and pondered major life questions. One question returned again and again: Where is security? She thought that she had found it in her marriage. "People with a lot of money can lose it overnight," she realized, and "you can have the greatest love in the world, and death can take it from you." The search for an answer brought her a deepening spiritual awareness. At night, she had many out-of-body experiences and visions, and she received numerous lectures from the spirit realms. As Eloise emphasizes to her students, she was particularly receptive to spiritual experiences at that time, because she was not dating. Since her emotions were not entangled in a personal relationship, nothing interfered with the transmission of information from the world of spirit.

Eloise pursued these experiences and visions. She loved the moon, and so she asked: "What's up there? I wish I could know." One night during that period of introspection, she traveled in her astral body through space and landed on the moon. She saw no greenery or trees and began to walk. The sensation was of "walking on air." The ground was soft, and she sank into it. She felt a certain lightness and buoyancy. Many decades later when the astronauts landed on the moon, she believed she "knew what the astronauts felt."

One of her visions would change the whole pattern of her life. Still nineteen,

Eloise had a striking vision of a slender, quiet man with a gentle face and penetrating gaze. She was told by another man's voice that "this man will become your teacher, and will be sent to you." This vision "was so vivid it startled me." Seven years would pass before she met him.

In the meantime, Eloise married Karl Black, after almost a year of insistent courtship. Eloise recalls, "I knew I was not in love with him. . . . I agreed out of loneliness." Within three years, Karl was seeing other women. Eloise also had an odd feeling that he was making more money than he admitted to, which proved to be the case. They divorced when she was twenty-six, in 1936.

While still living in the house she had rented with her husband, Eloise answered the doorbell one day, expecting a man from the power company. "I know you!" she exclaimed to the man standing there, who replied, "I know you, too." Although quite ill at the time, Eloise immediately recognized the man in her vision. Recalling his penetrating eyes, she felt she had known him forever. The man was E. B. Page. He sat down and looked at Eloise with "his eyes going clear through me." With her second divorce, Eloise had become a "nervous wreck" who weighed only ninety-eight pounds. She had started going to a doctor, who diagnosed a thyroid condition.

E. B.'s words startled her: "You think you are sick, but you are not." He explained that her physical condition was "purely an emotional thing." E. B. psychically knew about all the trials of her life until then and took Eloise through everything she had experienced in her life, in particular the fact that she had been given away as a child. The emotions had made her "torn up," E. B. told her. "If you have faith in me, I will give you a practice in meditation, and you will not have to go back to the doctor." Because of her seven-year-old vision, Eloise had "perfect confidence in him." Every day she practiced at least a couple of hours. She began putting on weight, lost the trembling in her limbs, regained confidence, and never returned to the doctor. Six weeks later she was walking again and began studying with this gentle and mysterious man.

E. B. Page had studied with Paramahansa Yogananda in Boston, receiving training in a philosophy known as "Natural Law," which Eloise today describes as deriving directly from Yogananda's teachings. (She is not certain how many natural laws exist—"maybe 150"—and in her own lectures on the subject, she often condenses several into one.) E. B. was twenty-seven years older than Eloise, but Yogananda had told him that he would be taking Eloise on as a student, so Page recognized her immediately when they met. It dawned on Eloise later that he was a minister. She greatly enjoyed his classes, which dealt with learning to understand oneself spiritually and emotionally. It marked the beginning of seventeen years of training for her. (Eloise finds this seventeen-year cycle significant, pointing out that Jesus studied from age thirteen to thirty, when he came back as a teacher.)

For seven years after that momentous meeting, Eloise did not date. She became a sales clerk, then a buyer for a large store in Muskegon. She was making a "terrific" commission from sales. At one point, her boss refused to pay the promised commission. She stayed away for a week until he paid her, her assertiveness reflecting a new, increased self-esteem. Meanwhile, she religiously attended Rev. E. B. Page's classes on natural law once a week.

In 1943, Page was planning to move to Iowa, where a church requested his services. He asked Eloise to marry him. Page stated his goal clearly: He wanted to give her personal supervision, working on her psychologically. In August 1943, they were married by a justice of the peace. Eloise was thirty-three and Page was sixty. The day they wed, they moved by bus to Clinton, Iowa, where they would live for five years. During that period, E. B. Page was minister of the Spiritualist Church and established the Center of Liberal Thought. In addition to teaching classes in natural law over the radio, he lectured in Cedar Rapids and Maquoketa, Iowa. Eloise worked primarily as a buyer at J. C. Penney. It was a time of great learning for her. Although she felt unqualified to give private readings, E. B. Page encouraged her to come before the public more and give brief platform messages. With great gentleness and persistence, he insisted that she examine her reactions to events and to people so that she could progress toward greater self-awareness and understanding of spiritual truths. He would awaken Eloise in the night and say, "Let's go downstairs and talk." During these sessions, E. B. would draw Eloise out by posing a question regarding her depth of feeling about an issue and analyze her response. "He put me through mental gymnastics, he made me think for myself," Eloise explains, which in turn "brought out a lot of my own creativeness." On December 9, 1945, E. B. ordained Eloise under the auspices of the Center of Liberal Thought.

A Cassadaga board member from Mt. Pleasant, Iowa, loved E. B. Page's lectures and recommended that the association hire him as a lecturer at the church during February 1948. The Pages stayed in Cassadaga through March, since the person the camp had originally booked had canceled due to illness. Cassadaga then was mainly a winter camp, with a vibrant community in January, February, and March. E. B. held Sunday services, a midweek service, and a weekly class in natural law. He was so well liked that the community asked him to move to Cassadaga permanently. To that end, the Pages were offered a house to help defray moving expenses. E. B. felt he could greatly expand his teaching opportunities by moving to Florida, and, in November 1948, the couple moved permanently to Cassadaga.

E. B. saw great potential for spiritual expansion in the Cassadaga community. For five years, he served as minister, holding year-round Sunday services, midweek classes and services, and natural law classes. One day, when Eloise touched his hand, her hand passed through his, as if he were pure spirit, so she quickly asked him about his death. E. B. allegedly knew the date of his death but refused to tell her, saying gently, "No, honey, you're not ready for it yet." He assured her that she would be given prior knowledge. One night, while he was sleeping next to her, E. B. appeared to her in spirit form as she lay awake. Standing next to her bed, he said, "Honey, I'm sorry, but I have to leave you." He told her that he would die on Good Friday.

Since he wasn't ill at the time, she never mentioned this experience to him. A month later, E. B. Page had a severe stroke and could not speak. Two students helped Eloise with his care; he survived at home for another six weeks. Much to the doctor's surprise, E. B. died at the age of seventy, exactly as he had predicted, on Good Friday, April 3, 1953. Eloise felt such a closeness to her husband that "there was perfect acceptance." She never felt separated from him and therefore shed no tears at his passing. Ever since that Good Friday, Eloise has felt her late husband's ongoing presence in her life; she has seen him in visions and felt his guidance for her personal well-being.

In one of the greatest acts of faith in her life, Eloise followed her husband's guidance and quit her job as buyer for J. C. Penney in DeLand to devote her time to giving readings and teaching. Eloise openly admits to her talent at sales, yet in March 1954, exactly eleven months after his death, the spirit body of Page appeared to Eloise to urge her to overcome her natural shyness and carry on the spiritual work. Eloise sat up in bed and remonstrated with him, "I couldn't earn a living that way!" At that time, Cassadaga was not even on the map. "Do as I say, leave your job, and go into the work," the spirit firmly replied. Eloise was in turmoil: "I couldn't go back to sleep that night. I thought of all the teaching he had given me and I owed it to him to at least try." She also thought that he must know something that she did not. Next morning, she told her boss at J. C. Penney that she was going into spiritual work, but she also felt obligated to train someone for six weeks to replace her.

Doors began opening for Eloise in her new vocation. Shortly after the manifestation of E. B. Page's spirit, Lorna Carroll knocked on Eloise's door, introduced herself, and requested an interview. Eloise spoke with Carroll from six o'clock in the evening until two in the morning. She also asked Eloise for a reading. "I had never given a private reading," Eloise reports, explaining her hesitation, but when she succumbed, Carroll seemed very pleased with the result. Like so many others, Carroll was fascinated by the lifelike painting of E. B. Page on the wall. As she was leaving, Carroll confessed that she was a journalist sent by her editor at the *St. Petersburg Times* to write a negative article about Spiritualism. Instead, she asked Eloise to hold a prayer for her—because of what she learned, she refused to write that story. Carroll persuaded her editor to publish a supportive and long article on the Cassadaga mediums. The story appeared in the Sunday magazine section on April 4, 1954, a year after E. B. Page's death, under the headline, "Cassadaga, Florida's Spirit City." In it, Carroll described Eloise as "extremely attractive" and "serious," as well as the "youngest medium at Cassadaga." This article figuratively put Cassadaga on the map—and the town appeared on the county map the following year. Newspapers all over Florida began to show interest in the camp. Cartons of mail arrived with requests for interviews and readings. Eloise was swamped with work, and often stayed up until three in the morning answering mail.

E. B. Page's students had also implored Eloise to take over his class in natural law. The painfully shy woman had never taught, but they kept reminding her of her extensive training under her late husband. "They were so sincere" that Eloise consented. In her first class with his students, she started without notes, fumbling around for about ten minutes. All of a sudden, "a tranquillity came over me," Eloise relates, and her nervous shaking stopped as every thought came "as clear as a bell." She lectured for a whole hour, much to the students' delight. She began taping these lectures about fourteen years ago. To date, she has recorded seventy-seven audio tapes on individual natural laws. After moving to her new Cassadaga home in 1969, Eloise began to teach smaller groups in what she calls "visualization" in addition to the classes on natural laws.

A few years after Eloise began her new life as a full-time psychic medium and teacher, she underwent another major test. She met a gifted writer with whom she felt a very close bond. She realized, however, that if she spent her life with him, she would not be able to fulfill her promise to herself and to her late husband to continue his life's work, giving back to others all the care and attention he had given to her: "I couldn't pursue it, I had a mission to perform." In 1969, the year she built her house, Eloise made the decision once more that she would not date and henceforth would devote her life to the spiritual work. In the intervening years, in spite of many opportunities, she has never dated again.

A few years after E. B.'s death, Eloise was elected president of the Southern Cassadaga Spiritualist Camp Meeting Association (SCSCMA). For about a decade, she served the community also as pastor of the Spiritualist church. In 1968, Eloise went through another test of faith. She had just returned from the hospital to her home on Stevens Street in the camp, suffering from shingles. Furthermore, she was broke. One night, E. B. Page's spirit appeared before her again and told her, "Honey, sell the old house and build a new one!" She replied vehemently, "I'm so sick, I don't care whether I live or die." She also felt insecure about carrying out his advice and asked, "Why are you telling me this?" With those very piercing eyes, E. B.'s spirit replied: "You need a new incentive. Do as I say!" He then gave her complete instructions on how much to go into debt.

With growing enthusiasm, Eloise started drawing plans for her house. A contractor, who, following E. B. Page's advice, rose from common laborer to business owner, had loved Eloise's late husband very much. He offered to draw her house plans to scale and to build the house at cost. Since people in the camp do not own the land their homes stand on, selling her old house might have presented quite a challenge. But a week later, a friend of another medium bought the furnished house on the spot. Eloise kept only her husband's desk. Moving into temporary camp quarters, Eloise worked hard for six months to earn the money she needed; she counseled for people in real estate and construction and helped advise on deals. Once again, her faith in her husband's counsel and her own persistence resulted in new growth and prosperity.

Recent years have brought further tests, primarily with her health. E. B. Page's spirit appeared to Eloise in the 1980s and told her to see a doctor concerning an impending stroke. With the help of her beloved former student Rev. Marie Lilla, she went to the doctor, who sent her home. Fifteen minutes after Marie left her home, Eloise had a stroke and Marie rushed her to the hospital. Eloise was paralyzed on the right side and her speech had become garbled. She could not control it and became terribly upset, so she decided she would say no more than yes or no. After five weeks of determined self-healing visualization, she regained her ability to speak.

Eloise has since had recurring health concerns, including a fall in November 1996 that fractured her ankle and thigh. When I visited her, she was lying on her bed, leg in the air, unable to move without assistance. Yet she radiated interest in her surroundings and energetic optimism about her own condition. Her recovery was swift, but niggling health problems recur. Still, they do not keep her down for long, and soon she is again giving four to five readings a day, receiving visitors, and staying vigorously active in her house and yard. As she frequently says to those of us who cannot keep up with her, "I've always had lots of energy."

## The Gifted Medium

Over the years, Eloise has taught and lectured extensively on natural law to groups around the country. In many locations, her sincerity and her psychic abilities have won the day. When she gave two seminars for graduate students and faculty in education at the University of Florida, a woman tested her by asking if everyone in the group had specialized in education. Eloise calmly replied that three people were in another field entirely. Sure enough, three of the group were M.D.s from Shands Hospital.

Eloise has given readings for thousands of people. Students and people she has read for stay in touch, supplying the childless woman with an extended family stretching throughout the country and abroad. To many, she has been a surrogate mother and grandmother.

It took a calamity in my own life, as for so many others who turn to Spiritualist mediums, to drive from Gainesville, Florida, to see the Reverend Page. On a late June morning in 1988, my mother died. I missed her with such grief that

*The Reverend Eloise Page, 1995.*

after two months I finally overcame my own resistance and decided to take the insistent advice of the Gainesville-based artist William Schaaf to "go see Eloise." Having received mediocre psychic advice and a reading in Washington, D.C., when I was younger, I was wary of asking for any more psychic help. I also believed in self-determination and resisted the idea of being influenced. But I was desperate—I longed to gain a deeper understanding of my mother's passing.

Eloise's home on Emmel Road is a simple concrete-block dwelling with large windows, situated between two lakes on an unsurfaced road behind the camp. I arrived on September 16 and was struck by how Eloise—a quick, slender, gray-haired woman with twinkling eyes—seemed considerably more spry than her seventy-seven years. She welcomed me warmly and, in her office, invited me to sit in an olive leather chair on one side of a large wooden desk, facing a painting of E. B. Page that vividly depicted his penetrating eyes. She sat on the other side of the desk, smiled at me, and said, "Every psychic reads differently, I read by symbols, just let me read right through for you, dear, then I am open to your questions. So let's see what we have here. . ." She laid her hands on her face, covering her eyes, and, obviously concentrating, began to speak: "Now, as I enter into your vibration . . ."

Eloise knew only my first name and nothing else about me, but for the next half hour, she spoke not only of my mother's passing, but of other significant and very private events in my life. During the reading, her brown eyes were sometimes open, her gaze darting over my shoulder, perceiving what I could not. She tilted her head like a sparrow. Eloise used visual metaphors to describe certain situations happening in my life. Since I was being trained as an art historian, these images proved particularly potent, encompassing more subtle layers of meaning than words alone.

For example, Eloise saw that a man with the initial *R* would soon enter my life and would be a "nice influence" with much sharing. Three months later, after an art lecture, I unexpectedly met a man named Randy Miller, which resulted in a wonderfully healing, deeply spiritual, and creative relationship that involved living together and making innovative art documentaries. We will always be close friends. Eloise also saw that I had come through a rough period four years earlier with strong feelings of "emptiness" and had "rounded a turn," which was precisely the time I was divorcing, moving, and changing career directions. She knew as well that I had made "a resolve" to withdraw "from the personal aspect of my life" by not dating for several years after the divorce.

To my surprise, Eloise rceived an "unusual image" that she had "never seen before." She described "little green elves" around me that were "so cute." She felt they were constructive forces that gave me a feeling of lightheartedness and helped me put thought into action. During my mother's long fight with cancer, I had begun drawing spontaneously onto wet porcelain, creating unknown faces that puzzled me greatly as to their origin yet made me laugh at their oddity. A few weeks after Eloise's reading, I suddenly realized that they bore a striking resemblance to the quirky faces of elves.

After her remarkably accurate and informative reading, she gave me plenty of opportunity to ask questions, to clarify what I might not have understood. From my very first reading with Eloise, and in every reading I have heard about from others, it has been clear that Eloise never abuses her psychic ability. She always maintains a high ethical level. This alone is remarkable, since many of us at some time in our lives have received destructive "psychic" guidance. It is tempting to tell people certitudes and what they *must* do. Eloise, instead, describes states of being, talking of stages of growth and areas of potential. The accuracy of her reading for past events and forthcoming ones was impressive. Her earnest simplicity and humility, coupled with wisdom gained from a rich life, were even more so.

That encounter eleven years ago represented for me the beginning of an extraordinary adventure in learning. That first reading led to more five-hour round-trip drives to take friends—in particular skeptical male friends—to meet Eloise and have readings. Invariably, skepticism would become respect and they would inevitably ask, "How does she do it?" It was a question I also wanted an answer for. So I began to attend her classes.

Like many of Eloise's students, my path has been one of unlearning, followed by learning a new language. Although some of my art classes emphasized the value of imagination, I had primarily been trained as a social scientist, with an education that stressed objective research based on large-scale statistical analyses of data involving controlled studies. This background naturally led to a skeptical attitude, a desire for concrete proof, and, more specifically, the need to find a way to analyze quantitatively if not qualitatively this world of mediumship. However, in Eloise's class, students learn about powers of communication that have nothing to do with intellectual processes such as reasoning, analysis, or rationalization, but rather depend on an intuitive creative process. Eloise pointed out that "we are not trained in this at school." She asserted, much to my surprise, that "any person, who has a longing, can develop their own psychic faculties."

## Beginning with Healing

In 1969, Eloise started holding small classes in her home for "visualization," training students to read for others. Thirty years later, Friday evenings in the fall, winter, and spring continue to find her moving all her chairs into her spacious sitting room as an ever-shifting assortment of people gathers for the class. Some live in or near Cassadaga and are mediums themselves. Others commute from Orlando, Daytona Beach, Tampa, Lakeland, and Gainesville. The process of unlearning and learning can begin at any age, but middle-aged and older women, often freed from child-rearing responsibilities, predominate. The classes usually include from seven to sixteen participants.

Many of Eloise's students have had considerable life experience. Besides the practicing mediums, some are healers trained in techniques from past-life regression to massage therapy or ministerial work. Others are artists or educators. Patrick Sullivan began coming to Eloise's classes in January 1998, driving two and a half hours each way from Lakeland. A series of "coincidences" led Patrick, raised a Baptist, to Eloise. Patrick has natural psychic ability; he receives clear, detailed images and also hears names. Eloise is certain that one day he will be a medium himself, if he wishes.

Some students leave to pursue other interests and then come back to attend the classes years later, using Eloise's teachings to enrich their lives, whatever work they do. Others become practicing spiritual mediums.

Eloise begins her Friday night class by reading out the names of persons on a long healing list, meticulously describing each of their afflictions. While some on the list are personally known to her, most she has never met; a phone call puts them on the list. Problems range from cancer to accidents, surgery, mental distress, depression, cerebral palsy, and major life changes.

Eloise then asks the students to sit upright with their feet on the floor, close their eyes, and begin to visualize healing specific ailments. For example, she may name a person and then ask us to visualize the healing of the relevant body part. Or she may ask us to focus on all those with brain tumors and to see the tumors shrinking and brain function returning. For a person unable to walk, we visualize the circulation improving in the legs, the person rising out of a chair, putting weight on the feet, and taking steps. At the end of the healing session, which can last up to a half-hour, she always asks for God's will to be done. It comes as no surprise to hear that a person's health condition has improved greatly from one class to the next. Over the years, the results have been impressive; for instance, a very ill young boy had no seizures for more than a year after he was "held in the healing."

Eloise teaches that our visualizing healing is an act of creation. She often emphasizes the power of thought, as she did one evening in November 1991, when her focus was the power of aspiration and thought. "Nothing is impossible with spiritual healing." For true healing to take place, however, inner faith and confidence in God are essential. "With a positive frame of mind, you can overcome negativity." When doing visualizations for healing, we are "coming into contact with the energy force within" and giving some of our strength to the persons in need. Thought is both very powerful and creative, so it is vital to project only positive thoughts. She also explains that "every one of us has certain creative forces, according to our devotion, sincerity, and earnestness, that begins to show within us as a talent." She points out the importance of persistence and admonishes her students, "I want to see you develop that force within yourselves." We go through life with doubts and frustrations in relationships and in our jobs and thus we get discouraged; we run into negativity and experience difficulty maintaining a positive attitude. "You are giving your breath of life to a project," Eloise tells us, and in doing so, "you can give yourself the training, since teacher forces from Spirit are drawn to you, once you have the aspiration." She explained in a class I attended in March 1998 that there is a light within us, and as we advance, we are to say, "I see the light." That "I see," which is part of visualization, is the equivalent of light dawning, of a deeper dimension within.

## Natural Law and Prerequisites for Mediumship

In her Friday night class, after the healing session Eloise usually instructs students briefly on a natural law, such as the law of emotion, motivation, or attachment. Often she picks the topic based on her intuitive awareness of her students' needs. For example, on my birthday in June 1997, when she knew my father was critically ill and dying, she lectured on the law of diversion, which states that we need a diversity of interests to refresh us so that tensions in our lives do not overtax us. While Eloise's talks on many of these natural laws have been taped and are available for purchase, each lecture is fresh, with new insights. If the class exceeds a certain number of participants, she spends the entire session teaching a natural law in depth, saving the practice in visualization for a smaller group. She talks without notes, using examples from nature and her own life to illustrate the concepts.

One of the first laws that Eloise teaches is the law of neutrality. To read for other people with accuracy, or to receive accurate spiritual guidance for ourselves, we must first achieve a state of complete neutrality or detachment. We have to release our preconceived notions or opinions about the person or the question for which we are seeking guidance. Eloise compares the ability to accurately receive guidance to the workings of a camera: To take an accurate picture, one's film cannot have a previous image or impression. "When we know the person, or have a prior opinion about them, we often react to that information, instead of mentally and emotionally standing aside in order to receive spiritual messages." By observing the law of neutrality, we can pick up on what a person is feeling, not on his or her desires, in essence gathering information from that person's soul level.

As a beginning student, I wondered why Eloise emphasized this law. Then I realized that I could lead a much healthier, more constructive life if I put this law into practice every day, whether dealing with my own issues or the problems of others.

Another crucial law that Eloise speaks of is the law of emotions. She suggests that during the rather painful process of growth, we do not realize the impact of our emotions, and we later have regrets. She quotes two axioms from her husband: "Before the voice can speak in the presence of the Masters, it must have lost the power to wound. Before the eyes can see, they must become incapable of tears." Not only is it important to think twice before speaking, but emotions can hide spiritual truth by impacting the medium's circulation and pulse.

Eloise distinguishes between having sympathy for someone and feeling compassion for them. She admonishes students not to yield to sympathy, because it will intensify the other person's feelings, stirring them up more emotionally. "By expressing sympathy, you are identifying on the level that that person is at, which precludes your giving any help. Sympathy is getting absorbed in the other person." While compassion is vital, Eloise notes that a medium must "see the problem and yet stand back and see beyond it." She warns her students that "not until you obtain that stage of objectivity can you really help." Sympathy tends to increase self-pity. When we identity with another person's feelings, "it's confirming something" for that person. In contrast, using empathy, "you're perceiving it but not identifying with it on that person's level."[3] When asked what to pray for, Eloise replies, "Light on your path."[4]

On a practical level, Eloise offers her students three axioms. First, "suspend thought" when confronted with emotion or even physical pain. Second, she quotes: "Be still and know that I am God." She commands herself to be still, and that suspends pain. Third, "before you stand in the presence of the Master, the feet must be washed in the blood of the heart." Our understanding must be clarified; we need to go through a purification of mind and heart. Our purity of heart—of our motives—is crucial. When we dwell on feelings of rejection and hurt, we experience intense pain. By "mastering" the emotions, we can let go of feelings of inadequacy, uncertainty, insecurity. Clarity of vision comes when a thought is pure and the mind is clear of previous events. Vision, creativity, comes from a new perspective, not from dwelling on the past.

Eloise often warns her students against a tendency to "intellectualize." By this she means that in the process of mentally analyzing information received, we tend to "override our hunches, our perceptions." She says that we have certain energy centers in the body, or chakras, that act as transformers carrying an electrical current. When we intellectualize, we are "breaking that current." We lose that energy at the solar plexus level, like a broken circuit. Often the process of intellectualization involves "drawing comparisons," rather than letting each moment be creative and fresh. "When we intellectualize, we tear down creative thought," Eloise contends.

As a student, I went to Eloise with great self-doubt. I felt that I lacked the inherent talent to receive psychic information for myself. The thought of receiving information for other people was even more scary because of the potential for harming someone with misinformation. Unlike some of Eloise's students, who had benefited from a more artistic or freer education than my own at the French Lycée, two universities in Vienna, and the University of Florida, I felt constrained by an education that had devalued intuition. It was particularly helpful to me when Eloise, in one of her classes, distinguished between "fantasy" and "imagination." Fantasy is what many describe as imaginary, illusionary, or wishful thinking; imagination, or the "power of creativity," a very real and concrete force, is the skill used to read for others.

Eloise compares the ability to read for someone with choosing a television channel. While reading, Eloise is picking up on vibrations that create images with symbolic meaning to interpret, as if she is tuning into a television station. Eloise does not want the people she reads for to talk or ask questions during the process: "If they start talking, they will talk about what they want, not about what *is*." Their questions might also lead Eloise to "intellectualize" during the reading itself. In the last ten years, Eloise has discovered not only that she can read for someone over the phone, but that such readings are far easier than those she gives in person, when she must neutralize her reactions to the person she is reading for. Over the phone, she can simply tune in to the person's tone of voice, which offers fewer personal distractions.

She further explains that the process of reading or visualizing for someone else begins with inspiration—literally, "the *first* thought that comes to mind"; what we might suspect to be imaginary or inaccurate is not. One of the aims of

Eloise's classes in visualization is in fact to test this out so that students realize from their own experience how accurate these received first thoughts and images are.[5] The way to practice concentration and seeing in detail, Eloise teaches, is to close one's eyes and visualize the human foot, the toes, or an object in great detail, thus focusing the mind.

In learning how to tune in to others, Eloise stresses to her students, we must remember all thoughts and images in detail, even if they seem ludicrous. Equally important, we need to remember them in sequence, because even though they may seem distinct, they often tell a story. Eloise notes too that the student is relaying a message to the person he or she is reading for; it is really not the student's business to know what it means. To precisely understand what one is seeing as a medium is the equivalent of "reading someone else's mail," she suggests. While students are trained to interpret accurately the images that they have received, they rarely understand, and indeed should not know, what the interpretations mean in the client's life. As Eloise proved over and over again in her classes, the message almost always has a specific and relevant meaning for the recipient. Gradually, as I learned the new language of tapping into my own psychic abilities, I was weaned from my habitual doubt regarding my ability. I learned over time that, if I practice detachment and let go of "intellectualizing," I am indeed able to tune in to others with accuracy.

In learning to observe every detail of a received image and, even more daunting, to remember them, we are training our minds to become more aware of where our thoughts lead us. As Eloise puts it, "We often cannot remember in everyday life where our minds were five minutes ago, let alone two hours before." By learning to trace the path that our minds take during the day, we gain greater awareness of and more control over our thoughts. In addition, our memory improves greatly.

Examples of the way Eloise continues to train her mind include her remarkable facility for crossword puzzles and for games that involve thinking of all the possible permutations of a set of letters. A striking example of her precise mental control occurs when in the middle of a reading she is interrupted by a phone call, which she answers since she is her own secretary. Caught in midsentence, she is warmly and fully responsive to the caller, and then resumes her reading exactly at the point where she left off.

Although she speaks repeatedly of the Christ light in her lectures and readings, Eloise embraces other spiritual traditions, in particular the Hindu/Christian tradition as taught by Yogananda. When asked what books she particularly recommends for personal study, she names two that she found beneficial to her own growth: *The Impersonal Life* (1941), and *Cosmic Consciousness: A Study in the Evolution of the Human Mind* (1901). Both predate the New Age movement. Eloise notes that the first book's author was so "impersonal" the book was published anonymously.

## Reading for Others

In her Friday night classes, after the healing session and a brief talk on a natural law, Eloise teaches visualization. She explains the process to newcomers in the class, many of whom have never tried to read for others. Eloise asks us to select someone in the room without their knowledge, preferably someone we do not know, and read for them. Then, eyes closed, we are to forget that person and return within ourselves. At times, Eloise simply guides us to open up our awareness to receive thoughts and images, without any judgment about their validity or their meaning. Other times, she leads us through guided imagery. (For example, she once guided us mentally up a mountain to the top, where we found water, met someone, and then descended, all the while observing every detail.) We then sit in silence with eyes closed. After about ten minutes, Eloise asks us to open our eyes, and one by one to identify the person we read for and tell the class what we have seen or heard.

After each of us speaks, Eloise helps us interpret what we have received, both by explaining the meaning of symbols and by adding her own impressions or insights. Repeatedly in her class, three or four students will have chosen the same person to read for, as if that person needed particular guidance, usually someone in need who shows no outer signs of distress. We also have the opportunity to learn from each other, not only by reading for others and being read for, but also by listening to the readings of others and Eloise's interpretations.

Some students tend to receive vivid, involved images with great clarity of detail that prove both informative and accurate for the persons they have chosen. Others, like me, at their first attempt saw almost nothing. Eloise feels we all have the potential to receive complex imagery, but that we often cannot pick up on others because we doubt our ability to do so. By practicing in her class and by hearing afterwards the often astonishing confirmations from the people we chose, we begin to develop confidence. Eloise closes the class with her own images and a minireading for someone in the class. By now, it is after eleven o'clock, and we are tired and filled with new insights. Yet Eloise, "a night owl," will stay up at least another three hours; she often gives phone readings for people all over the world at ten or eleven at night.

## Training in Symbology

In her classes on visualization, Eloise devotes a large portion of time to training in symbology: learning to interpret the symbols in the images we "see," largely in the form of still or moving images. She likens this to learning the alphabet in order to make words. While a few students "hear" words in their minds, most receive visual images, many of which seem completely unintelligible and disjointed until Eloise begins interpreting them.

Eloise explains how our five senses correspond to five spiritual senses: for sight there is vision; for hearing, clairaudience; for feeling, intuition; for touch, sensitivity; for smell, an awareness of attraction or repulsion. When the primary sense is vision, readers see a series of images; others are more likely to hear in their minds words, phrases, or even sentences. Some use all the spiritual senses when they read for someone. Eloise primarily uses vision, although she "hears" names. In the process, she identifies with that person: "It's like losing myself in them." At times, the images are repeated as if "the Forces feel that I haven't clarified enough."

In the interpretation of symbols, the natural elements play a major role. Water, for example, is always a symbol of the emotions. In an image with water in it, we learn the importance of observing exactly *how* the water looks, whether the surface is ruffled or smooth, whether it has currents or waves, is stagnant or flowing; whether it is dark, murky, or a clear blue; and whether the body of water is vast and overwhelming, or small and gentle. Equally important is the viewer's relationship to the water, whether one stands before it fearfully, plunges in, or steps over it. Similarly, snow can mean illness, and ice a serious illness.

Fire connotes the energy force related to physical, mental, emotional or spiritual endeavors and may be healing but also overwhelming. Just as fire can purify or warm, it can also burn. The warmth or friendliness of a person is a manifestation of that energy force. When we touch a person, there occurs an exchange of the energy, just as a cat receives energy from the person stroking it. In the course of spiritual development, one focuses on getting this energy under control. In the early years of life, most feelings, including pain, hurt, and being upset, are connected with the solar plexus or abdomen. We learn to gain control and to channel the force from the lower regions of the body to the heart, mental, and spiritual centers.

The elements of air and earth are equally powerful symbols. The earth symbolizes our material efforts—both the color of the soil and its fertility are important variables. A rich loam implies fertility with our material endeavors. The kinds of plants growing in the earth connote personal growth. Wilted plants suggest that the state of growth of the person being read for is stymied and malnourished. The element of air relates to aspirations and to clarity. Again, the state and kind of air, from a light, fresh, invigorating breeze to a gusty storm, implies the state of the person's aspirations.

Colors play a crucial role in interpreting images, especially shades of color. Following the law of opposites, the lighter, pastel tones are the more spiritual shades of each color. The darker shades indicate the same feelings on the negative pole. Although, for example, purple in general symbolizes the spiritual, light lavender indicates the highest spiritual qualities, whereas deep purple signifies spiritual nostalgia, wistfulness, or frustration.

Similarly, though red generally connotes love and a purity of emotion, light red symbolizes love, and dark crimson indicates hatred. While the color blue generally means self-confidence, aspirations, eagerness, and enthusiasm, light blue indicates optimism and encouragement, and dark blue signifies despondency and discouragement. Yellow relates to mental forces; for example, seeing yellow butterflies for someone can mean that the person is coming into "mental flexibility." Brown refers to material circumstances. White indicates purity of motive and purpose, as well as wholesomeness. Gold signifies the spiritual and mental activity or processes, so, for example, golden hair is interpreted as spiritual strength. Black is the color of power and also the ability to absorb. Orange usually means pride, so white orchids with orange specks can mean that the person has spiritual motivation with tints of pride. Green, the color of growth, comes in many shades that qualify the state of growth. Light green implies new growth, and richer greens connote healthy growth or confirmation of things learned, whereas very dark brownish green is a symbol of death. A green turtle symbolizes slowness and dependability. Colors that combine several colors reflect the meaning of their component parts. Pink, a blend of red and white, connotes a childlike outlook on life, simplicity. Teal, a mix of blue and green, represents a combination of strength or confidence and growth. Turquoise, which contains more blue than green, symbolizes development of faith and confidence in the self, or a development that lies more on the spiritual plane.

A body-part interpretation that intrigues me concerns the feet: According to Eloise, feet symbolize the mind. If a person is wearing boots, his mind is in a state of preparation.

The quantity of things or objects also changes the interpretation of an image. Golden wheat, for instance, is a sign of ripeness and productivity, whereas an entire field of wheat connotes unlimited productivity.

Animal and birds appear regularly in the visualizations and can be interpreted quite specifically.[6] When Diane read for Lee Ann, the first image she saw was of a small black dog, with lots of happy energy, running and jumping. The dog seemed shiny, clean, and healthy. Diane next saw the dog on a leash walking on the pavement, calm and obedient. Then she saw Lee Ann sitting still, putting on reddish-brown lipstick and fluffing up her hair, which was very soft. After hearing these images, Eloise explained that the dog is a symbol of a friend. So in this context, there is a lot of activity for Lee Ann around a friend, with new things developing and a sense of freedom for her. Yet, because the dog was later on a leash, Eloise explained that the friend was tied to something, tied in with someone else, not Lee Ann. And for the final image, Lee Ann was displaying an attitude of "accept me as I am" by paying some attention to herself, not for show, but with more of a sense of simplicity.

Another often visualized animal, the horse, Eloise explains as a symbol of communications, activity, news. David saw the following images for Lee Ann. At the edge of a forest, which was a little dark, with bumpy ground, Lee Ann sat on a horse. David then saw that the horse was excited, and it went galloping off. Next, he saw them riding through woods and down a path to a hidden pond or small lake that was calm. The horse had calmed down, and the trees cast many shadows. Lee Ann sat down at the edge of the lake and contemplated things. She decided to dive in and then came up and floated gently on her back downstream. She got back on the horse and was much calmer. There were now fewer trees, and it was more hilly, with miles of twisting fences that fell down one after the other like dominoes. It became brighter, the hills were at the foot of a mountain, and Lee Ann went peacefully up the hills and to the mountain.

Bearing in mind the symbology of the horse, Eloise interpreted these detailed images as follows. David first saw that material conditions and aspirations are unsettled for Lee Ann and that something needs to be worked out or examined. Then, there is an eagerness, an enthusiasm, about news, communications, or a trip. Here, her emotions are connected with the trip; there is enthusiasm, but it is somewhat disturbed. Lee Ann's attitude is not animated; she is quiet as though analyzing things. Then she experiences emotional relaxation away from material problems. There is again news, another trip or a project, which, coupled with her enthusiasm, means she may be getting good news. With the final image, the barricades and obstacles will fall down, and she will have new aspirations and more news.

Birds can symbolize a variety of things. In Lee Ann's reading for Jimmy, she saw an eagle holding arrows in one set of claws. In her interpretation of this image, Eloise saw Jimmy, who is partly Native American, as having a guiding force by the name of Big Eagle. In another instance, a streamlined orange bird meant that the man who was being read for had pride in something, since the color orange connotes an attitude of pride. In another case, a tiny owl emerged in a circular motion and flew up. The owl signifies wisdom, and the image as a whole implies further growth. Finally, when a white bird with smooth feathers landed on a hand, this implied a softness, confidence, and tranquillity with someone. As these examples indicate, the context and action as well as the species and color influence the specific meaning of a bird. In general, birds unconfined to the earth symbolize loftiness, creativity, and more flexibility.

A single symbol may be interpreted in several ways. For example, a snake may embody wisdom, but a threatening snake may represent a warning. One can also interpret a snake as a serpentine force, such as the energy force of the body, similar to the concept of kundalini in Yogic traditions.

Eloise emphasizes that students should observe very carefully the images that they receive and where an object, action, or detail of a landscape is in relation to a student's viewpoint when the student is reading for someone. To illustrate her point, if a river is flowing serenely on the left side of one's field of vision (the side symbolizing the heart and emotions), there would appear to be an underlying serenity in the emotional state of the person being read for. In contrast, all that appears on the right side of the student's field of vision symbolizes the mental and the material.

Eloise also teaches the significance of each number. The number *seven*, for example, symbolizes spirit. A cluster of seven butterflies would imply a lightness of spirit or a transformation of the spirit, and also an element of time, since all numbers can indicate time spans as well. The number *one* symbolizes creation, *two* connotes birth, and *three* represents air or the aspirations. *Four* is the symbol for water and thus the emotions. *Five* stands for fire or the energy force, while *six* signifies the earth and all that is material. *Seven* is the symbol for spirit. *Eight* means magnetism or attraction. *Nine* symbolizes power, and nine times any other single-digit number still returns to its source, *nine*; for example, nine times three is *twenty-seven* (*two* and *seven*, which added equal *nine*). When interpreting an image, it is important to observe the number of like objects or animals.

All of these images and their interpretations are part of learning the language of Spirit, whose vibrations we see symbolically in images, from which we in turn create a story. While the images may invite literal interpretation, it is the symbolic interpretation that communicates the more subtle information.

## Life Lessons

In her classes and in the audio tapes of her lectures on natural law, Eloise teaches much more than how to become aware of one's own psychic abilities and how to train them effectively. She talks about how to lead a life of ever increasing self-awareness that in turn leads to inner security and greater happiness. Without judgment, she speaks of the effect of our thoughts and actions, and suggests ways to bring them into greater harmony or better balance. Eloise can see in a person's aura—the colors around the body—whether balance has been achieved. The darker shades depict depths of negativity or a state of imbalance.

Although she does not practice meditation in her class, Eloise emphasizes its importance. It gets us into an attitude of quietude, so that we "learn to gain control over a nervous pattern, instead of the mind going around a topic." In her regular meditation, she visualizes her solar plexus as a pool of water and sees it becoming very quiet and serene, in the process gaining mastery over the nervous system.

Eloise shares with her students many insights about life, illustrating some with examples from her own experiences. In talking about motivations and emotions, she encourages us to look at and understand our motives for certain actions. She recommends lying in bed at the end of the day and going over our own actions and words for that day, asking ourselves what motivated our actions and speech. She suggests that we often expect too much of others whose level of maturity may not match our expectations. With spiritual training comes an inner security that we often mistakenly seek outside ourselves. By learning detachment from these external expectations, we also bring our emotions under control.

In her readings and lectures, Eloise often speaks of "pliability and flexibility." Frequently, the outcome of a situation differs from our preconceived notions of what should occur. Some of these outcomes offer us the opportunity to transform our lives for the better, if we are pliable and flexible in responding to unpredictable or unexpected events. For example, the death of my mother, which first brought me to Eloise, completely changed my everyday life on a very practical level. The more flexible and pliable I became, the more I could adapt to these changes.

In addition to shifting attitudes, another major opportunity for growth occurs through relationships. A crucial role in relationships is played by the law of blending, which Eloise defines as our absorbing "talents and capabilities" from the people we associate with. "When we can relax," she explains, this breaks down our reserve and "then we can blend." She uses herself as an example: although she grew up painfully shy and inarticulate, she absorbed the ability to speak and teach students from her teacher and husband, E. B. Page. From a subsequent great love, she absorbed a far greater ability to write. Although she had written poems since her twenties, her talent increased and blossomed through that association. Indeed, her poem "Remembering," written in January 1969 in honor of her late husband, is one of fluid writing and clarity of feeling; one of her many poems inspired by natural law, "Remembering" appears in her book of poetry, *The Path*. We often learn of our own potential talents and capabilities from those with whom we have identified and bonded.

In forming our relationships with others, the law of attraction is at work. That is, when we meet someone, we receive much more about the other person than our conversation with them would suggest. We exchange energy with that person, and we are drawn to those with whom we have something in common. We can also magnify that energy and project a certain magnetism, particularly if we are "fairly active." Eloise points out that there is something "very magnetic in each of us."[7]

Eloise repeats the phrase "Let go, and let God" frequently. She teaches us to release anxieties as they arise in order to live in the moment, where there is great power of creativity and inspiration. Eloise warns that worry, anxiety, and concern can deplete the physical body: One hour of anxiety effectively burns eight to twelve hours of physical energy, a staggering loss of life force.

Eloise made up her mind that she would not bring a child into the world "to go through what I have gone through," but "rather use the experience in guidance and counseling others." She is referring to karmic conditions that impelled her to follow her mother's pattern of early marriage, divorce, and remarriage. To explain this general phenomenon of family karma, Eloise quotes Scripture: "The sins of parents can be visited on the children even onto the tenth generation." For example, the children of divorced parents frequently go through divorce themselves and see the other side of the coin, which produces an internal "mellowing." This reliving of family karma generates a richness on the soul level, a tolerance.

Concerning the ancient past and the concept of reincarnation, Eloise believes that "Atlantis existed"; she also says, "I felt like I had lived before." In general, she believes, we lose the memory of past lives through the trauma of birth. Evidence for past lives can be found in the "thread of a talent," such as a longing for music that cannot be explained otherwise. When she met E. B. Page, she felt that she "had known him forever." Similarly, she felt an awareness about her own parents that was not "very distinct" and believes that her distress as a child may be due to some past karma with them.

Ultimately, Eloise has found, life is about learning to overcome challenges, to master defeats, frustrations, and feelings of disharmony, rising above them to gain a deeper understanding of oneself. She uses her own life to illustrate these points. When as a teenager she wished to become a nun, she was seeking a sense of belonging that she failed to find in her own family. Having failed to find security without—in the Catholic church and then in her early marriage—she turned within and spent years exploring the question, "Where is security and where does it come from?" As she repeatedly claims, the tumultuous events in her life brought her great spiritual growth. Even in extremes of emotional despair, we touch heights. Like the swing of a pendulum, one can move "from misery to the point of bliss." Eloise has observed this, for example, with alcoholics, who have gone from the depths to a total transformation.

In listening to Eloise's life story, her students gain greater perspective on their own difficulties. Those who have experienced divorce or a broken romance need to rebuild self-confidence and to begin to reevaluate their personal qualities. Out of that process of evaluation, Eloise insists, people gain a better knowledge of self that can then be put to good use. Challenges can bring all of us greater self-knowledge and greater inner fortitude. Finding the strength within ourselves, we can then change our lives. Her own life serves as prime example of turning what were exceedingly painful events into very positive outcomes. For every person, Eloise explains further, there is a time when momentous things happen. Often it is the birthday. For Eloise however, rather than October 15, her time of major shifts is mid-August. This is the time she divorced and married.

## Eloise As Friend

Eloise can be found mopping her spotless floors at three in the morning. Her house is meticulously neat, with a bedroom always available for guests. Her person is carefully dressed and coifed. A delightful side of Eloise is just how much *fun* she is to be with. She has a vivid sense of humor, and her curiosity is unabated. Even her business card reflects her talent for whimsy; in addition to MEDIUM, COUNSELOR AND ADVISOR, her occupation reads: PROFESSIONAL ROLE MODEL.

Following her own teachings about the importance of balancing work and play, Eloise takes time off for recreation. She loves to play cards, attend jai alai, and gamble for small amounts in Las Vegas, pastimes that offer relief from the serious nature of her work. She uses her highly trained memory to focus on numbers, yet her talent for winning varies. One week she will win only $40, a week later $1,400. But as Eloise herself puts it, her desire for winning can effectively block any intuition she may have about the winning numbers or the right cards. Before she goes to jai alai, she often plays Yahtzee to come up with numbers to bet on. An overnight stay at Eloise's frequently includes a game of cards such as Kings in the Corner.

After the seriousness of the spiritual work, the games bring her enjoyment: "It's a carefree thing." Several times a year she joins friends and goes to Las Vegas or Biloxi, Mississippi, from which she returns refreshed, even if she has slept only a few hours every morning. She also tests her abilities, just as when she reads for others, she gets feedback from them about her accuracy. "Generally, we can't pick up on things for ourselves," Eloise explains, "because it's too personal." So she feels elated when she is accurate.

In February 1996, I flew out to Las Vegas with Eloise and her good friends Bill and Betty Enright. We stayed at the Lady Luck Hotel, downtown. Eloise dressed with her usual care, and off we went to the slot machines and various card tables. I followed her like a dog, eager to learn and watch. She picked slot machines carefully, switching between them with amazing timing. At the card tables, she moved from game to game according to how she felt about them. She never grew discouraged.

Remarkably energetic, Eloise is certainly living proof of the law of friction. By walking and moving, she explains, we build up energy within. Running is also good, as long as we do not overdo it and thus burn up the acquired energy. Although the word *friction* can imply problems between people, here it deals with the actual movement of the body; the friction with the ground sends energy through the body. Eloise embodies a remarkable dual strength of mind and body. She darts about, vigorous mentally and physically. Her metaphor of a tree applies here. As she points out, a tree doesn't need external support, even though nature provides nourishment in the form of water, sunlight, and clean air. Rather, a tree is rooted in itself. We would do well to emulate trees.

## Eloise's Views on the Future

The devastating fires in Florida and earthquakes and floods elsewhere in May and June 1998 deeply disturbed Eloise. She spoke with great concern about the contamination of our universe and about the depletion of the ozone layer. The

1998 events that devastated the ecosystem remind her of what we are doing to the "body of the universe," just as the chemistry within our own body is altered by what we are doing to it, creating fevers. She sees a similarity between the dehydration of the physical body and that of the earth. With all that we are sending up into space, we are altering the air we breathe. "The chemistry of the earth is changing," she says, and the situation is "scary." She warns we may only have pavement and pollution in place of greenery.

Eloise is uncertain about an actual doomsday occurring. Yet she feels "a sense of suspense" about the manner in which scientists and others are experimenting with and exploring space. She feels "concern" about what they are contaminating; they are not looking at the scientific damage of the experiments. She points to the damage to the ozone layer and asks, "Are we learning from it? Are they just blindly carrying ahead with overenthusiasm for new discoveries?" She laments that "we can't think ahead." The situation is not hopeless, however. Eloise feels that as humankind looks more closely at what is unfolding, "it can bring a new understanding and new approach."

Eloise is also concerned about our children and what they absorb from television. That a young person can kill dozens of people reflects "a demand for attention" without concern for how he or she gets it. The cycle is clear: After "seeing so much violence on TV," they behave similarly and then get attention on television for doing something so violent. Overall, Eloise feels there is too much negativity shown on television. She feels that "kids shouldn't have so much exposure." Children are "very creative," yet they "build from their imaginations without reasoning, so they grow into that violent role and beyond."

As for the political future of the United States, she does not think "we will lose power. Eventually, there may be more of a balancing between nations." This is hard to predict because "so much depends on leadership." She foresees "a little struggle for power yet." Eloise also sees that "we will reach out and other nations will reach out, too, in a conciliatory manner." Some nations and leaders, of course, "don't reason at all," which make predictions for the world as a whole difficult. "Hopefully, as we come more into a spiritual age, that spirituality will touch those that we bring into the guardianship of our country," Eloise concludes.

All this environmental, economic, political tension "is making a lot of people think in terms of the spiritual." In Cassadaga alone, Eloise has noticed significant changes. Interest in the spiritual and in Spiritualism "has grown tremendously." There is a greater openness in all professions toward the spirit world and mediumship, as evidenced by an invitation that Eloise received to lecture at an Episcopal church.

The structure of our society is also shifting, as Eloise has noticed in her work. Of the apparent increase in the number of gay people, she observes that people are "seeking more understanding, and finding it more among their own sex than from the opposite . . . I think everyone has to follow what gives them a sense of peace within themselves and a sense of unfoldment. I don't criticize it, because I don't know. Unless you've been there, you don't understand it." She has noticed a companionship, sensitivity, and similarity of emotions among lesbians. She reminds us that in the world of Spirit, there is a "blending of the male and female within us," and "soul feelings" replace "physical feelings." She does not think that gender in a given incarnation is a choice. Gender is karmically determined; if a female soul experiences bitterness toward a male or father in one life, then that soul will incarnate into a male body "to see the other side of the coin."

Eloise notes the extraordinary knowledge of young children today and "how little we knew compared to what they know today." She feels that "every generation is coming up smarter" and that "the mental plane is expanding tremendously."

Finally, Eloise sees a shift "with our own spiritual movement" of "coming into an inner plane of understanding and a lot of soul knowledge." Generally, this is a "more spiritual cycle," with more practice in "meditation and yoga." She notes that "many other churches are taking up on that."

## The Power of Humility and Simplicity

At times of great distress, people seek Eloise out for guidance and help. She brings visitors to her sitting room to experience the serenity and quiet of her house and its tranquil vistas. She observes that many people feel such a sense of comfort and ease that they lean back on one of the couches and fall asleep waiting their turn for a reading.

When people become so dependent on her that they come continually to her for guidance, she points out the importance for them of coming into greater self-reliance or, as she also phrases it, "learning to appreciate one's own sense of individuality." Constantly running to Eloise for guidance can weaken one's sense of self.

Throughout all the years of being Eloise's student, I have gained tremendous respect for her ethics as well as for her psychic abilities. I have never heard her say anything to someone that was not in some way constructive. When a person is going through difficulties, she always talks of the process in a helpful and positive manner. In sincere humility, Eloise always expresses her gratitude for the teachings she has received and for the blessings and talents that have expressed through her life. Before eating, she always prays aloud.

Having attended many of her classes and witnessed the transformation of my own abilities and those of others in the class, I found my scientifically trained mind assuaged. Eloise is right; there is proof that with desire and focus one can learn to train psychic abilities.

Eloise explains, "My main goal with the teaching and with the reading has been that I wanted to share what my teacher gave to me." The guidance in her life, both on this plane and from the spirit world, has been extraordinary. Around the time she first met E. B. Page, Eloise's spirit guide, a Native American called White Feather, appeared to her in visions in which he was wearing a headdress of long white feathers. She received many different impressions from him, including intuitions of things that were about to happen. She has also felt her husband's teacher Yogananda around her at times.

One of the most important visions of her life was an out-of-body experience Eloise had shortly before she met E. B. She was lying awake at night when a rush of wind pulled her soul out of her body. The power was "terrific," but she "never lost consciousness, remaining totally aware." After her soul lifted out of her body, she experienced "a feeling of exhilaration" as she went rapidly through strata of colors and consciousness, reaching "a plateau with millions of colored threads, all moving, all intermingling." There was no space between the threads, and all the different colors were electrical and vibrant. The final plateau was one of "extreme quietude, with a serenity that is very hard to achieve here." This peacefulness radiated from a "supreme quietude." While she was experiencing this unearthly peace, her gaze shifted: "Then I saw the Master. He was sitting in a chair, and he held out his hand to me. In his hand, he had a white lotus flower. He spoke about the opening of it and the unfolding of it, and the power of love." The figure of Jesus Christ was "so beautiful, and the awe was so great." For three days, "I didn't feel like I was on earth . . . With the knowledge that was being revealed to me . . . I was coming in touch with my own soul. The soul was that flower that is unfolding." She realized this is true for every person: "We are still in the bud stage; we are beginning to unfold."

In spite of the extraordinary visions, teachings, and guidance she has received in a very full lifetime, Eloise remains simple and humble. She receives continued attention from the press. In June 1998, she was interviewed at length by *People* magazine and ABC television. The camp has also celebrated her by creating a meditation garden in her honor adjacent to the camp's hall and bookstore. Yet Eloise reiterates, "I am only a channel to convey something."

On Eloise's eighty-fifth birthday, Rev. Marie Lilla organized a surprise birthday party in the camp auditorium. Many friends and students from out of town attended in addition to members of the camp. We came to celebrate Eloise, with her unusual combination of great wisdom and youthfulness. A high school dropout who has been invited to teach at Stetson University, she reminded us that "there is no limitation on what we can learn, where there is a heart interest in wanting to know."

Eloise teaches us to "keep an open mind, for each day is a new discovery."[8] Even in her own life, she feels, "There is still something for me to unfold."

## Notes

1. My warmest thanks to Melanie Almeder, Gael Morgan, Elisabeth Rush, and William Schaaf for their comments and suggestions for this chapter.

2. Eloise Page, interviews by the author, Cassadaga, Florida, September 1995. Unless otherwise noted, subsequent quotations or information in the text attributed to Page are taken from this interview and others by the author, from January to July 1998, and from classes attended by the author between November 1991 and March 1998.

3. Eloise made the last two remarks when Elisabeth Rush read a draft of this chapter to her on June 15, 1998.

4. From notes taken by William Schaaf, September 1998.

5. This practice resembles that reported by Thurston in *Experiments in a Search for God,* in which students conduct specific experiments on a regular basis to prove for themselves certain spiritual truths.

6. In the examples that follow, I have changed names but not genders.

7. Eloise Page, audio tape on the Law of Fire, 1988.

8. This quotation is from a dedication Eloise inscribed for me in my personal copy of *Cosmic Consciousness* by Richard Maurice Bucke, M.D.

# Photographic Images of the Camp

## *Activities, Ceremonies, and Rituals*

GARY MONROE

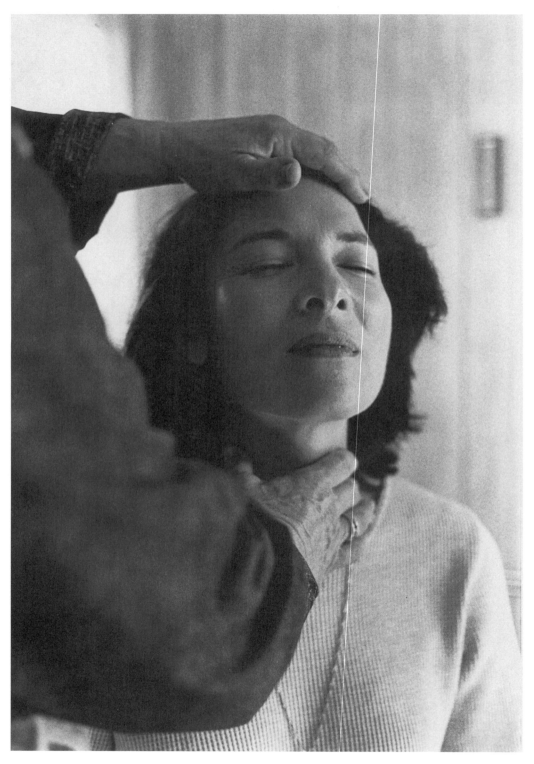

*Healing, Caesar Forman Healing Center, 1995.*

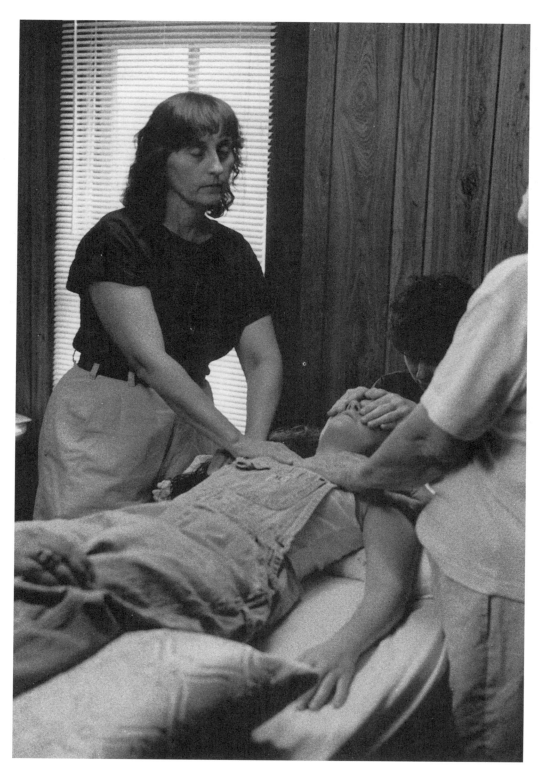

*Reiki healing group at a private residence, 1997.*

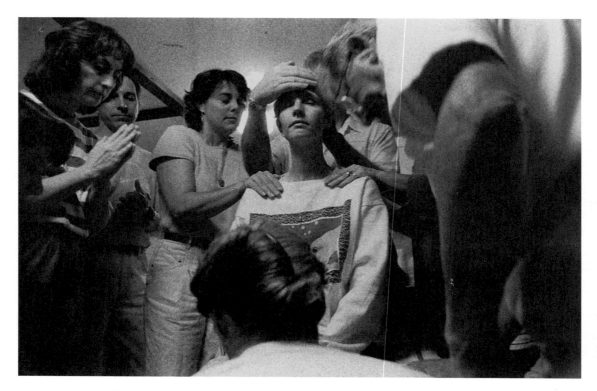

*Reiki healing group at a private residence, 1997.*

*Healing circle, Colby Memorial Temple, 1996.*

*Christmas Candlelight All-Message Service, Colby Memorial Temple, 1996.*

*Healing circle, Colby Memorial Temple, 1996.*

*Christmas Candlelight All-Message Service, Colby Memorial Temple, 1996.*

*Christmas Candlelight Message Service, Colby Memorial Temple, 1997.*

*Candlelight Healing Service, Colby Memorial Temple, 1996.*

*Candlelight Healing Service, Colby Memorial Temple, 1997.*

*People waiting for laying on of hands, Colby Memorial Temple, 1996.*

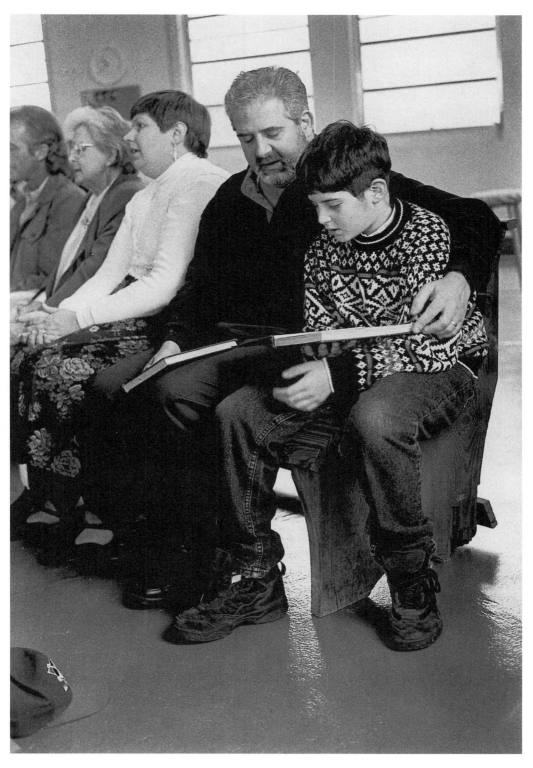

*Family at Sunday church service, Colby Memorial Temple, 1995.*

*Singing during Sunday church service, Colby Memorial Temple, 1995.*

*Women meditating, Colby Memorial Temple, 1996.*

*Group healing, Colby Memorial Temple, 1995.*

*The Reverend Kenneth Custance, 1995.*

*Camp elder Julia Slater, 1996.*

*Chauncey Street, 1994.*

*Seneca Park at Spirit Pond, 1994.*

*Séance in the Séance Room in Colby Memorial Temple, 1996.*

# SELECTED BIBLIOGRAPHY

Abzug, Robert A. *Cosmos Crumbling: American Reform and the Religious Imagination* New York: Oxford University Press, 1994.

Akin, Edward N. *Flagler: Rockefeller Partner and Florida Baron.* Kent, Ohio: Kent State University Press, 1988.

Alduino, Frank. "The Noble Experiment in Tampa: A Study of Prohibition in Urban America." Ph.D. diss., Florida State University, 1989.

American Association for State and Local History. *National Register of Historic Places, 1966–1991.* Nashville: American Association for State and Local History, 1991.

Atterbury, Grosvenor. "Model Towns in America," *Scribner's,* July 1912, p. 26.

Baker, John Milnes. *American House Styles.* New York: Norton, 1994.

Ballou, Adin. *History of the Hopedale Community.* Lowell, Mass.: Vox Populi Press, 1897.

Bednarowski, Mary Farrell. *New Religions and the Theological Imagination in America.* Bloomington: Indiana University Press, 1989.

———. "Nineteenth-Century American Spiritualism: An Attempt at a Scientific Religion." Ph.D. diss., University of Minnesota, 1973.

Beecher, Jonathan. *Charles Fourier: The Visionary and His World.* Berkeley: University of California Press, 1986.

Bledstein, Burton. *The Culture of Professionalism.* New York: Norton, 1976,

Block, Marguerite Beck. *The New Church in the New World: A Study of Swedenborgianism in America.* New York: Holt, Rinehart, and Winston, 1932.

Blumenson, John. *Identifying American Architecture.* Nashville: American Association for State and Local History, 1977.

Boles, John B., and Evelyn Thomas Nolen, eds. *Interpreting Southern History: Essays in Honor of Sandford W. Higginbotham.* Baton Rouge: Louisiana State University Press, 1987.

Braude, Ann. "News from the Spirit World: A Checklist of American Spiritualist Periodicals, 1847–1900." *Proceedings of the American Antiquarian Society* 99 (1989): 399–462.

———. *Radical Spirits: Spiritualism and Women's Rights in Nineteenth-Century America.* Boston: Beacon, 1989.

Brown, Burton Gates, Jr. "Spiritualism in Nineteenth-Century America." Ph.D. diss., Boston University, 1972.

Brown, Michael F. *The Channeling Zone: American Spirituality in an Anxious Age.* Cambridge: Harvard University Press, 1997.

Bucke, Richard Maurice, M.D. *Cosmic Consciousness: The Classic Investigation of the Development of Man's Mystic Relation to the Infinite.* New York: Penguin, 1901.

Bureau of the Census. Department of Commerce and Labor. *Religious Bodies: 1906* (Washington, D.C.: GPO, 1910), 1:102–104, 1:402, 1:526, 2:269.

Bush, George. *Mesmer and Swedenborg; Or, the Relation of the Developments of Mesmerism to the Doctrines and Disclosures of Swedenborg.* New York: John Allen, 1847.

Butler, Jon. *Awash in a Sea of Faith: Christianizing the American People.* Cambridge: Harvard University Press, 1990.

Carroll, Bret E. "Spiritualism and Community in Antebellum America: The Mountain Cove Episode." *Communal Societies* 12 (1992): 20–39.

———. *Spiritualism in Antebellum America.* Bloomington and Indianapolis: Indiana University Press, 1997.

*Centennial Book of Modern Spiritualism in America.* Chicago: National Spiritualist Association of the United States of America, 1948.

Chalmers, David. "The Ku Klux Klan in the Sunshine State: The 1920's." *Florida Historical Quarterly* 43 (January 1964): 209–15.

Conover, Jewel. *Nineteenth-Century Houses in Western New York.* Albany: State University of New York Press, 1966.

Conser, Walter H., Jr. *God and the Natural World: Religion and Science in Antebellum America.* Columbia: University of South Carolina Press, 1993.

Croce, Paul Jerome. *Science and Religion in the Era of William James.* Chapel Hill: University of North Carolina Press, 1995.

Cross, Whitney. *The Burned-Over District: The Social and Intellectual History of Enthusiastic Religion in Western New York, 1800–1850.* New York: Harper and Row, 1965.

Cummings, Abbott. *The Framed Houses of Massachusetts Bay, 1625–1725.* Cambridge: Harvard University Press, 1979.

Curl, James Stevens. *The Victorian Celebration of Death.* Detroit: Partridge, 1972.

Darnton, Robert. *Mesmerism and the End of the Enlightenment in France.* New York: Schocken, 1970.

Davis, Andrew Jackson. *The Harmonial Philosophy: A Compendium and Digest of the Works of Andrew Jackson Davis.* London: William Rider and Son, 1917.

———. *The Principles of Nature, Her Divine Revelations, and a Voice to Mankind.* New York: Lyon and Fishbough, 1847.

DeLand, Helen. *Story of DeLand and Lake Helen.* Norwich, Conn.: Louis W. Walden, 1928.

Delp, Robert W. "American Spiritualism and Social Reform, 1847–1900." *Northwest Ohio Quarterly* 44 (Fall 1972): 43–56.

———. "Andrew Jackson Davis: Prophet of American Spiritualism." *Journal of American History* 54 (June 1967): 43–56.

———. "Andrew Jackson Davis and Spiritualism." In *Pseudo-Science and Society in Nineteenth-Century America,* edited by Arthur Wrobel, 100–21. Lexington: University Press of Kentucky, 1987.

———. "Andrew Jackson Davis's *Revelations,* Harbinger of American Spiritualism." *New York Historical Society Quarterly* 55 (June 1971): 211–34.

———. "The Harmonial Philosopher: Andrew Jackson Davis and the Foundation of Modern American Spiritualism." Ph.D. diss., George Washington University, 1965.

———. "The Southern Press and the Rise of American Spiritualism, 1847–1860." *Journal of American Culture* 7 (1985): 88–95.

Dietrich, T. Stanton. *The Urbanization of Florida's Population: An Historical Perspective of County Growth, 1830–1970.* Gainesville: University Presses of Florida, 1978.

Douglas, Ann. *The Feminization of American Culture.* New York: Knopf, 1977.

Downs, John P., and Fenwick Y. Hedley, eds. *The History of Chautauqua County, New York, and Its People.* 3 vols. New York and Chicago: American Historical Society, 1921.

Duino, Russell. "Utopian Theme with Variations: John Murray Spear and His Kiantone Domain." *Pennsylvania History* 29 (1962): 140–50.

Ellwood, Robert S. Jr. *Alternative Altars: Unconventional and Eastern Spirituality in America.* Chicago: University of Chicago Press, 1979.

"The E. W. Bond Company Mill," *Logging* 5, no. 8 (August 1917): 247–63; 5, no. 9 (September 1917): 266–91.

Federal Writers' Workshop Project. "Lake Helen's Southern Cassadaga's Spiritualist Camp." February 1, 1939. Document on File at P. K. Yonge Library of Florida History, University of Florida, Gainesville.

Ferraro, Sharon. "*Ladies' Home Journal* Houses, 1895–1919." *Old-House Journal* 26 (April 1998): 52–57.

*Fire Insurance Map of Cassadaga, Volusia County, Florida.* New York: Sanborn, 1915 and 1925.

Fitzgerald, T. E. *Volusia County, Past and Present.* Daytona Beach: Observer Press, 1937.

Flynt, Wayne. *Duncan Upshaw Fletcher: Dixie's Reluctant Progressive.* Tallahassee: Florida State University Press, 1971.

———. "Religion at the Polls: A Case Study of Twentieth-Century Politics and Religion in Florida." *Florida Historical Quarterly* 72 (April 1994): 469–83.

Fogarty, Robert S. *All Things New: American Communes and Utopian Movements, 1860–1914.* Chicago: University of Chicago Press, 1990.

Fornell, Earl Wesley. *The Unhappy Medium: Spiritualism and the Life of Margaret Fox.* Austin: University of Texas Press, 1964.

Foster, Lawrence. *Religion and Sexuality: The Shakers, the Mormons, and the Oneida Community.* Urbana and Chicago: University of Illinois Press, 1984.

Fowler, Orson Squire. *A Home for All: The Gravel Wall and Octagon Mode of Building.* New York: Dover, 1853, 1973.

Frankiel, Sandra Sizer. *California's Spiritual Frontiers: Religious Alternatives in Anglo-Protestantism, 1850–1910.* Berkeley: University of California Press, 1988.

Frazer, William, and John J. Guthrie, Jr. *The Florida Land Boom: Speculation, Money, and the Banks.* Westport, Conn.: Quorum, 1995.

Fuller, Robert C. *Mesmerism and the American Cure of Souls.* Philadelphia: University of Pennsylvania Press, 1982.

Gannon, Michael. *Florida: A Short History.* Gainesville: University Press of Florida, 1992.

———, ed. *The New History of Florida.* Gainesville: University Press of Florida, 1996.

Garrett, Clarke. *Spirit Possession and Popular Religion: From the Camisards to the Shakers.* Baltimore: Johns Hopkins Universty Press, 1987.

Gold, Pleasant Daniel. *History of Volusia County, Florida.* Daytona Beach: Pleasant Daniel Gold, 1927.

Gould, Joseph. *The Chautauqua Movement.* Albany: State University of New York Press, 1961.

Grantham, Dewey W. *Southern Progressivism: The Reconciliation of Progress and Tradition.* 2d ed. Knoxville: University of Tennessee Press, 1987.

Grismer, Karl. *Tampa: A History of the City of Tampa and the Tampa Bay Region of Florida.* St. Petersburg: St. Petersburg Printing Co., 1950.

Guarneri, Carl. *The Utopian Alternative: Fourierism in Nineteenth-Century America.* Ithaca: Cornell University Press, 1991.

Guthrie, John J. Jr. *Keepers of the Spirits: The Judicial Response to Prohibition Enforcement in Florida, 1885–1935.* Westport, Conn.: Greenwood, 1998.

Haase, Ronald. *Classic Cracker: Florida's Wood-Frame Vernacular Architecture.* Sarasota: Pineapple, 1992.

Hagon, Zoe. *The Spiritual Connection.* Dorset, England: Prism, 1989.

Hammond, Charles. *Light from the Spirit World: The Pilgrimage of Thomas Paine, and Others, to the Seventh Circle in the Spirit World.* Rochester, N.Y., 1852.

Hanegraaff, Wouter J. *New Age Religion and Western Culture.* New York: Brill, 1996.

Hare, Robert. *Experimental Investigation of the Spirit Manifestations.* New York: Partridge and Brittan, 1855.

Harrold, Robert. *Cassadaga: An Inside Look at the South's Oldest Psychic Community.* Miami: Banyan, 1979.

Hatch, Nathan O. *The Democratization of American Christianity.* New Haven: Yale University Press, 1989.

Hayden, Dolores. *Seven American Utopias: The Architecture of Communitarian Socialism: 1790–1975.* Cambridge, Mass.: MIT Press, 1976.

Hebel, Ianthe Bond. "Florida's Bonds: Men Who Made Lumber History." *Southern Lumber Journal,* March 1951, pp. 24–25.

Heelas, Paul. *The New Age Movement.* Cambridge, Mass.: Blackwell, 1996.

Henderson, Janie. *The Story of Cassadaga.* Cassadaga, Fla.: Pisces, 1996.

Hess, David J. *Science in the New Age: The Paranormal, Its Defenders and Debunkers, and American Culture.* Madison: University of Wisconsin Press, 1993.

Higham, John. *From Boundlessness to Consolidation: The Transformation of American Culture, 1848–1860.* Ann Arbor, Mich.: William L. Clements Library, 1969.

Hofstadter, Richard. *The Age of Reform: From Bryan to FDR.* New York: Vintage, 1955.

Hovenkamp, Herbert. *Science and Religion in America, 1800–1860.* Philadelphia: University of Pennsylvania Press, 1978.

Humez, Jean M. *Mother's First-Born Daughters: Early Shaker Writings on Women and Religion.* Bloomington and Indianapolis: Indiana University Press, 1993.

*Impersonal Response.* Marina del Rey, Calif.: DeVorss, 1941.

Isaacs, Ernest. "A History of Nineteenth-Century American Spiritualism as a Social and Religious Movement." Ph.D. diss., University of Wisconsin, 1975.

Jackson, Kenneth T. *The Ku Klux Klan in the City, 1915–1930*. New York: Oxford University Press, 1967.

Jakle, John, Robert Bastian, and Douglas Meyer. *Common Houses in America's Small Towns: The Atlantic Seaboard to the Mississippi Valley*. Athens: University of Georgia Press, 1989.

Johnson, Allen, and Dumas Malone. *The Dictionary of American Biography*. Vol. 6. New York: Scribner's, 1931.

Johnson, Curtis D. *Islands of Holiness: Rural Religion in Upstate New York, 1790–1860*. Ithaca: Cornell University Press, 1989.

Johnson, K. Paul. *The Masters Revealed: Madame Blatvatsky and the Myth of the Great White Lodge*. Albany: State University of New York Press, 1994.

Jones, David E. *Visions of Time: Experiments in Psychic Archeology*. Wheaton, Ill.: Quest, 1979.

Judah, J. Stillson. *The History and Philosophy of the Metaphysical Movements in America*. Philadelphia: Westminster, 1967.

Karcher, Janet, and John Hutchinson. *This Way to Cassadaga*. Sanford, Fla.: John Hutchinson Productions, 1980.

Kelly, J. Frederick. *The Early Domestic Architecture of Connecticut*. New Haven: Yale University Press, 1924.

Kennedy, Roger. *American Churches*. New York: Stewart, Tabori, and Chang, 1982.

Kerr, Howard. *Mediums and Spirit Rappers and Roaring Radicals: Spiritualism in American Literature, 1850–1900*. Urbana: University of Illinois Press, 1972.

Kerr, Howard, and Charles L. Crow, eds. *The Occult in America: New Historical Perspectives*. Urbana and Chicago: University of Illinois Press, 1983.

Kimball, Fiske. *Domestic Architecture of the American Colonies of the Early Republic*. New York: Scribner's, 1922.

King, Anthony. *The Bungalow: The Production of a Global Culture*. New York: Oxford University Press, 1995.

Kyle, Richard. *The Religious Fringe: A History of Alternative Religions in America*. Downers Grove, Ill.: Intervarsity, 1993.

Lasley, Joseph. *Names and Places: A Lake Junaluska Cyclopedia*. Lake Junaluska, N.C.: Joseph Lasley, 1993.

Lawton, George. *The Drama of Life after Death: A Study of the Spiritualist Religion*. New York: Holt, 1932.

Lehman, Neil B. "The Life of John Murray Spear: Spiritualism and Reform in Antebellum America." Ph.D. diss., Ohio State University, 1973.

Lempel, Leonard R. "Race and Politics in Daytona Beach, Florida, 1876–1937." 1999. Photocopy in possession of John J. Guthrie, Jr.

Lewis, James R., and J. Gordon Melton, eds. *Perspectives on the New Age*. Albany: State University of New York Press, 1992.

*Light of Truth Album: Prominent Workers in the Cause of Spiritualism*. Columbus, Ohio: Light of Truth Publishing, 1897.

Link, Arthur S. *Woodrow Wilson and the Progressive Era*. New York: Harper and Row, 1954.

Link, William A. *The Paradox of Southern Progressivism, 1880–1930.* Chapel Hill: University of North Carolina Press, 1992.

Lucas, Phillip Charles. "The New Age Movement and the Pentecostal/Charismatic Revival: Distinct Yet Parallel Phases of a Fourth Great Awakening?" In *Perspectives on the New Age,* edited by James R. Lewis and J. Gordon Melton, pp. 189–211. Albany: State University of New York Press, 1992.

———. *The Odyssey of a New Religion: The Holy Order of MANS from New Age to Orthodoxy.* Bloomington: Indiana University Press, 1995.

MacLean, Nancy. *Behind the Mask of Chivalry: The Making of the Second Ku Klux Klan.* New York: Oxford University Press, 1994.

Maddex, Diane, ed. *Master Builders: A Guide to Famous American Architects.* Washington, D.C.: Preservation, 1985.

Mattson, Richard. "The Gable Front House: An Historical Geography of a Common House Type." Ph.D diss., University of Illinois, Urbana-Champaign, 1988.

McAlester, Virginia, and Lee McAlester. *A Field Guide to American Houses.* New York: Knopf, 1986.

McCandless, Peter. "Mesmerism and Phrenology in Antebellum Charleston: Enough of the Marvelous." *Journal of Southern History* 58 (May 1992): 199–230.

McCluskey, Audrey Thomas. "Mary McLeod Bethune's Impact on Daytona." *Florida Historical Quarterly* (October 1994), 200–20.

McMurry, Sally. *Families and Farmhouses in 19th-Century America.* New York: Oxford University Press, 1988.

Miller, Ernest C. "Utopian Communities in Warren County, Pennsylvania." *Western Pennsylvania Historical Magazine* 49 (1966): 301–17.

Moore, D. D., ed. *Men of the South.* New Orleans: Southern Biographical Association, 1922.

Moore, R. Laurence. *In Search of White Crows: Spiritualism, Parapsychology, and American Culture.* New York: Oxford University Press, 1977.

———. *Religious Outsiders and the Making of Americans.* New York: Oxford University Press, 1986.

———. *Selling God: American Religion in the Marketplace of Culture.* New York: Oxford University Press, 1994.

Morita, Sally Jean. "Modern Spiritualism and Reform in Modern America." Ph.D. diss., University of Oregon, 1995.

Morley, John. *Death, Heaven, and the Victorians.* Pittsburgh: University of Pittsburgh Press, 1971.

Morris, Christopher. *Becoming Southern: The Evolution of a Way of Life, Warren County and Vicksburg, Mississippi, 1770–1860.* New York: Oxford University Press, 1995.

Owen, Alex. *The Darkened Room: Women, Power, and Spiritualism in Late Victorian England.* Philadelphia: University of Pennsylvania Press, 1990.

Ownby, Ted. *Subduing Satan: Religion, Recreation, and Manhood in the Rural South, 1865–1920.* Chapel Hill: University of North Carolina Press, 1990.

O'Neill, William. *The Progressive Years: America Comes of Age.* New York: Dodd, Meade, 1975.

Padelford, Philip Sidney. "Adin Ballou and the Hopedale Community." Ph.D. diss., Yale University, 1942.

Page, Eloise. *Natural Law by Rev. Eloise Page: A Series of Inspirational Lectures.* Cassadaga, Fla.: Southern Cassadaga Spiritualist Camp Bookstore, prior to 1988. Published by Eloise Page 1988 to present.

———. *The Path: Inspirational Poems.* Cassadaga, Fla.: n.p., 1999.

Palliser, George, and Charles Palliser. *Palliser's American Cottage Homes.* Bridgeport, Conn.: Palliser, Palliser and Co., 1878.

Peat, Wilbur. *Indiana Houses of the Nineteenth Century.* Indianapolis: Indiana Historical Society, 1962.

Perry, Lewis. *Radical Abolitionism: Anarchy and the Government of God in Antislavery Thought.* Ithaca: Cornell University Press, 1973.

Pillsburg, Richard, and Andrew Kardus. *A Field Guide to the Folk Architecture of the Northeastern United States.* Hanover: Dartmouth University Press, 1970.

Podmore, Frank. *Modern Spiritualism: A History and a Criticism.* 2 vols. London: Methuen, 1902.

Porter, Katherine H. *Through a Glass Darkly: Spiritualism in the Browning Circle.* Lawrence: University of Kansas Press, 1958.

*Preliminary Report of the Seybert Commission for the Investigation of Modern Spiritualism.* Philadelphia: Lippincott, 1887.

*Proceedings of the National Delegate Convention of Spiritualists of the United States of America.* Washington, D.C.: Stormont and Jackson Printers, 1893.

Reps, John. *The Making of Urban America: A History of City Planning in the United States.* Princeton: Princeton University Press, 1965

Rerick, Rowland. *Memoirs of Florida.* 2 vols. Atlanta: Southern Historical Association, 1902.

Riasanovsky, Nicholas. *The Teaching of Charles Fourier.* Berkeley: University of California Press, 1969.

Robinson, Charles. "New Dreams for Cities." *Architectural Record* 17 (May 1905): 410.

Roof, Wade Clark. *A Generation of Seekers: The Spiritual Journeys of the Baby Boom Generation.* San Francisco: Harper and Row, 1993.

Roth, Leland. *A Concise History of American Architecture.* New York: Harper and Row, 1979.

Schene, Michael G. *Hopes, Dreams, and Promises: A History of Volusia County, Florida.* Daytona Beach: News-Journal Corporation, 1976.

Scott, Mel. *American City Planning since 1890.* Berkeley: University of California Press, 1969.

Shofner, Jerrell H. "Custom, Law, and History: The Enduring Influence of Florida's 'Black Code.'" *Florida Historical Quarterly* 55 (January 1977): 277–98.

Southern Cassadaga Spiritualist Camp Meeting Association. *Annual Convention Programs,* 1903–98.

Spann, Edward K. *Hopedale: From Commune to Company Town.* Columbus: Ohio State University Press, 1992.

Spear, John Murray. *Twenty Years on the Wing: Brief Narrative of My Travels and Labors as a Missionary Sent Forth and Sustained by the Association of Beneficents in Spirit Land.* Boston: William White, 1873.

Spurlock, John C. *Free Love: Marriage and Middle-Class Radicalism in America, 1825–1860.* New York: New York University Press, 1988.

Stark, Rodney, and William S. Bainbridge. *The Future of Religion.* Berkeley: University of California Press, 1985,

*State of Florida, ex rel. Charles T. Ford, George A. Dimmick, Joseph F. Snipes, A. B. Gaston, F. W. Mack, Charles Coolidge and T. Babcock v. Joseph Slater, Melvin J. Holt, E. P. Sully, Herbert Hollely, William Critchley, E. E. Hopkins, and A. Cowcroft.* Seventh Judicial Circuit Court of Volusia County, Florida, 1918.

Stein, Stephen J. "Shaker Gift and Shaker Order: A Study of Religious Tension in Nineteenth-Century America." *Communal Societies* 10 (1990): 106.

Stevenson, Katherine, and H. Ward Jandl. *Houses By Mail: A Guide to Houses from Sears, Roebuck and Company.* Washington, D.C.: Preservation, 1986.

Swank, Scott Trego. "The Unfettered Conscience: A Study of Sectarianism, Spiritualism, and Social Reform in the New Jerusalem Church, 1840–1870." Ph.D. diss., University of Pennsylvania, 1970 .

Tebeau, Charlton W. *A History of Florida.* Coral Gables: University of Miami Press, 1971.

Thurston, Mark A. *Experiments in a Search for God: The Edgar Cayce Path of Application.* Virginia Beach: A.R.E. Press, 1976.

U.S. Congress. House Subcommittee on Judiciary of the Committee on the District of Columbia. *Fortune Telling: Hearing before the Subcommittee on Judiciary of the Committee on the District of Columbia.* 69th Cong., 1st sess., February 26, May 18, 20, and 21, 1926.

Vaught, Paula M., and Joyce LaJudice. *Lily Dale Proud Beginnings: A Little Bit of History.* Lily Dale, N.Y.: Lily Dale Spiritualist Association, 1984.

Vaux, Calvert. *Villa and Cottage Architecture: The Style-Book of Hudson River School.* New York: Harper, 1864.

Volusia County Courthouse, Deland, Fla. Deed Book, Map Book, Miscellaneous Book, Quit Claim Book, Plat Book.

Wessinger, Catherine, ed. *Women's Leadership in Marginal Religions: Explorations outside the Mainstream.* Urbana: University of Illinois Press, 1993.

Whiffen, Marcus. *American Architecture Since 1780.* Cambridge: MIT Press, 1969.

Whiffen, Marcus, and Frederick Koeper. *American Architecture, 1607–1976.* Cambridge, Mass.: MIT Press, 1981.

White, O. Kendall, and Daryl White, eds. *Religion in the Contemporary South: Diversity, Community, and Identity.* Athens: University of Georgia Press, 1995.

Wilson, John F. "A New Denominational Historiography?" *Religion and American Culture* 5 (Summer 1995): 249–63.

Wilson, S. B. "Plan of the Camp Grounds of the Southern Cassadaga Spiritualist Camp Meeting Association," 1902.

Wilson, William. *The City Beautiful Movement.* Baltimore: Johns Hopkins University Press, 1989

Withey, Henry F., and Elsie Rathburn Withey. *Biographical Dictionary of American Architects (Deceased)*. Los Angeles: Hennessey and Ingalls, 1970.

Woodward, George E., and Edward G. Thompson. *Woodward's National Architect*. New York: G. E. Woodward, 1869.

Works Progress Administration. *New York: A Guide to the Empire State*. New York: Oxford University Press, 1940.

Wright, Gwendoyn. *Building the Dream: A Social History of Housing in America*. Cambridge, Mass.: MIT Press, 1981.

Wunderlich, Roger. *Low Living and High Thinking at Modern Times New York*. Syracuse: Syracuse University Press, 1992.

## Newspapers

*Banner of Light*, 1893–1907.

*The Cassadagan*, 1938–39.

*Daytona Beach News-Journal*, 1993–98.

*Daytona Morning Journal*, 1921.

*DeLand Daily News*, 1903–33.

*DeLand News*, 1903–33.

*DeLand Sun News*, 1928–33.

*Florida Times-Union*, 1895

*Jamestown (New York) Evening Journal*, 1923–26.

*New York Times*, 1952.

*Orlando Sentinel*, 1993

*Palm Beach Life*, 1975.

*Progressive Thinker*, 1926.

*Tampa Morning Tribune*, 1926.

*Volusia County Record*, 1893–1914.

# ABOUT THE EDITORS
# AND CONTRIBUTORS

BRET E. CARROLL is assistant professor of history at California State University, Stanislaus. He earned his M.A. and Ph.D. degrees at Cornell University. Carroll is the author of *Spiritualism in Antebellum America* (1997) and several articles on nineteenth-century American Spiritualism.

ANN JEROME CROCE is associate professor of American studies at Stetson University. She graduated from Yale University and earned her M.A. and Ph.D. degrees at Brown University. She has published on a wide variety of topics, including American fiction, sentimentalism, and the religious dimensions of alternative medicine.

PAUL JEROME CROCE is associate professor of American studies at Stetson University. A graduate of Georgetown University who holds a Ph.D. from Brown University, he has published *Science and Religion in the Era of William James* (1995).

JOHN J. GUTHRIE, JR. (1955–2000) was associate professor of history at Daytona Beach Community College. A graduate of Radford College, Guthrie earned his Ph.D. at the University of Florida. He had published *Keepers of the Spirits: The Judicial Response to Prohibition Enforcement in Florida, 1885–1935* (1998) and (with William Frazer) *The Florida Land Boom: Speculation, Money, and the Banks* (1995).

SIDNEY P. JOHNSTON operates a historic preservation and historical consulting business in DeLand, Florida. He holds an M.A. degree in history from the University of Florida and is the author of *Paper, Presses, and Profits: A History of the E. O. Painter Printing Company* (1996) and "The Historic Stetson University Campus in DeLand, 1884–1934," *Florida Historical Quarterly* (January 1992).

PHILLIP CHARLES LUCAS is associate professor of religious studies at Stetson University and general editor of *Nova Religio: The Journal of Alternative and*

*Emergent Religions.* He received his Ph.D. degree from the University of California at Santa Barbara. Lucas has published *Prime Time Religion: An Encyclopedia of Religious Broadcasting* (1997) and *The Odyssey of a New Religion: The Holy Order of MANS from New Age to Orthodoxy* (1995).

GARY MONROE is professor of art at Daytona Beach Community College's Southeast Museum School of Photography. He holds an M.F.A. degree from the University of Colorado at Boulder. Monroe has published his photographs in several books, among them (with Jerry Stern) *Florida Dreams* (1993), *Haiti* (1992), *Miami Beach* (1990), and *Life in South Beach* (1988).

ANNE BARCLAY MORGAN is an independent writer who has a doctorate in psychology from the University of Vienna and an M.A. in art history from the University of Florida. Besides publishing over 170 items, Morgan has produced and directed award-winning documentaries in the arts, including *Video Art to Virtual Reality*, which aired in cooperation with the PBS Adult Learning Service.

# INDEX

out-of-body experiences, 157
Owens, Vince, 59

Page, E. B., 176–178, 180, 186, 195, 200
Page, Eloise: 58, 60, 67, 75, 157; author's
    reading with, 182–183; early life, 173–176;
    life in Cassadaga, 177–180; poetry, 195;
    meeting E. B. Page, 176; out-of-body
    experiences, 175, 200–201; residing in
    Iowa, 177; teachings on natural law, 185–
    187, 195–197; views of the future, 197–199
Paine, Thomas, 50
Palmer, James D., 106–107
parapsychology, 21, 150
Parcell, C. E., 100
Peat, Wilbur, 115
Peebles, James M., 21
Peck, William F., 34, 37
Peltz, Paul, 98
Pennsylvania Dutch, 161, 167
Perry, Abby, 166
Pettengill, Abby, 109
Phelps, Frank and Mary, 105
Philadelphia, 13, 19, 20, 50
Phillips, Wendell, 35
phrenology, 2
physical phenomena, 22, 70–71, 88
physics, 150
Pierce, George and Anna, 118–119; Cottage
    described, 118–119
Pillsbury, Parker, 28
platform test mediums, 35
Post, Amy and Isaac, 3
Powell, James H., 15
Practical Christian, The, 19
Principles of Nature, The (Davis), 5, 7
Proctor, Samuel, 32
Progressive Era reforms, 41
Progressive Spiritual Church, 22
Progressive Thinker, 48
Prohibition, 34, 105
Prospect Hill, 109
Protestant American traditions, 27–28, 42
psychic readings, 58, 68, 88–89
Psychical Science Congress, 21
psychology, 154

Quakerism, 3, 7, 8

reading for others, 187, 188, 189
Reid, Gladys, 138–142, 168–170
reincarnation, 22, 23, 61–62, 195–197
Religio-Philosophical Journal, 19
religions, Asian. See Asian religions
republicanism, 8, 9, 10, 14
revivalism, 2, 8, 15, 16
Riffle, Mable, 47
Rochester, N.Y., 2, 3, 13, 20
Romanticism, 8, 9
Roof, Wade Clark, 85
Rosicrucianism, 61, 75
Rowley, W. S., 31

San Francisco, 13
Schaaf, William, 182, 202
science, authority of, 2, 8, 10–11, 12
Scientology, 23
Scott, James L. 18
séances, 10, 12, 14–15, 22, 33, 35, 36, 47
Sebring, contrasted with Cassadaga, 108
Seneca (spirit guide), 32
Seneca Falls Convention, 3
Seneca Street, 107, 109
Seybert, Henry, 12
Seybert Commission, 12
Shakers, 2–3, 8, 14
Shalam colony, 18
shamanism, 7
Sheets, Abbie E., 37–38
Sherman, Ray B., 118; cottage described,
    118, 118
Skidmore, Marion, 33–34, 77, 97, 103;
    library named for, 98, 103
Slater, Joseph, 43, 104, 123
Smith, Joseph, 2, 3, 10
Snipes, Joseph, 44, 45, 124; house
    described, 124–125, 124
Society for the Diffusion of Spiritual
    Knowledge, 14
Sourant, Jean, 147–154, 169
Sourant, Nick, 147–154, 168, 170
South, xi, 13, 27, 30, 32, 34, 37, 102, 111,
    120

Vogt, Julia, 105

*Volusia County Record,* on allegations of fraud against Spiritualists, 30, 35; and other matters, 96, 100

Volusia County, development of, after the Civil War, 32; Protestant churches in, 38

Waidelich, Janie, 84, 88

Ward, Mae Graves, 166, 169

Warren, Josiah, 17

waterworks at Cassadaga, 45, 109

Watson, Jim, 67, 73–74, 76

Washington, George, 10

Wednesday All-Message Service, 81, 89

Weigl, John, 162–63

Weigl, Lillian (Lollie), 160–166, 168–170

West Virginia, 18

White, J. D., 116; cottage described, 116

Wisconsin, 13, 19, 32, 99, 109

witchcraft, 12

women, as mediums. *See* mediums, women as

Women's Christian Temperance Union, 34

women's rights, 3, 8, 10, 20

women's roles in Spiritualism. *See* Spiritualism, women's roles in

Woodhull, Victoria, 20

World Parliament of Religions, 21

World War I, 45

World War II, 145

World's Columbian Exposition in Chicago (1893), 107–108

World's Congress of Religions, 38

Wright, Frank Lloyd, 120

Wright, J. Clegg, 27, *41*, 42

Yogananda, Paramahansa, 79, 176, 188

Zanghi, Don, 70, 90